THE INDIV
MULTI-SOCIO-CULTURAL-REALITIES

Culture Analysis as a Reading Strategy

Judith G. Campbell
Guenter G. Pfister

University Press of America,® Inc.
Lanham · New York · Oxford

Copyright © 2002 by
University Press of America,® Inc.
4720 Boston Way
Lanham, Maryland 20706
UPA Acquisitions Department (301) 459-3366

12 Hid's Copse Rd.
Cumnor Hill, Oxford OX2 9JJ

ISBN 0-7618-2230-5 (pbk. : alk. paper)

To Myrtle and Richard Campbell

Contents

List of Figures

Chapter 1

Introduction

To enter the dimension of culture pedagogy presupposes an approach or conception of culture, a method for teaching about culture compatible with this conception, and materials that correspond to both the method and approach. Hence, at issue for twenty-first century language study functional-relevance is an as yet to be formally established autonomous dimension of foreign language programs, namely culture pedagogy.[1] The main focus of culture pedagogy will be to establish approaches and methods, as well as techniques[2] for implementing cultural awareness through foreign language programs:

> In this perspective the learner is encouraged to learn 'language for cultural understanding' which embraces both 'language for reading' and 'language for touring'. The learner's ultimate goal is to achieve a capacity for cognitive analysis of a foreign culture, people and its artefacts –whether intellectual or other– and for affective response to experience of another culture which neither hinders his perceptions of self and others nor prevents his adaptation to new environments.[3]

The revision suggested in this study thus follows Byram and other methodologists who are working for the development of culture pedagogy as an independent –autonomous– component of foreign language study and not just an aspect of, or context for, situational language and literature studies. The future functional-relevance of language study necessitates a programatic shift which would fully establish culture pedagogy within the realm of foreign language study, altering the paradigm from foreign language study to foreign-language-culture study.

That this pedagogical shift is underway is apparent in publications of the past two decades. Foreign language professionals during the eighties and nineties began to realize that culture models and teaching methods were becoming increasingly unsatisfactory at meeting/developing the functional aims/cognitive strategies of Global-Information Age learners.[4] The informative and/or comparative methods of teaching culture in the (Pre-)Tourism Age(s) were not intended to promote critical thinking or analytical skills; the processes engaged by these approaches to culture develop the cognitive skills of knowledge, comprehension, and application.[5] However, the new intercultural competence functional aims of learners requires methods designed to promote strategies that impart the critical thinking skills of analysis, synthesis, and evaluation.

In the Global-information Age, the teacher, as a facilitator of cognitive-intellectual growth, must move away from the role of an information conduit. Effective critical skills for (inter)cultural competence can be developed and promoted within the realm of a foreign language program that sets cultural awareness/literacy as its culture proficiency goal. And, a culture pedagogy that seeks cultural awareness/literacy as its proficiency goal, will, in turn, promote strategies and methods that teach such critical thinking skills as analysis, synthesis, and evaluation.

At present, the goal to develop and implement culture pedagogies designed to enable students to address the pragmatic analysis of culture as it relates to communication remains. As Kramsch and Koope[6] have noted, future culture pedagogies must consider as culture the larger scale of propositional knowledge underlying institutions, behaviors, and artifacts. To do this, culture pedagogy must incorporate recent theoretical advances in anthropology and move the foreign language approach to culture *from* behavior-based cultural knowledge *to* cognitive-based cultural awareness.

The Three Ages of Foreign Language Pedagogy

When the historical development of foreign language pedagogy as three ages,[7] incorporating the proposed new dimension of foreign language-culture pedagogy, is depicted in a timeline the progression toward the revision presented in this work is clear. On the timeline given in figure 1.1, each age is listed with its core theoretical foundation and corresponding learner's functional aim in parentheses (i.e. Humanist Tradition and translation/reading), followed by the pedagogical approach (i.e. literary language), name of the age (i.e. Pre-Tourism Age), and finally proficiency goals of the pedagogy (i.e. written competence and language for reading).

Figure 1.1 The Three Ages of Foreign Language Pedagogy

Humanist Tradition (translation/reading)	Behavioral Sciences (speaking/touring)	Cognitive Anthropology (cultural awareness)
_____/_____/_____		
1900 1945	1970	1999
Literary language	Added situational language	Added culture culture pedagogy
Pre-Tourism Age	**Tourism Age**	**Global-Information Age**
Written competence/ Language for reading	Spoken competence/ Language for touring	Intercultural competence/ Language for cultural understanding

Cultural Awareness Through Culture Pedagogy

In order to forge a new and functionally relevant relationship between foreign language-culture study and students' experience in this Global-Information Age, foreign language programs must broaden to encompass a new and substantive culture dimension via an independently developed culture pedagogy. In the words of Kramsch and Nolden, we are striving for "a new type of literacy centered more on the learner, based more on cross-cultural awareness and critical reflection."[8] The new culture pedagogy will promote an understanding of the nature of culture within the context of a chosen language program.[9] Imparting this type of "understanding" necessitates a change in the current practice of supplementing distilled, culture-based information, as the perception of studying a foreign language changes from coping with "alien behaviours and objects" ("training for the predictable") to interacting "with individuals who have a different set of values and meanings" ("preparation for the unpredictable"). Byram and Esarte-Sarries diagnosed this new functional relevance of foreign language-culture study as "language for cultural understanding". And, the work of Kramsch, Pfister and Poser[10] represent the beginning of methodologies designed to support and promote this notion.

Just like the adjustments from the Pre-tourism to Tourism Ages, the current adjustment to the Global-Information Age represents a marked change in focus. But, unlike the previous shift, 'language for cultural understanding' does not necessitate a change in language materials or language teaching methods (i.e. language pedagogy). Rather, this new shift necessitates a change in approach toward cultural content as Kramsch, Pfister and Poser have recognized.[11] In order to develop a culture pedagogy for foreign language-culture study which is representative of the new advancements in cognitive anthropology, methodologies based-in cognitive-approaches to culture are needed. Such methodologies should move beyond identification of cultural issues and aim to help learners create an understanding of the foreign framework of ideas they have chosen to study. Such methodologies should also employ Nelson's 'Verfremdung'[12] idea by encouraging students to reflect on their own culture and perceive and understand it from the viewpoint of an outsider.[13] As foreign language methodologists work toward developing and implementing cognitive methods of culture analysis, they will endow learners with the potential for an "affective response to [the] experience of another culture which neither hinders his perceptions of self and others, nor prevents his adaptation to new environments."[14] Such affective responses are the reflections of (inter)cultural awareness and demonstrate intercultural competence.

Approach, Method and Materials for Culture Pedagogy

To distinguish between approach and method we follow the model of Edward Anthony[15] who relates these terms as levels of conceptualization and organization within an hierarchical scheme.[16] Accordingly, an approach "describes the nature of the subject matter to be taught." In this sense an approach is nominally axiomatic and, for the purpose of this present work, proposes a set of correlative assumptions about culture and the teaching of culture. While the approach is theoretical, the method enables the theory to be practiced and is thus procedural: "Method is an overall plan for the orderly presentation of material, no part of which contradicts, and all of which is based upon the selected approach. Within one approach, there can be many methods...".[17]

The current unsatisfactory methods for dealing with culture in foreign language programs do not result from failure to utilize anthropological approaches to culture, but rather from the choice of anthropological approach. Tourism methodologists had chosen to utilize the behavioral approach to culture which correlated with the 'language for touring' proficiency goals and functional aims of foreign language study during the Tourism Age. As the proficiency goals for a foreign language-culture pedagogy move from the predominate 'language for touring' and 'language for reading' paradigms to a new 'language for cultural understanding' paradigm the borrowings from approaches in the parent disciplines of anthropology and sociology must change also.

The behavioral focus, representative of Tourism Age language study, inevitably opted for behavioral based concepts of culture because the aim was to address surface cultural-phenomena for the purpose of *emulation*.[18] However, the emerging critical focus[19] representative of Global-information Age language-culture study necessitates a move to symbolic/cognitive based concepts of culture aimed at addressing surface cultural phenomena not as patterns to be emulated but as "expressions of meaning" to be translated and interpreted.[20] This more cognitive/semiotic approach to culture, occurring approximately three decades ago, is a recent development in the field of anthropology and centers on the work of Ward Goodenough, among others.[21]

Goodenough focused on models of perception and interpretation as the constitutive basis of culture. His cognitive definition of culture reads as follows: "A society's culture consists of whatever it is one has to know or believe in order to operate in a manner acceptable to its members."[22] Reading Goodenough, the shift in approach is clear. Cognitive conceptions of culture do not pertain to behaviors, but rather to the motivating thoughtforms behind the behaviors.

> Culture is *not* a natural phenomenon; it does *not* consist of things, people's behavior or emotions. It is rather an organization of these things. It is the form of things that people have in mind, their models of perceiving, relating, and otherwise interpreting them.[23]

The conception of culture outlined by Goodenough forms the base approach of cognitive anthropology. It is also the base approach to culture as we define it in Chapter 3 of this study.

Clifford Geertz was the other foundational theorist for our approach. The work of Geertz illustrates a concept of culture compatible to the cognitive approach in that it highlights the symbolic nature of culture as cognitive systems or models of perception, relation, and interpretation.

Geertz, as a cognitive anthropologist, pushed the interpretative dimension within the cognitive approach. Unfortunately, he never outlined his interpretative strategies.[24] But, the emphasis of his work on the expressive modes through which culture was transmitted or communicated have laid the foundations for symbolic anthropology. Geertz's 1973 definition of culture:

> an historically transmitted pattern of meanings embodied in symbols, a system of inherited conceptions expressed in a symbolic form by means of which men communicate, perpetuate and develop their knowledge about attitudes towards life.[25]

In his 1973 definition, Geertz is clearly cognitive in his use of the terms "pattern of meanings" and "inherited conceptions". Geertz, however, also adds the necessary elements for a semiotic understanding of culture by writing that it consists of "...meanings embodied in symbols...;" "...conceptions expressed in a symbolic form...".[26] His writings were instrumental in directing us toward a semiotic method of analysis for our cognitive conception of culture.[27]

In order to develop proficiency goals of 'language for cultural understanding' the work of cognitive and symbolic anthropologists must be acknowledged and utilized. Such acknowledgement renders the currently employed, yet outdated behavioral based definitions of culture and factual-situational methods for describing behaviors, artifacts and institutions incomplete because they focus only on the surface cultural manifestations without addressing the culture –or underlying meanings– embodied in and realized through these symbolic forms. What is needed now are teaching methods which promote an analysis and evaluation of culture as a meaning system contexted within a socio-cultural reality. Future methods for analyzing 'culture,' like the one presented in this work, should be grounded in the cognitive anthropological approach.

Considering approach, method and materials, a direction can be suggested for the paradigm shift that would address the goals of culture pedagogy and 'language for cultural understanding'. New approaches to culture in foreign language programs will not just conceive of culture as a 'behavioral way of life' or a 'national heritage' but, based on theoretical shifts and framework analyses provided by symbolic and cognitive anthropology, will conceive of culture as a shared meaning system or 'way of thinking about and interpreting reality.' Methods will not stop at the informative/comparative stages of cognitive awareness, but will need to help the student proceed onto the critical, evaluative stages of problem solving encompassing an opportunity to master both synchronic and diachronic analytical perspectives. Analytical procedures and frameworks will need to be developed to promote and facilitate students' mastery of these methods of critical evaluation. Materials will reflect an emphasis on primary sources, using secondary materials as a basis for reflective and/ or supplemental exercises which will prompt the students to compare their own analyses and evaluations with those of social historians.

Since the shift into the new Global-Information Age is well underway, the search for a new paradigm/pedagogy has, as witnessed in the methodological literature, already begun. Innovative methods and techniques have been developed from approaches and theoretical frameworks current in Cultural Theory, such as the Cultural Inventory developed by Pfister and Poser.[28] And, as with the work of Kramsch, methodologies have been inspired from the field of cognitive psychology. In developing this current contribution, we followed those who pointed the way to the field of anthropology, specifically its cognitive and symbolic branches.

Our research goal for this study focused on expanding and refining the Cultural Inventory developed by Pfister and Poser so that it would reflect, and teach, a cognitive-semiotic approach to culture and thereby address the revised pedagogical goals of twenty-first century, foreign language study; for, it is necessary to design pedagogical tools that will enable students to read, analyze and evaluate the 'deep' cultural content of texts from a symbolic/cognitive-anthropological perspective. The use of this revised Cultural Inventory will not only promote critical-analytical skills, but will also enable students to develop a symbolic-cognitive awareness of culture as the meaning systems by, and through which humans construct, and seek to maintain their respective socio-cultural realities. As such, our tool –the Cultural Inventory– will serve to teach a semiotic-based strategy for translating cultural phenomena and a method of analysis for determining and evaluating the "socio-cultural realities" -or ideologies[29]- present in these phenomena. The Cultural Inventory as an analytical, translation tool enables students to process data within a battery of theoretical filters created and arranged to facilitate critical reflection on the ideologies existent in primary texts of literature. Utilized as an instructional tool within foreign language programs, the Cultural Inventory also promotes student awareness regarding the elements and structure of a cognitive-anthropological conception of culture.

The Four Phases of an Anthropological Study

The anthropological perspective serves as our approach to culture. There are generally four phases to an anthropological study of culture. The initial phase is theoretical and functions to develop a concept of culture. The study's concept of culture thus impacts the choice of anthropological approach, research method and analytical technique. In most cases, the initial phase also determines the extent of the fieldwork by establishing temporal and spatial parameters of the study.[30]

From a concept of culture, then, a study model of culture (what culture is and how it functions in human interaction) is designed. The study model operates as a focus mechanism for directing the collection of data in the field. It further reveals the anthropologist's research approach and determines the techniques which will be chosen for data collection. As such, the study model of culture enables the anthropologist to address issues of method and pose questions which the data, once collected, will be analyzed to answer. Hence, this first phase is theoretical, encompassing both a proposal for determining a culture research goal and an outline for focusing the collection of data to attain this goal.

Collecting field-data constitutes the second phase in an anthropological study of culture. Here the anthropologist gathers data utilizing a method (participant observation, surveys, interviews, etc.) corresponding to his/her theoretical proposal of what culture is. The third phase in an anthropological study constitutes an analysis of the data collected. And, the final phase consists of an interpretation or a write-up of evaluations in keeping with the initial concept of culture developed.

These four phases represent a time-consuming endeavor and one necessitating a number of years of study in the field of anthropology, as well as the logistical opportunity to conduct fieldwork. Since our conditions were quite different, the desire to mimic anthropological studies in foreign language programs required creative adaptations. Adapting the anthropological approach to study culture in the classroom required the first (concept-approach-method) and second (field-data) phases of the study to be "ready-made". In this way, student-centered learning at the third and fourth phases could be promoted; namely at the analysis and evaluation phases.

Our Adaptation of the Four Phases of an Anthropological Study

In comparing the four phases of an anthropological study of culture as outlined above with our vision of how such an approach could be utilized to integrate the study of culture into courses of foreign language programs the following adaptations to the anthropological model were determined:

Phase 1: theoretical approach and analysis technique
Phase 2: determination of data-field
Phase 3: data collection and analysis
Phase 4: interpretation and evaluations

Phase 1: theoretical approach and analysis technique

It was clear that an already developed model of culture, research method and analysis technique, addressing the areas covered in the first phase of an anthropological study, would have to be supplied to instructors and students; for, a method of analysis was needed which could be directly implemented in a classroom environment. The work presented in this book has focused on this phase. And, for our particular purposes the model of culture would have to present a conception of culture designed to be adapted to data collection from texts. It would address the questions of culture's ideational nature. With the Cultural Inventory developed by Pfister and Poser as our beginning framework, we set about the restructuring of the Inventory into an analytical tool to be utilized by students with no prior background in cultural studies, semiotics, anthropology, sociology.

The initial phase, representing theoretical concept, approach, and method of analysis, is thus pre-determined and supplied through the Cultural Inventory: designed to analyze cultural phenomena present in texts in terms of the evidence these phenomena reveal concerning the culture content and the socio-cultural reality which they materialize.[31] The components of the revised Cultural Inventory and the theories chosen to construct its components illustrate our theoretical concept and approach to culture. The Cultural Inventory therefore has been designed to facilitate a semiotic method of analysis in correspondence with our cognitive/symbolic concept and approach to culture.

Phase 2: determination of data-field

The second phase of an anthropological study, addresses the determination of a data field. As method of cultural analysis was intended to be implemented first in the Civilization courses of a foreign language program, an adjustment of the anthropological notion of fieldwork was necessary. There would be no physically designated field and hence no fieldwork in an orthodox anthropological sense;

instead, the fieldwork would be textually based, relying mostly on artifactual phenomena since students would gather data from primary texts; initially literary works.[32] And, although, from an anthropological perspective, the proposal for the use of texts as 'field' constitutes an unorthodox notion of fieldwork, mention has been made concerning the use of texts as source phenomena for anthropological studies of culture: "Moving from law to literature, one again finds a tremendous resource –a stockpile of cultural data– albeit raw data which must be mined and refined before their meaning is clear."[33] Technically, then, instructors would provide the *field* of the second phase; that is, the "raw data...[to]...be mined and refined" would exist in the form of selected course materials. In our model, the instructor would determine the data-field through his/her selection of texts. The course material would thus constitute the field. As such, cultural informants would not be existing social actors, but rather historical/literary fabrications.[34]

Phase 3: data collection and analysis

The third phase, the actual collection and analysis of data would be completed by the students employing our analytical method: The Cultural Inventory. Fieldwork as the collection of data would occur through interaction between the student-analyst and the chosen text. The Cultural Inventory would be utilized as a tool to facilitate this interaction. Thus the Cultural Inventory as a tool for mining the cultural content(s) of a text guides the analysis process through analytical categories arranged in stages. The method has been designed in a format to facilitate a cognitive analysis of cultural phenomena, the translation of these phenomena into etically comparable data, and finally the contexting of this data within a typology of cultures. Thus, phase 3 is completed by the student as s/he works through the text with the Cultural Inventory.

Phase 4: interpretation and evaluations

Because the Cultural Inventory guides the analysis process in its provision of set categories, the student interpretation is generated by working through the Inventory's stages. In other words, the completion of each stage represents an interpretation. The final interpretation and evaluative write-up provided by the student constitutes an account of the choices taken while progressing through the Cultural Inventory analysis; a cultural interpretation of a text complete with textual evidence. Phase 4 is thus a student generated narrative.

In the next chapter we will discuss our theoretical choices within the context of anthropological approaches to culture, as well as the theories chosen to address the problem of contexting cultural data within social structures. In chapter 3 we discuss Melford E. Spiro's conception of culture and his 'Hierarchy of Cognitive Salience' as these two contributions came to be foundational for determining the nominal concept of culture we employed to develop the Cultural Inventory. In the second half of chapter 3 we explain our nominal conception of culture, the model of culture which the Cultural Inventory has been designed to analyze. In chapter 4 the semiotic basis of our analysis design is explained. Chapter 4 also addresses how we have employed semiotic design to develop the translation-filter structure of the Cultural Inventory. In chapter 5 we define the parameters of an action sequence as a unit of cultural communication and provide a brief theoretical overview of the semiotic processes underlying the symbolic analysis presented by the first four Inventory filters. In chapter 6 we present Level 1 of the Cultural Inventory. In this chapter, the stages of the symbolic analysis are given with definitions and explanations of all the categories, filter by filter. To illustrate the symbolic analysis, an example analysis is performed for each filter explanation using a sample text. In chapter 7 we present Level 2 of the Cultural Inventory. In this chapter, the stages of the contexting process are outlined with definitions and explanations of all the categories. The contexting process is illustrated by continuing the example analysis on the sample text from chapter 6. In chapter 8 we present a summary of our conclusions and a complete worksheet copy of the Cultural Inventory.

Notes

[1] This understanding of culture pedagogy follows the suggestions of Byram who refers to the dimension as 'Cultural Studies': "Thus under the term 'Cultural Studies' we refer to any information, knowledge or attitudes about the foreign culture which is evident during foreign language teaching. 'Cultural Studies' is taught and learnt both overtly and implicitly, both consciously and incidentally, in much the same way as other components of the overt and hidden curriculum, and thus merits thorough discussion in curricular terms. It is an important feature of the viewpoint taken here that Cultural Studies should not be considered merely as incidental to the 'real business' of language teaching. To discuss its significance as part of the general education curriculum from this basis is therefore to venture a step beyond the dominant philosophy in

much foreign language teaching.[...we must...]seek to establish that Cultural Studies has a rightful place as part of language teaching, not just as an adjunct to language learning, not just as a means of creating better communication but as an integral component with appropriate aims and methods." Byram 3-4. We differ from Byram in our method for teaching cultural understanding and hence achieving cultural awareness. Byram and Esarte-Sarries choose a method that would develop the language learner as ethnographer, Byram and Esarte-Sarries 10-11.

[2] "The difficulties will arise from problems of practice, from issues in implementation, from the introduction of an additional discipline for teachers who were themselves taught to be linguists and literary critics rather than sociologists or social anthropologists.[...]We are at the moment not concerned with methodological techniques or theories of learning, although these will have to be dealt with in the course of time." Byram and Esarte-Sarries 11;13.

[3] Byram and Esarte-Sarries 11.

[4] The processes engaged by these approaches to culture remain at cognitive levels of knowledge, comprehension, and application. Keller points out that a behaviorist model [of culture]is unsatisfactory because it deals with surface phenomena, and suggests functional and Marxist models [of culture]for older pupils. In the course of this shift, pupils will move from the 'knowing how' – pragmalinguistic, competence oriented– to 'knowing that' which makes the learner conscious of the knowledge which the native has both consciously and unconsciously. But because Keller, with Kramer (1976), believes that cultural studies should have an emancipatory function, the knowledge that the learner acquires should also include a critical dimension, an understanding of underlying factors which goes beyond the everyday knowledge of the native." G. Keller, "Grundlegung einer neuen Kulturkunde als Orientierungsrahmen für Lehrerausbildung und Unterrichtspraxis," *Neusprachliche Mitteilungen aus Wissenschaft und Praxis* 4: 200-209, as noted in Byram 68.

[5] The reference here is to the lower and upper levels of cognitive awareness outlined in Bloom's and Krathwohl's Taxominies for the writing of educational objectives as printed in James W. Van der Zanden and Ann J. Pace, *Educational Psychology in Theory and Practice*, 2nd ed. (New York: Random House, 1984) 377-379. The lower three levels include knowledge, comprehension and application. The mistake might be located in some misconceived parallel between the target language ability of our students and their cognitive awareness. Although they may not be able to form a sentence in the target language they are capable of performing the cognitive skills of analysis, synthesis, and evaluation -Bloom's higher three levels. Our jobs as instructors is also to facilitate the perfection of these higher skills through our subject matter.

[6] Claire Kramsch, "Culture and constructs: Communicating Attitudes and Values in the Foreign Language Classroom," *Foreign Language Annals* 16(1983): 437-448. Pamala Koope, "Hints from the Classroom: Teaching

Culture and Language in the Beginning Foreign Language Class: Four strategies that Work," *Die Unterrichtspraxis* (Spring 1985): 158-169.

[7] The historical division of foreign language pedagogy into a 'Pre-Tourism and Tourism Age' is first noted in the work of Michael Byram and Veronica Esarte-Saaries. The forces behind the 'pre-tourism and tourism age' changes are socio-economic as explained by Byram and Esarte-Sarries. We add that the current age change, i.e. Global Information Age, has been brought on by the technological revolution. Language learners and their aims can be classified historically according to these ages. See Michael Byram and Veronica Esarte-Sarries, *Investigating Cultural Studies in Foreign Language Teaching: A Book for Teachers*, Multilingual Matters 62 (Philiadelphia: Multilingual Matters Ltd., 1991) 2.

[8] Claire Kramsch and Thomas Nolden, "Redefining Literacy in a Foreign Language," *Die Unterrichtspraxis* (Fall 1994): 28.

[9] Culture pedagogy within a FL program represents the ideal learning environment from which to impart cultural awareness and literacy. It could be argued that culture pedagogy would best be imparted through undergraduate courses in anthropology or sociology. Yet these courses are often structured around a series of disjointed case studies. FL programs, on the other hand, offer the continuity of studying one evolving system of meanings in its complexity providing a unique opportunity to explore culture from non-historical, historical, and trans-historical perspectives of analysis. Moreover, there is the issue of learner preference; for, in opting to study a foreign language, learners have already made an affective choice -based on their own interests and functional aims- to concentrate on a particular language-culture. Thus, the most affective environment, and therefore effective arena for promoting cultural awareness and literacy remains the FL program.

[10] The reference here is to the need recognized by Pfister and Poser to develop a culture analysis and measurement tool for use in foreign language classrooms. Guenter G. Pfister and Yvonne Poser, *Culture, Proficiency, and Control in FL Teaching* (Lanham: University Press of America, Inc., 1987) 43.

[11] Byram and Esarte-Sarries 10.

[12] See G.E. Nelson, "Focus on Undergraduate Programs: The German Major as Education," *Die Unterrichtspraxis* 7 (Spring 1974): 1-7.

[13] Byram and Esarte-Sarries 11.

[14] Byram and Estarte-Sarries 11.

[15] Richards and Rogers 63-67.

[16] As a linguist, Anthony applied his scheme to the subject of language, we have altered his model in reference to the subject of culture.

[17] Cited in Richards and Rogers, 15. From E. M. Anthony 1963, "Approach, method and technique in English Language Teaching" 17: 63-67.

[18] Byram and Esarte-Sarries: Rather than drawing on the products of ethnography and social anthropology –as it currently the case with sociology

and history– teacher and learner should become acquainted with the procedures and processes of this other discipline, 10.

[19] The focus is founded in the realization that there is a present need to attend to the three higher levels of Bloom's Taxonomy; namely, to teach the critical thinking skills of analysis, synthesis and evaluation across the curriculum.

[20] Byram 81. Here he follows the work of Williams and Leach in locating his concept of culture within the theories that consider culture as "expression of meaning".

[21] As Byram has noted D'Andre semi-humorously attributes the change to an afternoon in 1957: "We went from 'let's try to look at behaviour and describe it' to 'let's try to look at ideas'. On, I think, the same afternoon in 1957 you have papers by Chomsky and Miller and, in anthropology, Ward Goodenough. All signal an end to the era of 'Let's look at people's behavior and see what they do." Byram, 81. Quoted in Schweder and LeVine, 1984, 7.

[22] Ward Goodenough as cited in Byram 81.

[23] Ward Goodenough as cited in Byram 81-82.

[24] Clifford Geertz, *The Interpretation of Cultures* (New York: Basic Books, Inc. Publishers, 1973) 26.

[25] Geertz 89.

[26] Geertz 89.

[27] Geertz 24. Geertz refers to his interpretative approach as a semiotic approach. For our application of semiotic theory to our method of analysis see Chapter 4 of this study.

[28] See Pfister and Poser's Cultural Inventory in Pfister and Poser 66-67.

[29] We use the term 'ideology' here as described by Winfried Nöth, *Handbook of Semiotics* (Indianapolis: Indiana University Press, 1995) 377. Nöth writes: "In a value-neutral sense, ideology is any system of norms, values, beliefs, or weltanschauungen directing the social and political attitudes and actions of a group, a social class, or a society as a whole. In this value-neutral sense, ideology is mostly defined by American sociologists". 377.

[30] Kenneth A. Rice, "Culture and the Anthropology of Clifford Geertz," in *Geertz and Culture*, Anthropology Series: Studies in Cultural Analysis, ed. Vern Carroll (Ann Arbor: The University of Michigan Press, 1980) 3-23.

[31] We describe culture etically as an intellectual formation, and emically as an ideational system. This system manifests itself semiotically or as a symbolic system in varying degrees of explicitness. And, from a synchronic perspective we see a reciprocal relationship between this intellectual formation (culture) and the social formation (society). When the two are perceived as a 'gestalt' unit then the whole can be termed a socio-cultural system. As Geertz writes: "Culture is the fabric of meaning in terms of which human beings interpret their experience and guide their action; social structure is the form that action takes, the actually existing network of social relations." 145.

[32] Should the Inventory be utilized in language courses, then the "field" data might approach that of more traditional anthropological proportions for an

analysis of customs or descriptions/depictions of social rituals to actual participant observations. Byram and Esarte-Sarries suggest the use of more anthropological data collection procedures involving trips to the target culture countries; however, the logistical constraints of foreign language study in the United States greatly hamper such efforts.

[33] Hall, *Beyond Culture* 114.

[34] How far reaching the conclusions of the cultural analysis are will depend on the determination of the texts chosen. The analysis of texts which have a documented widespread social history (i.e. folksongs, legends, fairy tales, myths) might illustrate the more dominant socio-cultural reality of a particular period; while, a cultural analysis of texts from the "avant-garde" of a given period might illustrate a less dominant or minority reality. As many have shown, film and other non-print media also provide intriguing texts for cultural analysis. These are all issues pertaining to the future pedagogical applications of Cultural Inventory analysis.

Chapter 2

The Theoretical Approaches Represented in the Cultural Inventory

By observing material evidence and considering environmental factors, the materialist seeks to determine why meanings constitutive of a particular ideology take the form they do. Materialist approaches, following the scientific standards of replicability, favor the 'hard'[1] and empirically verifiable evidence of material products to support their anthropological inferences. The cultural content of these data is evaluated according to the explicit function of culture as a psychological adaptive system or socially sustaining ideology.

Idealist approaches view all cultural phenomena as representations of culture. As such, idealist approaches aim to integrate the behavioral –"what people do"– perspective of culture with the cognitive/symbolic –"what people think"– perspective, placing emphasis on the latter. By gathering verbal evidence from respondents, the cognitivists seek to determine which meanings constitute a particular culture. The cognitive branch of idealist approaches counters the materialist perspective by asserting that, with carefully designed methods, 'hard' and empirically verifiable evidence to support anthropological inferences can be collected from verbal phenomena, to be comparatively analyzed against material phenomena.

By observing material evidence and by gathering verbal evidence from informants, the symbolist interprets significant meanings as they are articulated through cultural phenomena. This more 'intuitive' branch of the idealist approach explicitly expands the overall representative function of cultural phenomena to that of sign-vehicles through which components of the meaning system (i.e. a particular belief) are expressed. As such, symbolists gather data through observation and informants, and interpret the shared meanings embodied in these data-sign-vehicles. When the anthropologist, as symbolist, explains the cultural content of observed data in terms of its implicit meaning with regards to a shared ideational system, anthropology is employed overtly as an interpretative science. Cognitivists who also wish to explain the cultural content of observable data in terms of its meaning with regards to a shared ideational system, but are unwilling to make the interpretative leap[2] of symbolists, have developed analytical strategies and cognitive categories to 'scientifically collect' and evaluate verbally articulated meanings; i.e. linguistic phenomena and espoused beliefs.

Although ultimately all anthropological research aims at drawing conclusions about meanings 'not limited to individual minds' (i.e. the shared beliefs/values of a group), the materialists focus on empirically verifiable material data as evidence of these conclusions, while the cognitivists focus on empirically verifiable mental data as evidence of these conclusions. For the symbolists, however, who interpret in-the-field, the practice of paradigmatically collecting and categorizing 'hard' data whether behavioral, artifactual or mental, is bypassed as these cultural phenomena are rendered, from the start, articulations of ideational phenomena to be interpreted by the anthropologist.

The summary of the Materialist/Idealist Approaches given in figure 2.1 was generated by grouping these two differing theoretical perspectives on the function of a cultural system according to their attendant 1) perspectives on the causality and function of culture and 2) sources for data collection. Because any anthropological study addresses both the psychological and social-interactional spheres of human activity simultaneously, distinguishing between the materialist and idealist approaches to culture according to either a behavioral or mental emphasis masks the beneficial analytical results of both approaches and hampers efforts to reconcile them within the framework of an expanded, and integrated paradigm. Thus the debate can be bridged by placing the approaches within an alternative theoretical context.

Figure 2.1 Materialist/Idealist Approach Summary

Materialist Approaches

The ideological element of culture operates as an adaptive psychological system which functions to maintain a social formation.

Culture consists of technological, social and ideological elements-technological elements effect the social; ideological elements are introduced as shared beliefs and perspectives to support, rationalize and transmit established social formations.

The ideological element of culture is inferred from behavioral phenomena- which exist 'outside individual minds.'

Idealist Approaches

Culture operates as a meaning system which functions to satisfy the human psychological need for identity.

Culture consists of an intellectual formation which is articulated, both explicitly and implicitly, through beliefs, behaviors and artifacts.

Culture is inferred from both mental (verbal) phenomena- which exist 'inside individual minds' and behavioral phenomena- which exist 'outside individual minds.' [cognitivist perspective]

When these two phenomena categories are perceived as cultural symbols, or the embodiments of shared meanings 'not limited to individual minds,' they are grouped as ideational products and can be thus interpreted directly. [symbolist perspective]

In *The Human Enterprise*, James Lett suggests that the adaptive and ideational distinction in analysis is based upon the artificial division of life and identity maintaining activities and, therefore, can be transcended if an integrated research paradigm is utilized. He enables a shift in context by first changing the terminology of the debate:

The adaptive approaches regard culture as a *socio-cultural system* [a larger configuration] composed of behaviors and their attendant beliefs, while the ideational approaches regard culture as *symbolic systems* composed of beliefs and their attendant behaviors.[3]

He suggests that the debate be restructured by considering symbolic (read cognitive) systems as "subsets of socio-cultural systems."[4]

Adaptive perspectives on culture emphasize social structure and the material environment as the generators of culture. Anthropologists who follow this branch of anthropology focus on 'culture' as it is determined in the elements of the social sphere. Observable data pertaining to social structure provides explicit evidence from which to infer descriptive and normative propositions as they pertain to a social actor's role and group membership; i.e. his/her function to adapt, or develop social identity. If the adaptive and ideational approaches are combined, as Lett suggests, then 'culture' as a cognitive/belief system can be viewed as a subset, perhaps core, of social systems. From this perspective, culture can be perceived as *one* of the strongest aspects contributing to the construction of social reality.[5] When this cognitive understanding of culture is combined with a social system, its relation to the social system appears close to the materialist notion of ideology; yet, the difference in conception developed for the Cultural Inventory analysis is that *all* cognitive systems perform equally as ideologies.[6]

When 'culture' is perceived as a cognitive system symbolically articulated through phenomena as cultural symbols and is thus analyzed according to its effect on the interpersonal relations of the social actor, one then speaks of the cognitive system as it is articulated, or externalized through a socio-*cultural* system. In this manner one can view 'culture' as a separate cognitive system on the one hand, while, on the other, conceiving of socio-cultural realities as the articulation of culture within patterned forms of human interaction.

From this view, it is possible –as Lett suggests– to reconcile the divisions between adaptive and ideational perspectives (materialist and idealist approaches) into one eclectic paradigm. A paradigm that employs materialist theoretical categories for analyzing cultural data in terms of adaptive questions, and idealist theoretical categories for analyzing cultural data in terms of ideational questions.

The separation of culture into physical-adaptive and psychological-ideational spheres is a theoretical construction designed to fit the limitations imposed by the act of analysis. But, the intertwining, in fact reciprocal relationship, of the life and identity spheres, with their corresponding behavior and thought dimensions, is more illustrative of the concepts socio-cultural realities and culture systems. Grasping the two levels of discourse existent in the study of culture becomes clearer when cognitive systems and socio-cultural realities are addressed separately. From this theoretical perspective we envisioned a method of analyzing cultural data first in terms of information pertaining to the cognitive or ideational formation of a social actor –his/her cognitive-culture system– and then in terms of how this objective content is, or is not reinforced within the context of the social actor's social formation –his/her socio-cultural reality.[7]

Our Theoretical Choices

The theories chosen as foundation for the Cultural Inventory as an approach to culture analysis were theories which 1) determine the elements and structure of culture systems, 2) determine the elements of socio-cultural realities, and 3) explain how these two systems interpenetrate. To determine the elements and structure of a culture system, theories from symbolic and cognitive branches of idealist approaches in anthropology were examined. And, to determine the elements of socio-cultural realities and their relationship to culture systems theories from functional approaches in sociology were examined.

The elements and structure of culture as cognitive systems

Both the symbolic and cognitive branches of anthropology,[8] although methodologically distinct, are compatibly linked in their orientation toward culture as a meaning system. In short, cognitivists view culture as cognitive codes which can be mapped through the collection and analysis of ethnographic data. They seek to analyze culture as the "patterned sets of meanings, learned and shared, that enable people to perceive, interpret and evaluate life."[9] Symbolic theorists interpret culture as meanings implicitly and explicitly embodied and expressed in beliefs, behaviors and artifacts. Focusing on culture as "public systems of shared meanings," symbolic theorists read cultural phenomena as texts.

In theory, the understanding of culture in symbolic anthropology, particularly in the work of Clifford Geertz, approximates a conception of culture which would correspond to what would be faced as source phenomena for the Cultural Inventory analysis; namely textual data.

Symbolist hold the premise that cultural phenomena can be read as texts, therefore texts could, in turn, be read as cultural phenomena. Because of their insistence on the symbolic nature of cultural phenomena, symbolists perspectives stretch the notion of culture beyond a system of actions and roles into a system of meanings embodied in actions. From the perspective of symbolic anthropology culture is, as Clifford Geertz's definition indicates,:

> an historically transmitted pattern of meanings, embodied in symbols, a system of inherited conceptions expressed in symbolic form by means of which men communicate, perpetuate and develop their knowledge about and attitudes towards life.[10]

In short, symbolists consider the behavioral, verbal and artifactual phenomena of man as symbols of culture. For symbolists, the task of anthropology is an interpretative, i.e. semiotic, endeavor. They read human phenomena as embodiments of values and beliefs which form the basis of a culture system:

> The concept of culture I espouse[...]is essentially a semiotic one. Believing, with Max Weber, that man is an animal suspended in webs of significance he himself has spun, I take culture to be those webs, and the analysis of it to be therefore not an experimental science in search of law but an interpretive one in search of meaning.[11]

Viewing culture as a system of meanings embodied in symbols corresponded to the Cultural Inventory analysis choice of source data – texts as artifactual elements of culture; perceiving anthropological analysis as an interpretive endeavor corresponded equally to the Cultural Inventory analysis pedagogical goals. However, further research found the symbolic approaches bereft of standardized analytical methods.[12] The 'symbolists' read cultural frames as texts, and explication comes through "thick description" but there are no reading strategies.[13] Instead, illations from observation are intuitive; the 'method' amounts to an interpretative description of cultural frames, and this lack of a 'systematic' method makes a replication of a symbolic analysis impossible.[14] Although symbolic analysis has added a more philosophical dimension to the field of anthropology,[15] it has been widely criticized for this lack of empirical validity.[16]

Therefore, for the Cultural Inventory method of analysis we adopted from symbolists, the hermeneutical premise that culture is, in fact, embodied in, and therefore symbolically mediated through altered and/or man-made phenomena. The adoption of this premise enabled texts, both historical and literary, to be considered as valid data sources for anthropological inquiry. But, the lack of a systematized procedure of interpretation and the lack of well-defined analytical categories made further use of symbolic analysis impractical for the pedagogical purposes of the Cultural Inventory.

Theories in the branch of cognitive anthropology were therefore examined. Cognitive theories supplied the analytical categories which helped determine the elements and structure of culture as meaning systems. As cognitive theorists analyze culture as cognitive codes, the usage of the term 'code,' in comparison to the symbolist term 'text,' indicates the systematizing goals of cognitive analysis. Like phenomenologists and symbolic anthropologists, cognitive anthropologists seek patterns of meaning or models of everyday cognition. But, their models are based on primary data, or what they term 'hard' ethnographic evidence collected in the field and, as Keesing states, their aim is to characterize these models in scientifically standardized, cognitive terms.[17]

> Cognitivists' engagement with such models does take them into domains already extensively explored by symbolists and others; but the insights this exploration is beginning to yield are complementary to, and in some important ways corrective of, those discovered along different paths.[18]

Unlike the symbolists, their work aims to provide systematic categorization of data. Such categorization, in turn, not only facilitates cross-study comparisons of data but also provides more explicitly verifiable evidential support for evaluative conclusions. As such, their studies satisfy the 'scientific' standards of empirical research in a manner in which the work of symbolists does not.

While both symbolists and cognitivist engage in interpretation –as do all anthropologists–, the symbolists' intuitive strategy of analysis could be surmounted by the cognitivists' paradigmatic analysis. It is, admittedly, a more 'scientific' procedure for dealing with culture as a meaning system. As Keesing's quote above explains, employing the terminology of cognitivists provides an additional structure to what has often been referred to as 'deep' culture.

We note, that from our perspective the conclusions drawn utilizing both cognitive and symbolic theories are equally 'scientifically' valid.

Symbolic analysis, however, is only generative for those who already possess a highly intuitive awareness and understanding of the elements, structure and cognitive function of culture. In other words, those who are already fluent in anthropological discourse. Since the method of analysis taught through the Cultural Inventory would have to rest on the assumption that students do not possess this training, the only viable theoretical approach to culture would be a combination of the symbolic and cognitive theories.

The problem of social context: elements of socio-cultural realities

The next task in developing a theoretical foundation for the Cultural Inventory involved choosing theories which both determined the elements of socio-cultural realities, and structurally explained how these elements interrelated with those of culture systems. It was clear that we would need to move beyond our chosen idealist approaches as one of the major criticisms of analyses within these approaches, whether cognitive or symbolic, is the failure of their study models and evaluative conclusions to relate "ideational" data back into the social – or human-to-human interactional– sphere.[19]

Even Geertz, as Wuthnow informs us, has conceded that a symbolic analysis of culture should always proceed in two stages, namely A) examining the symbols and B) relating the mentalist analysis to an overall social structure. Unfortunately, "the second of these [B], for whatever reasons has been generally ignored [by symbolists]."[20] And, commenting on the direction of cognitive analysis as it pertains to social theory, Keesing admits that "Cognitive anthropology grew up curiously innocent of social theory…".[21] Reminding cognitivist of their theoretical connections to phenomenology, Keesing suggests how theoretical paradigms from sociology might offer cognitive analysis additional frameworks within which to socially context ideational data:

> Past explorations of everyday cognition and common-sense constructions of reality include not only those of the phenomenological tradition and its off-shoots[…]but also those of the Marxist tradition and its off-shoots[…]. In this Marxist tradition, the realm of commonsense is viewed as refracting as well as reflecting[…]shaped by as well as shaping the realities of the social world.[22]

To address this deficiency in both cognitive and symbolic paradigms, sociological theories designed to investigate socio-cultural systems were consulted.[23]

In order to relate the Cultural Inventory's emerging cognitive-symbolic conception of culture to a social structure, it was necessary to locate a theory that would enable data collected and processed through a cognitive/symbolic analysis to then be contexted within a social structure: the A and B stages referred to by Geertz above. Thus, the ultimate goal for the Cultural Inventory as a student-centered analysis of cultural phenomena would culminate in the student determining an operative socio-cultural reality within which to context the data evidenced by the cultural phenomena; effectively combining the two spears noted by Wuthnow. As such, a theory was needed that would enable students to relate the conclusion of the cognitive-symbolic analysis to a social formation. But, this would require a theory which could match a cognitive(culture) system with a social structure thereby socially contexting the analyzed data. Such a theory would bridge the culture-social formation gap evident in cognitive-symbolic studies.

It was clear that a theoretical framework was needed to evaluate symbolic/cognitive findings within a social context, with culture as a cognitive system viewed not as equivalent to, but rather as a subset of a socio-cultural reality. Taken in this sense, a culture system could continue to denote a shared meaning system materialized through symbolic forms; while the prefix "socio-" (emphasizing patterns of human interaction) would provide a social context for such a meaning system.

The 'Grid-group Theory' originated by Mary Douglas[24] and expanded in the 'Cultural Theory' of Michael Thompson, Richard Ellis and Aaron Wildavsky[25] to suited the needs as listed above. For, in developing 'Grid-group Theory' Douglas' objective was to devise a method whereby the individual, or social actor, could be set in a social context. The theory then is,

> [...]a method of identifying cultural bias, of finding an array of beliefs locked together into relational patterns. [For,] The beliefs must be treated as part of the action, and not separated from it as in so many theories of social action. The action or social context, is placed on a two-dimensional map[...][26]

The two dimensions comprising Douglas' theory are referred to as 'group' and 'grid' and constitute the "two most general spheres of action limited by social order" namely, "whom one interacts with" as group and "how one interacts with them"[27] as grid. Accordingly, social environments can be classified "according to the degree to which individual freedom is restricted"[28] relative to these two dimensions or spheres of action. In this way, "the grid/group classification is intended to have the sort of general applicability necessary for analyzing the relationship of the social and symbolic orders."[29] Thus, Douglas' 'Grid-group Theory' and the typology it generates "accounts for the distribution of beliefs according to variation in social experience"[30] but taken from a Cultural Inventory perspective, use of the typology would enable cultural data to be socially context. For, when the social actor is analyzed within the dimensions of grid and group s/he is positioned within a quadrant of a typology. From the application of 'Grid-Group Theory' Douglas generated a typology of 4 cells, (A,B,C,D)[31] each representing a different cosmological possibility (see figure 2.2).

Figure 2.2 Grid-Group Typology

	grid -	grid +
group –	A	B
group +	D	C

The grid/group typology suggests that there are as few as four prototypical patterns of culture. Each consists of a characteristic behavioral pattern and an accompanying justificatory cosmology.[32]

Douglas' 'Grid-group Theory' was chosen for the Cultural Inventory because of the universal applicability of the dimensions grid and group; for, the four categories, or cells of the framework are formed from the theoretical dimensions of 'grid' and 'group' rather than derived "ad hoc from observation."[33] The uniqueness of the method as a typology is that it generalizes and limits the analytical possibilities without compromising the substance of the analysis: "...what the theory does mean is that the number of cultural packages among which people choose when they settle for any particular kind of social environment is limited."[34] Both the applicability of the dimensions grid and group to the analytical needs of the Cultural Inventory, and the generalizing aim of typology theory[35] made typologizing data the answer to determining a social context for culture. Indeed, Douglas captures the implications and benefits of 'Grid-group Theory' to the analysis method: "...the four extreme grid/group positions on the diagram are liable to be stable types,[...]their way of life [...] is at the same time inevitably a way of thought."[36] And, while 'Grid-group Theory' provides a generalized and universal structure with which to categorize the 'culture' of social actors, it was not developed as sociological determinism. It, rather, simply reveals the chosen social context as reflected through analysis of data within the two dimensions: "As a theory it [grid-group theory] has very little to say about people's choices between social forms; [...] All that and more has to be filled in for any particular historical case."[37] For, as Gross and Rayner continue:

> What grid/group analysis does assume, however, is first, that cultural bias is unavoidable and second, that there is a limited number of cultural packages from which people are free to choose when they settle for any particular style of social organization.[38]

Finally, and most importantly, in the choice to incorporate 'Grid-group Theory' were Douglas' comments on what typology analysis could achieve:

> It [grid-group theory] can expose the normally invisible screen through which culture lets options be perceived. It [grid-group theory] means that most values and beliefs can be analyzed as part of society instead of as a separate cultural sphere.[39]

From cells to socio-cultural realities

With Douglas' 'Grid-group Theory,' cultural data gathered from a symbolic analysis using the first level of the Cultural Inventory could be socially contexted. However, the typology is meant as a method for only determining, and not defining a particular social context. Therefore, locating a theory that had expanded the A-B-C-D cells of Douglas' 'Grid-Group Theory' into socio-cultural realities would make it possible for students *to define* a social context for data gathered from a cultural analysis.

The 'Cultural Theory,' or rather 'Sociocultural Viability Theory' of Thompson, Ellis, and Wildavsky presented definitions for the quadrants of Douglas' 'Grid-group typology.' Defining the quadrants was key to their theory since their goal was to "present a theory of sociocultural viability that explains how ways-of-life (i.e. the quadrants) maintain (and fail to maintain)themselves."[40] To define the 'ways of life' upon which their theory of socio-cultural viability is based they applied the theory of Douglas' typology in the following manner:

> *Cultural bias* [grid] refers to shared values and beliefs. *Social relations* [group] are defined as patterns of interpersonal relations. When we wish to designate a viable combination of social relations and cultural bias we speak of *a way of life*. [cell A, B, C, or D][41]

For the analytical and pedagogical purposes of the Cultural Inventory, the 'ways of life' upon which their theory is based, provide the four combinations of culture and social formation used to define the four typology quadrants:

> The term *sociocultural viability theory* has the advantage of indicating to the reader that ways of life are composed of both social relations and cultural biases (hence socio-cultural) and that only a limited number of combinations of cultural biases and social relations are sustainable (hence viable).[42]

In their theory they set out to prove the "compatibility condition;" namely, that "The viability of a way of life[…]depends upon a mutually supportive relationship between a particular cultural bias and a particular pattern of social relations…".[43] By so applying the Douglas' typology, Thompson, Ellis, and Wildavsky were able to determine operative 'ways of life' –in the Cultural Inventory they are referred to as socio-cultural realities– for each of the four cells[44] located within Douglas' scheme. And, from the "compatibility condition" noted above, Thompson, Ellis and Wildavsky found that…

> Five and only five ways of life –hierarchy, egalitarianism, fatalism, individualism, and autonomy– meet these conditions of viability.[45] […For, as they show,…]biases and relations cannot be mixed and matched.[46]

The diagram depicted in figure 2.3 represents Thompson, Ellis, and Wildavsky's expansion of the 'Grid-group Typology'[47]: Incorporating the vignettes from the theory of Thompson, Ellis, Wildavsky as quadrant definitions for the Cultural Inventory produced socio-cultural-realities with which to replace Douglas' cells.

Figure 2.3 Way of Life Vignettes

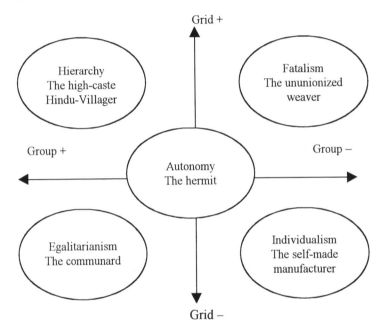

The 'Theory of Sociocultural Viability', and the vignette definitions do not address the origin of a particular 'way of life.' The vignette definitions are rather aimed at description and bypass the materialist/idealist debate of anthropology therefore achieving an integrated paradigm,

> Causal priority, in our conception of ways of life, is given neither to cultural bias nor to social relations. Rather each is essential to the other. Relations and biases are reciprocal, interacting, and mutually reinforcing: adherence to a certain pattern of social relationships generates a distinctive way of looking at the world; adherence to a certain worldview legitimizes a corresponding type of social relations.

As in the case of the chicken and the egg; it is sufficient to show that cultural biases and social relations are responsible for one another, without confronting the issue of which came first.[48]

Moreover, as Thompson, Ellis, and Wildavsky note, Douglas' 'Grid-group Theory' and the typology method/framework it enables is a superior sociological theory because it allows for five modes of organization. And,

> Although 5 may seem [...] an impossibly small number of ways of life, this number more than doubles the amount of conceptual variety available in existing theories of social organization.[...]the great social theorists of the past rarely went beyond the development from hierarchy to individualism.[49]

The application for the goals of textual analysis involving the Cultural Inventory rests in the "requisite variety condition" of 'Cultural Theory' which argues that:

> [...]each way of life depends upon each of the four rival ways of life for survival,[...]there must be at least five ways of life in existence. This we refer to as the requisite variety condition, that is, there may be more than five ways of life, but there cannot be fewer. [However]That no way of life can exist alone does not mean that every way of life will be equally represented within a single [textual work] country at a given point in time.[50]

This 'requisite variety condition' of 'Cultural Theory' is particularly intriguing for it provides the basis and categories for enabling students to analyze and ultimately translate cultural misunderstandings, as misunderstandings between vying socio-cultural realities. As such, the method put forth in the Cultural Inventory would move the level of students' culture consciousness beyond that of surface particularities, as the Cultural Inventory has been designed to first facilitate an analysis of culture as the cognitive system underlying human interactions and to secondly enable the analysis to be contexted within socio-cultural realities. For, in learning the Cultural Inventory as an analysis method, it becomes apparent that the basic convictions underlying human interactions, i.e. core assumptions, are reducible to five viable ways of life. Thus, through employing the Cultural Inventory method to analyze culture students will develop an awareness that "...although nations and neighborhoods, tribes and races, have their distinctive sets of values, beliefs, and habits, their basic convictions about life are reducible to only a few cultural biases."[51]

Having thus decided on a symbolic-cognitive approach to culture and having located sociological theories that would enable social context, via grid-group, to be determined and then via ways-of-life to be defined as socio-cultural realities, the Cultural Inventory was constructed as an analysis method designed to address human interaction as symbolic manifestations of culture and social actors as manifestations of socio-cultural realities. The method of analysis present by the Cultural Inventory therefore views culture as systems of meanings embodied in symbols, and socio-cultural realities as systems of interpersonal relations which originate from, and reciprocally reflect their respective culture.

Notes

[1] While the insistence that hard evidence may be considered more appropriate for anthropological inquiry from the viewpoint of scientific discourse strategies, it should be noted that interpretation is inherent in anthropological method. Therefore, conceptions, models and studies of cultures will vary depending on the interpreter until, or unless some standard format of interpretation procedure is devised. Until this point, it is only necessary that the interpretations be supported by the evidence gathered whether 'hard' or otherwise.

[2] This leap is viewed by cognitivist and materialist as intuitive and non-verifiable therefore non-scientific. That is not to say however, that the evaluations and conclusions made by symbolists are found to be incorrect.

[3] Lett 59. It should be noted that Lett here refers to symbolic anthropology in general as the idealist approach. His usage of the term symbolic systems refers to culture as a meaning system and not necessarily the status of cultural phenomena as symbolic-vehicles, although this is implied.

[4] Lett 59 "[...]the symbolic anthropologists have a strong argument in their favor for calling symbolic systems 'culture' and sociocultural systems 'sociocultural system' –after all, it is the human capacity for symbolic communication [read culture] that distinguishes human sociocultural systems from other primate social systems." Indeed, this is what Spiro also suggests as the strategy for reconciling the necessity to relate cognitive systems to larger configurations.

[5] Culture as a symbolically expressed intellectual formation is perhaps the single most important aspect. Experience could be named the second. For, experience provides the dialectical spark –often confronting us with an 'antithesis' to our cultural 'thesis.' Depending, this force can be perceived of as constituting a destructive or revelation nature. It is the potential catalyst of 'culture shock;' figuratively shaking the foundations of our cultural reality. This force of learning we have termed 'experience' can spring from three realms: environmental sources –that of the natural world outside the boundaries of the (human) socio-cultural worlds; human sources –that of alternate socio-cultural realities; or transcendental/mystical sources –that beyond what we currently perceive of the natural and human worlds.

[6] There is a tendency for Marxist theories to employ the term ideology for non-marxist cognitive systems. See Terry Eagleton "What is Ideology," *An Introduction to Ideology* (New York: Verso, 1994) 1-31. However, the term ideology as we employ it refers to all cognitive systems equally.

[7] Theories which address the mutually reciprocal relationship between these 'two' systems have appeared. We note particularly the 'Sociocultural Viability Theory' of Thompson, Ellis, and Wildavsky. But this theory was not designed to address the analysis of the cultural systems, instead its goal is to examine how socio-cultural realities operate. The theory thus presents pre-constructed cognitive-social formations, or as they are referred to: "ways of life." We have employed the 'ways of life' as a theoretical base for defining the 'socio-cultural realities' used to context the sequence actor(s) in the Level II Analysis of the Cultural Inventory. Thus, in an attempt to address both systems we have created 2 levels of analysis for the Cultural Inventory: Level I designed to analyze action sequences for their culture content-symbolic systems and Level II designed to analyze the social context of the culture in the action sequence-socio-cultural system.

[8] For convenience we refer to symbolic anthropology as a branch, but as Langness notes, "...there are no genuine schools of British, French, or American symbolic anthropology although individual scholars, Levi-Strauss and Schneider for example have attracted and influenced many others," 163. Symbolic Anthropology has also been referred to as semiotic anthropology –a clue which became highly influential in the structural design of our method.

[9] Lett 58.

[10] Clifford Geertz, *The Interpretation of Cultures* (New York: Basic Books, Inc. Publishers,1973) 89. "Expressed in symbolic form" is the key phrase here for our technique of cultural analysis. What culture truly is for the symbolist is the cognitive system of assumptions in tact below the conscious surface of the individual and from which are generated the 'sponsor thoughts' for the creation of actions, artifacts and verbalizations.

[11] Geertz 5.

[12] Langness 162. Langness writes: "Geertz's approach, whatever its elegance, is primarily descriptive and does not lead to much in the way of theoretical formulations.[...]His theory lacks criteria for evaluating interpretations. Thus, how would anyone know whether any given interpretation is good or bad, valid or invalid or even useful? And how would interpretive anthropologists be able to evaluate other interpretations or explanations of the same thing?"

[13] The only guidelines for thick description are noted by Langness: "Thick description is what an anthropologist does when he or she carefully analyzed ethnographic detail, breaking it down further and further to get at the meaning of it for the members of the culture- the native's point of view.[...]Geertz acknowledges that interpretation is not predicative, nor is it verifiable." 162.

[14] Robert Wuthnow, *Meaning and Moral Order: Explorations in Cultural Analysis* (Berkeley: University of California Press, 1987) 47. Wuthnow goes much deeper into the limitations of symbolic analysis however the main point to be stressed for our purposes deals with systematic analysis: "It is primarily as a basis of systematic inquiry, however, that the neoclassical tradition runs into difficulties. [...]The methodological frustrations derive from the fact that phenomenology and hermeneutics, as practices in sociology [and anthropology], have defied systematization and have explicitly denied efforts to arrive at replicable knowledge."

[15] Wuthknow 36-37; 42. Wuthnow writes: "In the work of theorists like Berger, Bellah, and Geertz, who led the way in articulating an alternative perspective on culture, the problem of meaning became the essential element salvaged from the classical tradition." 36. [Marx, Durkheim and Weber]...Neoclassical theorists in a sense circumvented the dualistic distinction between subject and object by emphasizing the 'symbolically constructed' character of all reality, both subjective and objective. This emphasis relativized the objectivity of the external world by demonstrating that it, no less than the subjective world, was created symbolically." 37. "The major methodological approaches that emerged within the neoclassical tradition were phenomenology and hermeneutics." 42.

[16] Some of the standardization problems with symbolic analysis are noted in Shweder and LeVine's "Preview" in *Culture Theory*– we will see that it is precisely these issues which cognitive anthropology seeks to address; Shweder and LeVine write: "...as Geertz himself has noted, 'terms such as meaning, symbol and conception cry out for explication [Geertz 1973:89]' Indeed it is around such questions -what kinds of meanings are there: what kinds of concepts are there, what kinds of symbols are there, how does historical transmission take place, is this or that meaning, concept or symbol historically transmitted or not, what is this or that person's or people's conception of this or that, how are ideas and symbols related to attitudes, feelings, and behavior- that all of the quarrelling, much of it fruitful, goes on." 7.

[17] Roger M. Keesing, "Models, 'Folk' and 'Cultural': Paradigms Regained?," *Cultural Models in Language and Thought*, ed. Dorothy Holland and Naomi Quinn (New York: Cambridge University Press, 1987) 375-376. Keesing writes: "A good deal of Geertz's work, and, of much of phenomenology (Husserl, Schutz, Heidegger, Merleau-Ponty) is precisely about models of everyday cognition: about what thinking, remembering, understanding, seeing, communicating, getting angry, the passage of time are, experientially, to human beings; and, more or less explicitly, how they are culturally constructed, how they are shaped by language and metaphor.[...]Are putatively cognitive accounts of models of the mind more perceptive, systematic, or powerful[...]? Where symbolists mainly view their task as interpretive, cognitivists mainly view theirs as scientific. For the latter, the primary data -transcribed tapes of interviews or other discourse or other "hard" records of the behavior of individuals- are crucial, and the inferences drawn from them systematic and explicit.[...]It is misleading that Geertz's metaphor of culture as text to be read suggests close convergence: The texts of the cognitivist exploring models of everyday reality mainly comprise what individual subjects said and did."

[18] Keesing 376.

[19] In terms of symbolic anthropology, Wuthnow writes: "...another limitation of neoclassical approaches, compared with classical approaches, has to do with reintroducing the relations between culture and social structure." 49.

[20] Wuthnow 49.

[21] Keesing 376.

[22] Keesing 377. It should be noted here that the references to Marxist traditions and its off-shoots pertains to one of the major contributions of Marxist analysis; namely the inherent reciprocal relationships between cultural and social systems and the factors which play in maintaining and/or altering these relationships.

[23] The reader should note that inherent in our use of the term socio-cultural systems is the fact that we did not move wholly to sociology and theories pertaining to social systems- but rather to those theories which attempted to address the combination of adaptive-ideational/ life-identity questions. We found our theories in what the British term social anthropology and its sociological counterpart in the U.S.

[24] Mary Douglas, "Introduction to Grid/Group Analysis," *Essays in the Sociology of Perception*, ed. Mary Douglas (Boston: Routledge and Kegan Paul, 1982) 4.

[25] Michael Thompson, Richard Ellis, and Aaron Wildavsky, *Cultural Theory* (Boulder: Westview Press, 1990).

[26] Mary Douglas, *Cultural Bias*, Royal Anthropological Institute of Great Britain and Ireland no. 35 (London: Royal Anthropological Institute, 1978) 14.

[27] David Ostrander, "One- and Two-Dimensional Models of the Distribution of Beliefs," *Essays in the Sociology of Perception* ed. Mary Douglas (Boston: Routledge and Kegan Paul, 1982) 14.

[28] Ostrander 14.

[29] Ostrander 14.

[30] Ostrander 15.

[31] We include here Douglas' short explanation of the cells in the typology. We have adapted descriptions of grid and group to suit an implementation of the typology for our method of analysis and pedagogical goals. As will be shown in Synthesis I, the Interpersonal Filter, and Synthesis 2 of the Cultural Inventory analysis (Chapter 7), the terms grid and group are sufficiently general so as to promote universal applicability. The inclusion of the cell descriptions here is to give the reader an indication of how the typology can function. Douglas writes: "Square A (low grid, low group) allows options for negotiating contracts or choosing allies and in consequence it also allows for individual mobility up and down whatever the current scale of prestige and influence. Square B (high grid, low group) is the environment which ascribes closely the way an individual may behave. In any complex society some categories of people are going to find themselves relegated here to do as they are told, without the protection and privileges of group membership. Square C (high grid, high group) is the environment of large institutions where loyalty is rewarded and hierarchy respected: an individual knows his place in a world that is securely bounded and stratified. Finally, square D (low grid, high group) is defined by the terms of the analysis as a form of society in which only the external group boundary is clear: by definition all other statuses are ambiguous and open to negotiation." Douglas, "Introduction to Grid/Group Analysis" 4.

[32] Mary Douglas, "Introduction," in Jonathan L. Gross and Steve Rayner, *Measuring Culture: A Paradigm for the Analysis of Social Organization* (New York: Columbia University Press, 1985) x.

[33] Thompson, Ellis, and Wildavsky 14.

[34] Douglas, "Introduction to Grid/Group Analysis" 3.

[35] As Douglas states: "...without typologising there can be no generalizing." Douglas, *Cultural Bias* 15.

[36] Douglas, "Introduction to Grid/Group Analysis" 5.

[37] Douglas, "Introduction to Grid/Group Analysis" 7.

[38] Gross and Rayner 18. The claims to the limited number of possibilities is what makes grid-group theory attractive, as well as its universal applicability. As Gross and Rayner explain: "General claims that social environment affect behavior and attitudes are unassailable, However, grid/group theory asserts a highly specific hypothesis, which leaves it accessible to challenge. This hypothesis is that different organizations with the same combinations of grid and group scores will reflect the same cultural patterns of behavior and

attitudes, whether the locality is an African village, a New York corporate office, or a submarine." Gross and Rayner x. And, although 4 prototypical patterns of culture seem a small number it doubles the patterns recognized in traditional sociology; see note 88 this chapter.

[39] Douglas, "Introduction to Grid/Group Analysis" 7.

[40] Thompson, Ellis, and Wildavsky 1.

[41] Thompson, Ellis, and Wildavsky 1.

[42] Thompson, Ellis, and Wildavsky note 5, 15.

[43] Thompson, Ellis, and Wildavsky 2.

[44] There is a fifth way of life which is defined as a negation of the other four. Because a fifth quadrant in not located on the "Grid-group Typology" we only adopted the four 'way of life' which corresponded to Douglas' theory.

[45] Thompson, Ellis, and Wildavsky 3.

[46] Thompson, Ellis, and Wildavsky 2.

[47] We present this version of the '5 ways of life' following the figure generated by Thompson, Ellis and Wildavsky 8. In terms of the Cultural Inventory, we have only chosen to focus on the four main quadrants, leaving out the 'way of life' classified as 'Autonomy'.

[48] Thompson, Ellis, and Wildavsky 1.

[49] Thompson, Ellis, and Widlavsky 3.

[50] Thompson, Ellis, and Widlavsky 4.

[51] Thompson, Ellis, and Wildavsky 5.

Chapter 3

A Conception of Culture: the nominal definition developed for the Cultural Inventory

In *The Study of Culture* L.L. Langness comments on the theoretical position of Melford E. Spiro's work by stating that it "offers what is now perhaps the most sophisticated means we have in psychological anthropology for attempting to actually relate the acts of individuals to culture."[1] Spiro's 'conception of culture' as discussed in *Culture and Human Nature: Theoretical Papers of Melford E. Spiro,* and particularly regarding the implications for what his conception does not designate as culture, provided the foundation for determining the form and content of the nominal concept of culture put forth in this current study. Therefore, to theoretically context the model of culture outlined in the second section of this chapter the axioms of Spiro pertinent to the conception in their entirety are included here. Spiro views culture as a cognitive system consisting of descriptive and normative propositions about reality:

> "culture" designates a cognitive system, that is, a set of "propositions," both descriptive (e.g., 'the planet earth sits on the back of a turtle') and normative (e.g., 'it is wrong to kill'), about nature, man and society that are embedded in interlocking higher-order networks and configurations.[2]

From this definition it is very clear that Spiro designates only a cognitive system as culture. We follow Spiro in this designation. Defining culture solely as a cognitive system then provides the basis for distinguishing between culture and the products of human interaction mediated by culture. To underscore the mediated essence of cultural products and to designate culture as *the mediation mechanism* of this essence, Spiro described the products of human interaction as being "culturally constituted," i.e. imbued with, or in a semiotic relationship to culture, but not culture per se: "The conflation of culture and culturally constituted phenomena is based on a confusion of logical types of cause with effect, structure with function, producer with product."[3]

The axioms used to develop the Cultural Inventory's nominal conception of culture are listed below in their relevance to what Spiro outlines as four categories of culturally constituted phenomena, namely behavior, social structure, thoughts and emotions. In order to illustrate the borrowings, each of Spiro's italicized points is cross listed with the nominal definition's corresponding component in brackets.[4]

A: *Actions*: [(non)verbal-behavioral products]

[…] although by this conception culture is obviously an important – though only one– determinant of behavior, culture as such does not consist of behavior.[5]

B: *Social Formation* [socio-cultural reality]

[…]although culture –to broaden this [behavior] implication– includes propositions referring to social structure, social organization, social behavior, and the like, culture as such does not consist of them.[6]

Thinking and Feeling [mediation, or the activity of sponsor thoughts]

Although not a part of culture, thinking and feeling are often determined by culture. That is, we most often think by means of the concepts comprising cultural propositions, and our emotions are often aroused by them; in short, many of our thoughts and emotions are (what might be termed) 'culturally constituted.'[7]

C: *Emotions* [mental products–sponsor thoughts]

[…]although many cultural propositions have emotional antecedents, and although others have emotional consequences –they arouse emotional responses in social actors– and although some even prescribe the proper conditions for the expression of emotions, culture as such[...]does not consist of emotions.[8]

D: *Thoughts* [mental products–sponsor thoughts]
[...]although I have defined 'culture' as a cognitive system– culture does not consist of thought (thinking) any more than it consists of emotion (feeling).[...]thinking and feeling are properties of persons[...][9]

As the preceding axioms state, culture does not consist of behavior, social formation, feelings/emotions or thoughts. It is, rather, the determinant of these human actions. For, Spiro, very clear in holding to a cognitive concept of culture, maintained this concept to refer only to a set of descriptive and normative propositions and was therefore able to explain the social, mental/emotional, and behavioral/emotional aspects of human interaction as generated from, or as consequences of these propositions. It is from these statements that one develops a distinction between culture as mediation mechanism (or cause – described as propositions when analyzed) and culturally constituted phenomena- as products; ideational, mental, (non)verbal-behavioral and artifactual.[10]

Most important for the development of a conception of culture, then, were Spiro's axioms regarding the distinction between culture and culturally constituted phenomena. And to further support a distinction between culture as a cognitive 'set of propositions' and beliefs, thoughts, behaviors, and artifacts as culturally constituted phenomena, it is helpful to note Spiro's theory of cultural acquisition as it is through his theory of cultural acquisition that the distinction between culture and culturally constituted phenomena can be best contexted and understood.

Spiro's theory of cultural acquisition, the 'Hierarchy of Cognitive Salience,' presents a description of the cognitive stages constituting the acquisition process by social actors of culture; i.e. the acquisition process of propositions as core beliefs/values.[11] Each stage of the 'Hierarchy' represents a different level of cognitive consequence and awareness relative to the social actor's internalization of any given cultural proposition. The 'Hierarchy' is arranged in descending intensity of cognitive saliency; that is, as the cognitive consequence, or saliency, of a proposition increases, the social actor's awareness of the proposition as a culturally generated belief/value decreases.

Figure 3.1 Excerpts from Spiro's Hierarchy of Cognitive Salience

> *Level I*: [least salient] As a result of normal enculturative processes, social actors, *learn about the propositions*, they acquire an "acquaintance" with them[...].
>
> *Level II*: In addition to learning about the propositions, the actors also *understand their traditional meanings* as they are interpreted, for example, in authoritative texts or by recognized specialists.
>
> *Level III*: Understanding their traditional meanings, the actors *"internalize" the propositions* –they hold them to be true, correct, or right. It is only then that they are acquired *as personal beliefs*. The transformation of a cultural proposition into a culturally constituted belief does not in itself, however, indicate that it importantly affects the manner in which the actors conduct their lives, which leads to the fourth level.
>
> *Level IV*: As *culturally constituted beliefs*, cultural propositions inform the behavioral environment of social actors, serving to *structure* their *perceptual worlds and* hence, to *guide* their *actions*.
>
> *Level V*: [most salient] At this level, *culturally constituted beliefs* serve not only to guide but to *instigate action*, that is, they posses emotional and motivational, as well as cognitive, salience.[12]

The descending order of the 'Hierarchy' captures what has come to be known as the surface-to-deep characteristics of culture; namely, the more internalized a proposition becomes, the deeper or less cognitively aware the social actor is of a distinction between that proposition and his/her own personal beliefs/values. This condition consequently presents the reason for the difficulty of analytically "getting at" deep-culture, its highly symbolic nature, and why Geertz referred to such analysis as "thick-description".[13] The condition also presents the basis for the filter structure of an analytical method- the Cultural Inventory.

We cite the stages of Spiro's 'Hierarchy' because his stages are helpful in understanding the semiotic nature of cultural communication; namely, how it is that social actors are the agents of culture. For, they are the route, the access to these core (deep) assumptions (propositions) which surface through their behaviors, verbalizations[14] and artifacts as culturally constituted phenomena. The stages are also instrumental in underscoring the difference between culture and cultural phenomena –often referenced as the distinction between surface culture (Spiro's culturally constituted phenomena) and deep culture (Spiro's culture proper –a cognitive system). And so, while Spiro's culture/cultural phenomena distinction was instrumental in the development of a form-content model of culture which maintains a distinction between culture and cultural products corresponding to Spiro's theory, his 'Hierarchy,' which explains the operative nature of culture as a cognitive system, was also instrumental in the development of an analytical method.

In addition, because Spiro's 'Hierarchy' explains the internalization of a proposition as a psychological event it provides the basis for illustrating how culture –when defined as a cognitive set of propositions– can be seen to serve both as an adaptive and ideational system:

> to say that the propositions comprising culture are "traditional" propositions is to say that culture is quintessentially a historical product. [adaptive system] [...]Nevertheless, once a cultural proposition is acquired as a personal belief by social actors, its acquisition is a psychological event, and that event requires a "psychological" explanation.[15] [...]When cultural propositions are learned by social actors, they become personal thoughts that, like emotions, are private; they are now "located" in the mind. However, because these private thoughts are derived from, though they may be less than isomorphic with, cultural propositions, they [i.e. the thoughts] are culturally constituted.[16] [ideational system]

By delineating the various levels of internalization whereby a cultural proposition is acquired as a personal belief, Spiro's 'Hierarchy of Cognitive Salience' provides the idea to approach culture analysis on various levels, and highlights the necessity to develop a nominal study model of culture that remains true to a cognitive understanding of culture while addressing the multiple levels by which it surfaces as manifested products. His 'Hierarchy' further provides an explanation for enculturation and conversely the process whereby a culture shift may occur: "To learn a culture is to acquire its propositions; to be enculturated is, in addition, *to* "internalize" them as personal beliefs, that is, as propositions that are thought to be true, proper, or right."[17] For analysis purposes Spiro's above description of enculturaltion points to the necessity to address the relationship between culture, as cognitive propositions, and the social context, or interactions, which either invest them with or divest them of meaning:

> In learning a foreign culture a non-native may acquire as firm a grasp of the meanings of culture as a native, but not having been socialized in the group, he or she has not had those social experiences that, alone,

serve to invest the culture with those surplus meanings [18] [i.e. serve to substantiate the propositions as part of a socio-cultural reality].

This quote from Spiro pertaining to the social experiences that serve to invest the culture corresponds directly to the 'compatibility condition' of 'Sociocultural Viability' as noted by Thompson, Ellis, and Wildavsky; namely, that..."The viability of a way of life[...]depends upon a mutually supportive relationship between a particular cultural bias and a particular pattern of social relations...".[19] The need to address the 'social context' in which culture is activated and reinforced was also instrumental in formulating the two main levels of Cultural Inventory analysis, Level I focuses on symbolic analysis and is designed to access 'culture' as cognitive propositions,[20] Level II focuses on socially contexting the results of a symbolic analysis and is designed to determine the social context in and through which it (culture) is tested as a reality.[21]

It remains, now to provide Spiro's theory on the relationship between culture and the social world, there is a clear distinction which we have chosen to follow:

> If "culture" refers to traditional propositions about nature, [time, space],[22] man, and society, then "society," as I am using the term, refers to traditional forms of social relations, in which "social" refers to a range extending from a dyad to a nation-state.[23]

In Spiro's work one finds the most compelling base argument for retaining the term culture to refer only to intellectual formations, or in his terms cognitive systems. And, we have adopted his term proposition, with both qualifiers: descriptive and normative, as analytical terminologies to refer to the structure, or component parts, of culture as a cognitive system. Further, one keeps the concept of social formation to reference the systems of interpersonal relations that provide the sphere, or context, in which culture is manifested and tested. Additionally, when the two are brought together, one can thus speak of a socio-cultural reality to use the term derived from Lett and implemented in the 'Theory of Sociocultural Viability' developed in the work of Thompson, Ellis, and Wildavsky.

A Conception of Culture

In an attempt to promote consistent base usage of the term 'culture' in anthropological studies, Kenneth Rice sought to determine the basic components which comprised anthropological conceptions of culture.[24]

> If every conception of culture contained certain basic components or aspects, components or aspects which made it a conception of culture and not a conception of something else, we could use these components as a framework for organizing our analysis.[25]

In his work, Rice proposed that anthropological studies address four different components of culture:

> I propose that we view culture concepts as having (at least) four components: the focal, the phenomenal, the temporal and the situational.[...] These components are not entirely separable parts,[...], but rather are "aspects" or "dimensions" of a concept of culture. Each aspect is the product of a different point of view, a different way of looking at a concept of culture.[26]

His findings lead to the formulation of a generic template, which he used to determine the theoretical orientation of various conceptions of culture. Rice's template is composed of a list of theoretical questions designed to aid anthropologists in formulating the focal, phenomenal, temporal, and situational aspects of their inquiries prior to fieldwork. The questions of the template have been formulated to distinguish "the essential points of a conception of culture without obscuring that conception's particular character and its particular implications for analysis."[27] Designed thus as a generic guideline, Rice's template represents the "skeletal form of *any* concept of culture."[28]

> At the focal dimension, the anthropologist delimits the group of people among whom he will look for culture.[...]On the phenomenal dimension, the anthropologist decides what it is he will look for:[...]He decides what the relations are between the elements of culture:[...]He also decides how cultural elements are related to non-cultural ones:[...]At the temporal dimension, the anthropologist decides whether a culture is best viewed in non-historical terms as static or stable or in historical terms as changing over time.[...] on the situational dimension, the anthropologist adopts a view of his relationship to, or with, the people whose culture he studies.[29]

The template can be characterized as a skeletal form for culture concepts because the dimensions outline the basic theoretical issues to be clarified in anthropological research prior to data collection in the field. As such, the dimensions outlined by Rice can be utilized to determine the essential areas to be addressed in any model of culture. Thus, although Rice's template was developed to compare anthropological concepts of culture, it can be used as a basic guideline for developing a conception of culture from which to organize the collection and evaluation of data. We have utilized Rice's dimension guidelines as a base direction in formulating a conception of culture and in choosing content theories for our analytical tool.

As we learned from Rice's work, a research definition of culture must be clearly set prior to designing a method and strategy for analyzing culture. This section is therefore limited to a discussion of the base, or nominal concept of culture for the Cultural Inventory following the theoretical guidelines set in Rice's 'phenomenal dimension.'

The distinction between culture and cultural phenomena provides a conceptual structure for discussing the initial theoretical questions faced when developing a model of culture for analysis. The phenomenal dimension guidelines gleaned from Rice amount to questions of approach, and address the issues of content and form which serve as heuristic pillars for establishing a nominal, or research definition.[30]

> When one asks the question "What is it we are looking for when we look for culture?" one is asking about the phenomenal dimension of a concept of culture. The phenomenal aspect of a conception of culture consists of an image, model, or conception of what culture is composed of and what the relations among its elements are: a conception of culture's content and its form.[31]

The first issue determines content; it corresponds to what phenomena will be considered elements of culture in a method. The second issue determines form; it corresponds to how the elements of culture are related in the research definition.

A conception of culture thus serves to design a theoretical model of culture as we will investigate it, addressing both elemental and structural aspects. The structural aspect, or form of a model of culture is directly related to the choice of elements. The more elements included in a conception, the more there exists a need to explicate the relationship among these elements.

Elements

The elements within anthropological conceptions of culture have been traditionally determined by dividing cultural phenomena into roughly three analyzable categories -ideational products, physical products and behavior. However, whether some or all of the elements are chosen to constitute the content of a particular conception of culture is a matter of study choice:

> If the anthropologist defines culture to refer only to *ideational products*, culture becomes 'mind,' esprit or Geist in opposition to everything involving substance, as in the Idealist/Materialist contrast. If *physical products* are added to culture, but behavior is not,[...]culture is not only what people think, but anything they make and use, whether mental or physical. Here, behavior constitutes culture's social context. Finally, if *behavior*, too, is added to culture, culture is lived,[...]In this case, all that remains outside of culture is the natural environment within which human beings live.[32]

Common Definitions

Two dictionary definitions have been chosen as a common starting-ground to frame the discussion of our conception of culture. *The American Heritage Dictionary* lists a two-part definition for the anthropological usage of culture. Its first entry defines 'culture' as an abstract social and intellectual formation. Its second, listing more tangible examples, defines culture as: "the totality of socially transmitted behavior patterns, arts, beliefs, institutions, and all other products of human work and thought characteristic of a community or population."[33] In *Webster's New Collegiate Dictionary*, a similar two-part definition for culture is found. Attempting to address three aspects of this term (behavioral, material and cognitive), the entry defines culture as: "a: the integrated pattern of human behavior that includes thought, speech, action and artifacts [...]b: the customary beliefs, social forms, and material traits of a[...]religious, or social group."[34] While, *Webster's* and *The American Heritage* reflect the common American usage of "culture," it is clear that neither provide a sufficiently developed concept from which to design a method/strategy for analyzing culture. For, although the definitions, replete with examples, cover the whole range of human phenomena –action and thought– they do not suggest a content-form model, or phenomenal conception of culture applicable for our analysis purposes.

The dictionary definitions denote 'culture' as a noun that in one respect refers to both a social formation and an intellectual formation, and in another encompasses the "totality" of humanly produced phenomena. If focus is placed on the phenomena, and thus regroup the phrases provided in the definitions, then the examples of culture listed span three major facets of human existence. There are phrases which focus on a) how humans interact and what they say;[35] phrases which emphasize b) the actual material things which humans make and use;[36] and, phrases which pertain to c) what humans think while interacting and producing.[37] By dividing the dictionary examples in this manner, the examples are regrouped under the following anthropological 'element' categories: a) behavioral and speech acts (actions)[38], b) material products (artifacts) and c) mental products (thoughts).[39] A restructured definition, substituting the anthropological categories for the descriptive examples would thus read:

> Culture: a: a social and intellectual formation
> b: the totality of customary behavior and speech acts, material and mental products characteristic of a community or population.

The above definition is still a two-part definition; "a:" addresses form, while "b:" addresses content. With these revised elements in mind, one can move to anthropological determinations of content.

Content Determination

Although "anthropologists formulate culture's content in a variety of ways," it is possible, as Rice concludes, to group the elements most often included in an anthropological conception of culture into two broad categories: 'behavior' and 'products of behavior'.[40] This division is also apparent in part 'b:' of the restructured definition above: b: the totality of customary behavior and speech acts, material and mental products characteristic of a community or population.

Leaving the behavior and speech acts category aside, Rice's work provides a more concise description on products of behavior. Accordingly, products of behavior may occur "within individual minds" as verbalized thoughts. These "Mental products include such things as ideas, beliefs, knowledge, cognitive structures...".[41] Products of behavior, however, may also occur "outside of individual minds" in which case they are termed "non-verbal" or physical. These "Physical products of behavior [include]...artifacts, and all other items of material culture."[42] From this perspective on content, behavior constitutes an element category of its own, while the two "product" categories are seen as derived from behavior. One can name this perspective 'Perspective A.' A summary of the elements of 'Perspective A,' is given in figure 3.2.

Figure 3.2 Elements of Culture Perspective A

> Elements of Culture (Perspective A)
> 1. Behavior
> 2. Products of Behavior (further subdivided into)
>   a. Mental Products
>   b. Physical Products

Culture from 'Perspective A' is thus seen as behavior which, in turn, generates mental and physical products.

Rice notes, however, that it is possible to hold another perspective whereby the three elements of culture listed above (see figure 3.2 – namely 1., 2a, and 2b) are seen equally as semiotic phenomena; in short as signs-vehicles performing simultaneously on the one hand as embodiments of cognitive meanings, and on the other as mental or physical realia. One can name this second perspective 'Perspective B'. In 'Perspective B' all three categories of phenomena: behavioral, mental and artifactual, are considered products "that contain, or at least express, [shared] concepts and ideas."[43] If attending to the semiotic function of these phenomena, the anthropologists is able to consider yet another 'deeper level' of analysis, a level of analysis that seeks to unveil the cognitive signification, or culture-based meanings that these phenomena are seen to represent.[44] In 'Perspective B' the earlier distinction between behavior and the products of behavior held by 'Perspective A' is collapsed; for, in 'Perspective B' behavior becomes a product.

In 'Perspective B,' all three categories of elements –behavioral and speech products, mental products and artifactual products– are viewed as vehicles through which culture-based meanings are objectified. In other words, they are utilized by human actors as the forms into which culture-based meanings are manifested, and through which such meanings are further communicated. Viewing the elements from 'Perspective B' thus recasts the former mental, behavioral and physical product categories into symbols, and opens the way for another type of product:

> If symbols mediate meaning between individuals, then shared knowledge, institutionalized norms and values, and conscience collective –ideational products that *are not limited to individual minds*– become possible [elements in a conception of culture].[45]

Within 'Perspective B', the term "ideational" is used to distinguish the deeper-level products (i.e. values and beliefs) from the surface-level mental, behavioral and physical products.

By viewing culture from 'Perspective B,' one has four possible elements in a conception of culture. Figure 3.3 gives a summary comparison of the elements of culture from the two perspectives.

Figure 3.3 Elements of Culture Perspectives A and B

> Elements of Culture (Perspective A)
> 1. Behavior
> 2. Products of Behavior (further subdivided into)
>   a. Mental Products
>   b. Physical Products
> Elements of Culture (Perspective B)
> 1. Values and Beliefs as Ideational Products
> ideational products objectified via
> a. Sponsor Thoughts as Mental Products
> b. Actions as Behavioral and Speech Products
> c. Artifacts as Material Products

The element categories of 'Perspective B' can be grouped according to physically observable characteristics. As such, actions and artifacts constitute the physical elements that can be observed "outside of individual minds;" sponsor thoughts constitute the non-physical elements that exist "inside of individual minds;" while values and beliefs, the deeper-level products, are interpreted as mediating "meaning between individuals" and therefore constitute elements that are "not limited to individual minds." In figure 3.4 'Perspective B' is diagrammed as a series of concentric circles:[46]

Figure 3.4 'Perspective B' Concentric Circle Culture Model

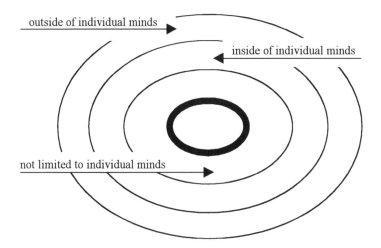

Returning to part 'a:' of the restructured dictionary definitions of culture one can add the two phrases "intellectual formation" and "social formation" to the above four content element categories of 'Perspective B.' In so doing, six components now comprise the reformulated definition. These six components will constitute the elements of the concept and study model of culture.

Figure 3.5 Elements of Culture: Cultural Inventory Perspective

> *Elements of Culture*: Cultural Inventory perspective
> I. Intellectual Formation   (cognitive system)
>   A. Ideational products   (values and beliefs)
>   1. mental products   (sponsor thoughts)
>   a. behavioral products   (actions)
>   b. material products (artifacts)
> II. Social Formation

The first task outlined by Rice's guidelines for creating a study model pertains to delineating the elements of culture, its 'content,' the second pertains to deciding how these elements are related, or the 'form' of a conception of culture. Grouping the elements of culture according to physical and non-physical characteristics –or the more colorful 'inside' and 'outside' the head dichotomy– represents the materialist/idealist contrast indicative of theoretical splits in the field of anthropology. And, the task of theoretically integrating culture's physical and non-physical elements is the central challenge common to the 'form' issue of all anthropological conceptions of culture. Therefore, in deciding the issues of form one determines which elements constitute culture 'proper' and which elements constitute cultural phenomena, or the products of culture.

Form Determination

A conception of culture's form theoretically stipulates 'how' the physical and non-physical elements of culture are integrated. For direction on how to design a relationship-model of these elements within a concept Rice's base guidelines can again be referenced:

> Anthropologists usually conceive of the form of a culture, the relations among its elements, whether these elements be behavioral, [verbal], ideational, or artifactual, in one of two ways. [...]The difference between these two views of a culture's form is a difference between a collection[...]into which various contents are placed, and a system[...]or structure in which the comprehended elements are not merely included but interact with one another, directly or indirectly.[47]

The structure of a concept of culture, or study model, is generated from the manner in which an anthropologist accounts for the relationships among its elements. Often, synchronic culture studies, having a limited descriptive purpose, approach the structure of culture as a collection. In these limited studies there is little need to address the interaction of elements, their goal is descriptive.[48] However, clearly specifying the theoretical issue of element relationship is important for any research conception of culture that attempts to enable diachronic studies addressing questions of culture shift or change; hence, for our pedagogical purposes, it was necessary to develop a form conception of culture following the second view. In this view, the elements of culture are seen to be related and "...belong[ing] to a living system which perpetuates itself and within which the various parts interact with one another."[49]

If the ideational, mental, (non)verbal-behavioral, and material products generated by a human group were to constitute the phenomena of that group's "culture," the adjective 'cultural:' meaning "of or relating to culture," can be employed to help determine the interactional relationship of these phenomena and thereby reach closer to a core concept of culture.

Figure 3.6 Products of Culture
    1. A. Ideational products (values and beliefs)
        mental products (sponsor thoughts)
           a. behavioral products (actions)
           b. material products (artifacts)

The hierarchical relationship of these products is articulated by qualifying ideational products as first order products realized with the term: (products); while, using the term (products^2), first order products materialized, to refer to the materialization of ideational products. The term (products^2) would then denote the sponsor thoughts, actions and artifacts through which ideational products are externalized (see figure 3.7).

Figure 3.7 Relationship Among Culture Products
    (Products)
    ideational products (values and beliefs)
        (Products^2)
        mental products (sponsor thoughts)
        behavioral products (actions)
        material products (artifacts)

The hierarchical relationship of these products is represented using concentric circles in figure 3.8.

Figure 3.7 Relationship Among Culture Products Diagrammed

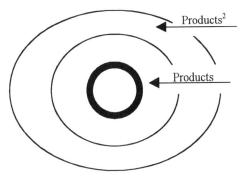

An examination of the mental, behavioral, and material categories listed under (Products[2]) determines yet another sub-relationship or grouping (see figure 3.9), as these products can be distinguished according to externalized form. For, while all three categories represent products generated from ideational products, there exists a sequence chain of materialization among them. The materialization of behavioral or artifactual products of culture requires that they first be realized as a mental products –with or without the conscious awareness of the social actor.[50]

Figure 3.9 Division of Products[2]

       (Products[2])
          mental products (sponsor thoughts)
             behavioral products (actions)
             material products (artifacts)

In other words, cultural behaviors and cultural artifacts represent physical manifestations of culture. The stage prior to this point of materialization, namely a cultural sponsor thought, would thus represent a mental manifestation of culture.

A cultural product in a realized state (a non-physical, non-materialized product) can be classified as a culturally generated, or as Spiro coined, "culturally constituted" thought. These will be referenced as "sponsor thoughts" to highlight their positioning between 'values and beliefs' on the one hand, and 'actions and artifacts' on the other. The relationship among these products is depicted in figure 3.10.

Figure 3.10 Sponsor Thought Positioning

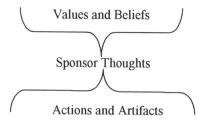

A cultural product in a physically materialized state –in the form of an artifact or action– represents a projection or further externalized version of a mental product. A physical product is then a mental product which has progressed into a physically discernible form either as an artifact (i.e. book, house, garden) or as a behavior (i.e. expression or interaction). One can revise the product division into the hierarchical scheme given in figure 3.11 and depicted as a concentric circle diagrams in figure 3.12:

Figure 3.11 Expanded Relationship Among Culture Products
   (Products)
  ideational products (values and beliefs)
    (Products^2)realized
   mental products (sponsor thoughts)
     (Products^3) materialized
    behavioral products (actions)
    material products (artifacts)

Figure 3.12 Emic and Etic Culture Models

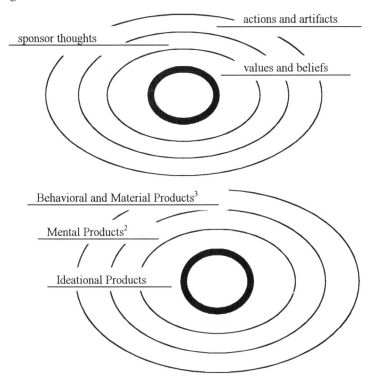

According to this conception of culture, speech and writing are also considered materialized artifacts, for the term "materialized" is here used to essentially denote that which is externalized so as to be discernible to the senses and not limited to the concrete tangible. Thus a cultural product or phenomenon of culture can be anything of human origin, or anything altered by human intervention.

Here 'values and beliefs' might seem a viable candidate for culture; for, cultural 'values and beliefs' could stand as the genesis of 'culturally constituted thoughts' which, in turn, would stand as the genesis of 'culturally constituted behaviors and artifacts:'

Figure 3.13 Outline of Culture Model

Values and Beliefs
(ideational products)=(products)
generate

Sponsor Thoughts
(mental products)=(products^2)
which, in turn, generate

Actions and Artifacts
(behavioral and material products)=(products^3)

When the generative meaning of "*of*" in the definition for 'cultural' is replaced with the phrases "based on, or derived from culture," then the term 'cultural' can be employed as an adjective to denote phenomena which are generated from culture, rather than that which constitutes culture at its core. From this vantage, ideational, mental, (non)verbal-behavioral, and material products are no longer seen as "culture," but are considered its products. Culture is thus the determinant of these products.

The above re-grouping of products then raised the following question for the study model: If behaviors, artifacts, and sponsor thoughts are products of ideational products (surface-level realized-products^2 and materialized-products^3) what, then, would generate 'ideational products,' hence what would be culture at core?

Within the model of culture 'values and beliefs' constitute group specific statements that the social actor employs to access the *axioms* (learned and/or adopted) with which s/he conducts life and by which interprets reality.[51] If one inquires as to the source of these 'values and beliefs' it can be concluded that they are generated from the axioms of a shared cognitive system/background, handed down through family, schooling, religious heritage, etc.[52]

With this inquiry the study model is moved back one level; for, values and beliefs are created and maintained on the basis of these shared, unconscious axioms which, when viewed from the perspective of a social actor, constitute his/her core assumptions about reality. Thus, values and beliefs are the surfaced ideational products of these axioms, or core assumptions. With the introduction of the term "core assumptions" a category is formed for the innermost section of the concentric circle diagram (see figure 3.14).

The distinction between culture as cognitive systems composed of core assumptions about reality on the one hand, and values and beliefs as the ideational products of cognitive systems is necessary for analysis purposes. First because one does not refer to values and beliefs as culture at base, and secondly, –a reason tied to the first– because the distinction indicates that values and beliefs are generated from cognitive assumptions about reality and therefore can be traced back to

Figure 3.14 Core Assumption Circle

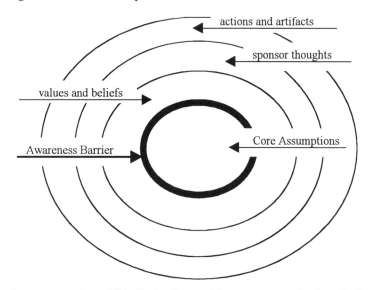

these assumptions. This distinction enables one to perceive how beliefs and values are heuristic in nature but factual in practice. Ideational products are thus the emic values and beliefs generated by emic core assumptions, i.e. culture.

Values and beliefs as the ideational products of culture can only be approached in their culturally specific form: i.e. "It is wrong to kill." However, when values and beliefs about reality are categorized by cognitivists into meaning systems composed of notions, an analytical translation occurs whereby the values and beliefs are rephrased into the etic discourse of anthropology. These notions, according to the work of Spiro, can be categorized as descriptive and/or normative propositions about reality. Core assumptions translated into their propositional form thus provide the descriptive and normative foundation for determining two groups of ideational products; namely, the beliefs and values of social actors. Following the definition outlined by Melford Spiro, an etic definition of the concept of culture at core designates:

> ...a cognitive system,[as] a set of "propositions," both descriptive (e.g., 'the planet earth sits on the back of a turtle') and normative (e.g., 'it is wrong to kill'), about nature, man and society that are embedded in interlocking higher-order networks and configurations.[53]

Thus, culture, as a meaning system, is a shared body of descriptive and normative propositions which exist for the social actor as the core assumptions that generate his/her cultural reality. These propositions, functioning as core assumptions, provide the often unconscious foundation for the ideational products –the values and beliefs– of the social actor.

Both propositions and assumptions are terms employed in the Cultural Inventory to refer to the constituent parts that comprise the actor's 'worldview'[54] or culture-at-base. Both terminologies –core assumptions and descriptive-normative propositions– are used in the Cultural Inventory analysis because the varied terminologies permits a flexibility to denote the perspective from which culture-at-base is being described. A proposition denotes a statement accepted or supposed true within a theoretical framework, while an assumption denotes a "statement accepted or supposed true without proof or demonstration."[55] When there is a need to emphasize the anthropological perspective of culture as a cognitive system, one refers to culture using etic terminologies, i.e. a set of descriptive and normative propositions. That is, when there is a need to describe the components of the cognitive system for the purpose of analysis the more scientifically precise terminologies, descriptive and normative propositions, are utilized. The term proposition maintains a heuristic, i.e. theoretically relative, connotation that the term assumption does not.

Employing the term 'core assumption' to refer to a descriptive-normative proposition underscores how a proposition unconsciously functions for the social actor because the term 'assumption' carries a connotation of being unconsciously generated; a connotation not connected with the term proposition. Therefore, to underscore culture from the perspective of the social actor its cognitive components – propositions– can be generalized as "core assumptions," and culture, as a cognitive system-at-base, is referenced as "worldview". The concentric circle diagram given in figure 3.15 represents the two, etic and emic, vocabularies employed to articulate culture and its products.

Figure 3.15 Etic/Emic Concentric Circle Model of Culture

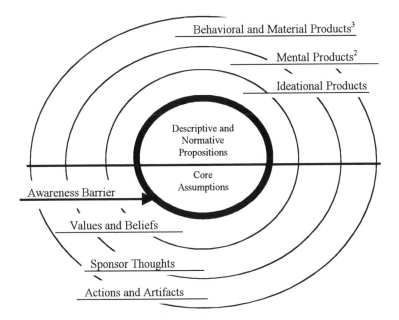

When surfacing, core assumptions-as-descriptive propositions can be/become articulated as beliefs, while core assumptions-as-normative propositions can be/become articulated as values. It is these propositions then, which serve as the mechanisms for cultural construction and interpretation of realities, and thereby create and maintain human cultural identities.

The distinction between values and beliefs and descriptive and normative propositions is a distinction of terminology and provides categories that enable the analyst to translate the culturally specific values and beliefs into the anthropological terminology of propositions. It is not simply a substitution of terms, but rather an analytical translation process which, when completed, transforms the value or belief in questions into a more universal and analytically comparable data. Culture-at-base is referenced using the term "core assumptions" when there is no need to analytically distinguish between the descriptive or normative content of the assumptions.

Core assumptions, then, are shared, have a tradition (i.e. exist prior to our entering the scene), and form a cognitive system, or as described by Edgar Schein a "mental map":

> Culture as a set of basic assumptions defines for us what to pay attention to, what things mean, how to react emotionally to what is going on, and what actions to take in various situations. Once we have developed an integrated set of such assumptions, [we could call this set] a *thought world* or *mental map*.[56]

According to this study the cognitive system is designated as "culture;" and, the realized or materialized phenomena that are generated from this system and that surface through the social actor are designated as "culturally constituted products." In this way, "culture" as a cognitive system functions as an internalized, automatic translator by, and through which 'thought worlds' are deciphered. As such, it constitutes a mechanism enabling social actors to simultaneously create and maintain way(s) of life via the ideational, mental, (non)verbal-behavioral, and artifactual products they employ as vehicles to communicate and access culture. The outline cited above is expanded in figure 3.16 to represent a complete nominal conception of culture.

On hand of this study 'model,' one can argue that 'values and beliefs' do not constitute culture, rather they too are generated by culture. And, culture thus can be conceived of as sets of core assumptions about reality which, for practical purposes, are described structurally as an intellectual, or cognitive formation. Culture as this cognitive back*ground* consists of meanings which function as a hermeneutic code for creating and interpreting human interactions. It is this cognitive definition of culture as a core assumption set composed of descriptive and normative propositions which constitutes the utilization of the term culture in this study.

The chain of relations is, in short: culture, as a meaning system, is composed of a core assumption set through which social actors interpret their realities. The core assumptions that comprise the meaning system can be divided into two scientific categories of propositions; namely, descriptive and normative. The core assumption set is the base, or generator of emic values and beliefs. The values and beliefs, in turn, perform as the base for generating sponsor thoughts. These sponsor thoughts, in turn, are the social actor's basis for interpreting the materialized products of others and for materializing his/her own products.

Figure. 3.16 Expanded Outline of Culture Model

Core Assumptions about Reality
(Worldview)=(Culture)
are organized into

A System of Meanings
(an intellectual -cognitive- formation)
which generates

Values and Beliefs
(ideational products)=(products)
that generate

Sponsor Thoughts
(mental products)=(products^2)
which, in turn, generate

Actions and Artifacts
(behavioral and other material products)=(products^3)

The tree diagram, given in figure 3.17, proves a useful visual image to depict this conception of culture.

Figure. 3.17 Tree Diagram of Emic Cultural Elements

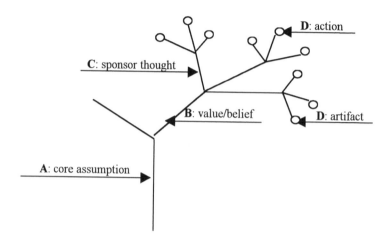

In conclusion, culture consists of A) shared core assumptions about reality formed and organized into cognitive meaning systems by and through which humans make sense of the world around them. Because the core assumptions that comprise the system are shared, they are learned and communicated. In order for this to occur, the core assumptions are translated into group specific terminologies (ideational products). In this way, the core assumptions surface emically, that is they are realized into the group specific terminologies B) values and beliefs. When taken to another level of realization, the ideational products surface as individual mental products in the form of C) sponsor thoughts. As mental products, sponsor thoughts act as the not-yet-materialized interpretations of reality; i.e. hypotheses and judgments about reality which appear to be Self but, which are part of the social actor's Cultural Self. The final level of surfacing involves an actual materialization of these mental products. In their materialized form, they become D) artifactual and/or (non)verbal-behavioral products. Thus, theoretically, artifacts and actions can be read as materialized core assumptions about reality. A pyramid diagram of this structure is given in figure 3.18.

Figure.3.18 Pyramid Diagram of Emic Cultural Elements

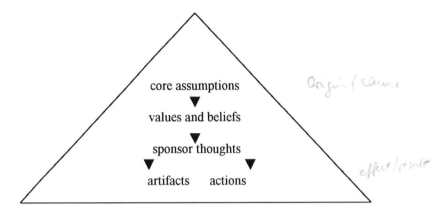

Or, this pyramid structure can depicted inversely beginning with the most externalized product as given in figure 3.19.

Figure. 3.19 Inverted Pyramid Diagram of Emic Cultural Elements

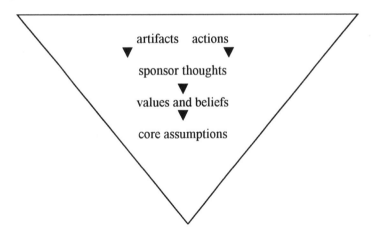

To recap, culture is a learned and hence shared meaning system. It is comprised of patterned sets of meanings that social actors use semiotically to construct and interpret the reality in which they live. As such, a social actor's culture constitutes his/her belief system, a portion of which is inevitably accessed to decode each behavior or other realized/materialized product with which the actor comes into contact. And, a portion of this belief system is conversely encoded into each thought and attendant behavior or other realized/materialized product that the actor produces. In this manner, materialized or realized products perform as signs of culture and therefore can be described as "culturally constituted" objectifications, but do not constitute culture as we approach the concept. Additionally, it stands, that these "culturally constituted" objectifications can be read for their cultural content. It is left then, to devise a method or strategy for reading such signs.

Notes

[1] Langness 118. We assume the reference is to Spiro's theory on the 'Hierarchy of Cognitive Salience' which explains how the propositions that comprise a cognitive system, or culture, become internalized and therefore indistinguishable from personal belief systems.

[2] Melford E. Spiro, "Some Reflections on Cultural Determinism and Relativism with Special Attention to Emotion and Reason," *Culture and Human Nature: Theoretical Papers of Melford E. Spiro*, eds. Benjamin Kilborne and L. L. Langness (Chicago: University of Chicago Press, 1987) 32. Additionally, Spiro's hint that the structural and content components of cognitive systems are "embedded in interlocking configurations" gives one the key for explaining the mutually reciprocal relationship between belief- or cognitive systems and systems of interpersonal relations highlighted in Thompson, Ellis and Wildavsky's rendition of Mary Douglas' sociological Grid/Group Typology; namely the 5 'Ways of Life'.

[3] Spiro, "Reflections" 34.

[4] Spiro's axioms did not address artifactual products which we incorporated into the conception from anthropological theories. Also, we have made distinctions among mental products, ideational products and core assumptions.

[5] Spiro, "Reflections" 32-33.

[6] Spiro, "Reflections" 33.

[7] Spiro, "Reflections" 34.

[8] Spiro, "Reflections" 33.

[9] Spiro, "Reflections" 34.

[10] For an explanation of cultural products see below.

[11] In our nominal conception of culture we have denoted Spiro's core beliefs/values as core assumptions; for, we found the term core assumptions more suitable as an emic translation of descriptive and normative propositions. In so doing, we were able to utilize the terms beliefs/values to

denote ideational products. This, in turn, enabled us to isolate the term sponsor thoughts, encompassing Spiro's emotions and thought categories, as mental products.

[12] Spiro, "Reflections" 38.

[13] Rice 140-149.

[14] We chose the term verbalizations here because thoughts, values and beliefs are expressed in words. Hence the term verbalization includes both internally and externally manifested verbal products of culture.

[15] Spiro, "Reflections" 37. Additionally, Spiro writes: "Again, in saying that the transformation of a cultural frame into a personal belief entails an explanatory shift from a historical to a psychological perspective, I am not saying that this represents a shift from a group to an individual level of explanation. For the psychological characteristics of social actors must also be explained by reference to a group phenomenon -[social formation]." "Reflections" 39.

[16] Spiro, "Reflections" 34-35.

[17] Spiro, "Reflections" 35.

[18] Spiro, "Reflections" 35.

[19] Thompson, Ellis, and Wildavsky 2.

[20] Level I of the Cultural Inventory contains the following analyses: Situational Filter, Interactional Filter, Application 1, Feedback Filter, Application 2, Notional Filter.

[21] Level II of the Cultural Inventory contains the following analyses: Application 3, Synthesis 1, Interpersonal Filter, Synthesis 2, and Evaluation Typology.

[22] Time and space have been added to Spiro's categories in order to correspond with the 5 areas of cognitive orientation as determined by Tinsley and Woloshin.

[23] Spiro, "Reflections" 39. Spiro also makes the following remarks pertaining to culture and social structure: "[...]Just because thoughts and emotions are culturally constituted, it is logically impermissible to conclude that culture, as such, consists of emotion or thought any more than it can be concluded that culture consists of behavior or social structure, although they too are culturally constituted [...rather...]cultural propositions serve to motivate behavior and to provide a model for social structure." Spiro, "Reflections" 34. And for the distinction between culture and social structure Geertz writes: "Culture is the fabric of meaning in terms of which human beings interpret their experience and guide their action; social structure is the form that action takes, the actually existing network of social relations." Geertz 145.

[24] Rice 4-5. Rice comments: "Recognizing the ambiguity of culture as a problem, we are obliged to respond to the problem, to decide just what we should do about it. In our own work, we can avoid the conceptual fog which

results from the ambiguity of 'culture' by defining culture in a particular way and using the term in strict accordance with this definition. This is not to suggest that there is only one way in which it is useful to define the term. Different definitions may be useful in different cases or for different purposes. But we will never find out which definitions are useful for which cases and which purposes unless we use one such definition at a time, following out its implications to see where it leads us, rather than use culture in a miscellaneous variety of ways within a single study.[…]The definition and consistent use of culture would aid anthropologists both to maintain logical consistency in their work and to make their works more readily comprehensible to their readers. Variation in the use and interpretation of culture can, if not perceived, lead to logically inconsistent thinking. Definitions of culture would help to limit such variation by making the intended meaning of the term explicit."

[25] Rice 10.

[26] Rice 10.

[27] Rice 23. Rice explains: "Each conception of culture has focal, phenomenal, temporal, and situational aspects, but each conception of culture presents a different image of what culture and the study of it are. A general framework consisting of focal, phenomenal, temporal, and situational components can be used to draw together the essential points of a conception of culture without obscuring that conception's particular character and its particular implications for analysis by forcing it into a narrow mold." 23.

[28] Rice 19.

[29] Rice 19.

[30] We stress that our definition is nominal and not essentialistic. As Rice explains: "To nominally define culture is rather to stipulate how one is going to use the term by using more common terms to attach a connotation to it. There is no question of truth or falsity in nominal definitions since they simply announce an intention to use a term in a particular manner (Cafagna 1960: 117)." 5.

[31] Rice 12.

[32] Rice 14.

[33] *The American Heritage Dictionary of the English Language*, ed. William Morris (Boston: Houghton Mifflin Company, 1981) 321.

[34] *Webster's New Collegiate Dictionary*, ed. Henry Bosley Woolf (Springfield: G. and C. Merriam Company, 1981) 274. Our emphasis. In the above noted definition of 'culture' the original concluding sentence ended "...and material traits of a racial, religious, or social group." We have eliminated the term "racial" from this list as we deem it an inappropriate and invalid category. And, in terms of the nominal definition of culture to be presented here it should be stated from the outset that any category derived from biological or

physical based characteristics, such as race, gender, etc., represents an invalid grouping according to the conception of culture to be developed in this work. Issues pertaining to race and gender are, as it will be seen, relegated to the ideological products of a particular 'culture' and should not be confused with or substituted for the term 'culture' as presented in this work.

[35] Namely, "speech," "action" and "social formation," see above.

[36] Namely, "artifacts," see above.

[37] Namely, "thoughts," "customary beliefs," "intellectual formations," see above.

[38] Rice notes the "overt behavior could be subdivided into *verbal* and *nonverbal* behavior, into 'speech' and 'act,'" 13.

[39] We have not compared Rice's elements –namely ideational products, physical products, and behavior– with the products listed here, as our conception of culture does not equate mental products and ideational products. As will be shown, a distinction in level of manifestation between mental products on the one hand, and ideational products on the other is foundational in our conception of culture.

[40] Rice 12.

[41] Rice 13.

[42] The whole quote in Rice reads: "Anthropologists often include products of human behavior in the content of culture. These products may be mental, occurring within individual minds; physical, occurring outside of individual minds; or both at once. Mental products include such things as ideas, beliefs, knowledge, cognitive structures, and intellectual competence. Physical products of behavior, like artifacts and all the other items of material culture, from agricultural implements to ceremonial masks or even body scars, may also be included in culture's content." 13.

[43] Rice 13.

[44] Hall, in *Beyond Culture*, conceives of the deeper level of culture in the following manner: "A first approximation of a definition of such systems would be as follows: The cultural unconscious, those out-of-awareness cultural systems that have as yet to be made explicit.[...]Such systems have various features and dimensions which are governed by the order, selection, and congruence rules. These rules apply to the formative and active aspects of communications, discourses, perception (in all modalities), transactions between people, and the action chains by which humans achieve their varied life goals." 166.

[45] Rice 13.

[46] We found the idea to depict the elements of culture using concentric circles in Jim Petersen's "True Spiritual Transformation," in *Lifestyle Discipleship: The Challenges of Following Jesus in Today's World* (Colorado: Navpress, 1994) 83. Regarding the concentric circle diagram he writes: "There is a

diagram anthropologists use as a descriptive device to study people. It separates out certain elements of culture. This enables them to study each part by itself." 83.

[47] Rice 13. Rice continues: "In the first case, the elements of a culture are related to one another like apples in a crate: they belong together because they share particular characteristics [...and hence, represent an artificial grouping] In the second case, a culture's elements are related to one another like apples on a tree:..."

[48] An example of culture viewed as a collection would be the familiar "culture capsule-culture cluster" taught in foreign language classes. The approach to culture in these instances is as behavior patterns. See H. Ned Seelye, "Culture Assimilators, Culture Capsules, Culture Clusters'" *Teaching Culture: Strategies for Intercultural Communication* (Lincolnwood: National Textbook Company, 1985) 116-139.

[49] Rice 13.

[50] We note, again, that when we speak of cultural phenomena, we are speaking of mediated phenomena. Such understanding follows the axioms of Symbolic Interactionism as Blummer writes after Mead: "The possession of a self provides the human being with a mechanism of self-interaction with which to meet the world- a mechanism that is used in forming and guiding his conduct.[...]With the mechanism of self-interaction the human being ceases to be a responding organism whose behavior is a product of what plays upon him for the outside, the inside or both. Instead, he acts toward his world, interpreting what confronts him and organizing his action on the basis of the interpretation.[...]The process of self-interaction puts the human being over against his world instead of merely in it, requires him to meet and handle his world through a defining process instead of merely responding to it, and forces him to construct his action instead of merely releasing it." Herbert Blumer *Symbolic Interactionism: Perspective and Method* (Berkeley and Los Angeles: University of California Press, 1986) 62-63.

[51] These axioms or 'system of meanings' as culture behind the 'values and beliefs' is usually so well learned (internalized) by adulthood, that, in most cases, an awareness of its existence requires a 'meaning-system-breakdown' commonly referred to as "culture shock." Unfortunately, anger rather than awareness usually results from such experiences.

[52] We should also note that we have excluded experience here for the simplicity of the argument. It is clear that experience is a great 'adjuster' of values and beliefs, as Spiro writes: "although by this [our] conception "culture" designated a cognitive system, it is not the only –though it is clearly the most important– source of cognitions and schemata held by social actors. The other source consists of their own experience." Spiro, "Reflections" 33.

[53] Spiro, "Reflections" 32.

[54] "A world view is linked to reality in two ways; first by regarding it, by forming more or less accurate images of it, images that mirror the world; and second, by treating these images through using them to guide action." Michael Kearney, *World View* (Novato: Chandler and Sharp Publishers, Inc., 1984) 5. "Images that mirror the world" correspond to our descriptive propositions, or emic beliefs; while, images that guide action correspond to our normative propositions, or emic values.

[55] Entry on the meaning of 'assumption' in *The American Heritage Dictionary*, 80.

[56] Schein 22. Our emphasis, the original reads "such assumptions, which might be called a thought world or mental map,…".

Chapter 4

Applied Semiotics:
A strategy of analysis for culture

In the fields of anthropology and sociology many have described culture as a set of regulative and constitutive rules; a cosmology; a worldview; even an ideology.[1] Despite differences in terminology, culture, when taken as these meanings, is seen to function as an internalized, conceptual apparatus that we, as humans, access to culturally interpret the reality around us.[2] When the term culture is limited to an internalized, conceptual apparatus only, there is a need to account for all the other material phenomena that traditionally have been referenced as culture; i.e. rituals, (social) behavior patterns, material artifacts.[3]

In the preceding section a model of culture was discussed which, following Spiro, holds culture to be a conceptual apparatus; more specifically a cognitive system composed of descriptive and normative propositions about reality. As Spiro's 'Hierarchy of Cognitive Salience' has shown, the descriptive and normative propositions that constitute culture function, for the social actor, as the core assumptions from which his/her acts[4] are generated. Reciprocally, these propositions also function as the core assumptions that structure how the social actor interprets such acts. For, the material objects of a social actor's environment will elicit in him/her some cultural (shared life-identity meaning) significance. From this significance the social actor, in turn, reacts as Spiro's description for the most internalized stage, level 5, on the 'Hierarchy of Cognitive Salience' indicates:

> Level V [most salient]
> At this level, culturally constituted beliefs serve not only to guide but to instigate action, that is, they posses emotional and motivational, as well as cognitive, salience.[5]

It is this interaction, based on core assumptions, that evidences the semiotic use of human acts, and that, in turn, enables these acts to be understood –be they behavioral, verbal, or artifactual– as cultural products (compare figures 4.1 and 4.2).

Figure 4.1 Non-semiotic Use of Human Acts

Figure 4.2 Semiotic Use of Human Acts

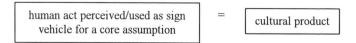

Thus, when core assumptions are considered the generating and/or interpreting principles for human acts, these human acts are called cultural products. Culture, therefore, can be accessed through these products; for, in the moment when human acts are attended to as representations for core assumptions they cease to be "just acts" and become articulations of culture; 'cultural' objects or cultural products.

The definition of culture, then, supposes a distinction between culture as a cognitive system constitutive of both normative and descriptive propositions, and cultural products as the embodiments or vehicles through which this system, when employed by social actors in human interactions, is expressed. Hence, when culture is defined as a cognitive system of core assumptions, human acts in themselves are not regarded as culture, but rather as cultural products. As such, cultural products (verbalizations, behaviors and artifacts) serve as signs of culture for the analyst.

In his *Glossary of Semiotics*, Colapietro defines the verb to mediate as "The process of bringing together things that otherwise would be unconnected;" and further defines mediation as "the result of such a process."[6] When social actors assign shared life-identity meanings to their own verbalizations, behaviors, and artifacts and to those of others, they are transforming these human acts into cultural products, utilizing a cognitive system of core assumptions as a mediation mechanism for this transformation/ interpretation. This process of objectifying the environment through the mediation of core assumptions constitutes an interpretative process through which social actors continuously rehearse and/or recreate their cultural identities. In assigning these core assumption meanings to human acts, social actors affirm or negate their cultural identity vis-a-vis others. Few, however, are conscious of the process. It stands then that an awareness that core assumptions constitute culture as a cognitive system, and an awareness of how culture is employed semiotically as a mediating mechanism for interpreting reality are both key factors for the development of cultural understanding and intercultural competence.

Fluency in Reading Cultural Signs

The approach presented here seeks to teach students a method for reading human acts as cultural products; as signs mediated by core assumptions. To read human acts as cultural products the student of culture must develop an ability to interpret the culture manifested in human acts. In order to develop this ability, the student of culture must be taught a method to consciously translate human acts as signs of culture. By learning and employing such a method, the student of culture will gain an awareness of how culture semiotically functions as a mediation mechanism including both an *understanding of culture* as a cognitive system composed of core assumptions and *an understanding of human acts* (i.e. verbalizations, behavior and artifacts) as the cultural products through which these core assumptions are expressed.

If one were to imagine a post-linguistic sign system [as Deely's tertiary modeling system][7] functioning through signs of all types, then the use of actions like tipping a hat or hugging; the use of artifacts like buildings or maps; and the use of verbalizations like "man is an animal" would be considered signs; would convey meanings beyond themselves; namely, they would convey information about the culture or core assumptions of their producer. It is this expanded concept of a 'language' which encompasses the notion of cultural communication whereby core assumptions are mediated through human acts performing as signs.

A language can be classified as a sign system or code used for the expression and interpretation of meaning. And, cognitive anthropologists speak of culture as a cognitive system or a code for the interpretation and expression of descriptive and normative meanings. Accordingly, one can learn to read human interactions (whether artifactual, behavioral or verbal) as core assumptions like one learns to read a foreign language.

A key factor of learning a foreign language rests in studying the rule system, or grammar of that language. In order to study the grammar of foreign language, the student must first master or possess a working knowledge of the terminologies developed to express and interpret these rules. The terminologies ('universal' concepts) of this vocabulary (metalanguage)[8] come from the field of linguistics. When a student becomes relatively proficient with the metalanguage of linguistics, s/he is able to attend to the sentences of a language using an analytical perspective that renders grammatical, rather than semantic meanings.

When a student employs the metalanguage of linguistics to elicit the grammatical meaning of a sentence s/he is, in effect, translating the words of a sentence into a different code;[9] a code of grammar. Thus, the sentence "I walk the dog" contains different types of information depending on the perspective or code employed by the reader/interpreter. If s/he were interested in the functions of words s/he could employ the metalanguage of linguistics to translate the sentence according to grammatical function:(Subject) verb (object). Or, if interested in the types or classes of the words, s/he could translate the sentence according to grammatical form:(1st-person-singular-pronoun) present-tense-active-indicative-1st-person-singular-verb-[definite article (noun- singular)].

By translating into a different code of grammar the student is able to focus on other meanings for the sentence. The choice of code (semantic, grammatical-function, or grammatical-form) and/or the need to code switch/translate depends on the 'meaning' sought. For example, if in reference to the above sentence we ask: "What are you walking?": the answer would read: "the dog": no code switch. However, if we ask: "What is the tense of the verb?": an answer to the question would necessitate a mental code switch/translation of the sentence from its current form into a grammatical-form code. From this example it is clear that the ability to access or elicit multiple levels of meaning, in turn, rests both on one's knowledge of codes and on one's ability to translate to, or among codes.

Translation as An Analysis Method

The ability to access descriptive and normative meanings from human acts depends on the ability to interpret these acts through, or in reference to codes designed to analyze culture.[10] In this way, cultural analysis is seen as an interpretation process (see figure 4.3). In designing the Cultural Inventory as a method of analysis, it was therefore necessary to examine interpretation processes. Once an interpretation process had been found, it was possible to implement the theoretical systems, or codes, which would support the process.

From the semiotic perspective of Roman Jakobson, an interpretation process is a translation process of which there are three types:

(1) intralingual translation or *rewording* is an *interpretation* of verbal signs by means of other signs of the same language;
(2) interlingual translation or *translation proper* is an *interpretation* of verbal signs by means of some other language;
(3) intersemiotic translation or *transmutation* is an *interpretation* of verbal signs by means of nonverbal sign systems (Jakobson, S.W. II. 1971:261).[11]

Figure 4.3 Interpretation Process in Cultural Analysis

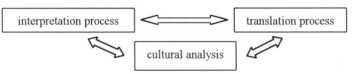

The use of the terms translation and interpretation as synonyms by Jacobson enables a more "user friendly" perspective on interpretation; for, if cultural interpretations are perceived as translation processes then to facilitate the act of a cultural analysis as translation –the goal of the Cultural Inventory project– it was left: a) to determine the steps of the translation process, and b) to choose the codes into which cultural data would be translated. Hence, in order to teach students how to translate human acts as signs of culture it was necessary to find and/or develop:

1) a metacode or codes for culture[12]
2) a method of translation that could potentially sustain interlingual, intralingual and intersemiotic translations.

Knowledge of a metacode

A major portion of cultural analysis method presented here rests in teaching students to consciously perceive human acts as cultural products and to decode –or translate– these signs through levels of meaning until reaching the core assumptions from which they have been generated. The ability to perform such interpretations, however, rests not only on a method of translation but also on the knowledge of 'metacodes' for translation.

In the end, the multiple levels of analysis which comprise the Cultural Inventory would consist of etic (i.e. meta-) terminologies drawn from the fields of cultural studies, sociology and semiotics, as well as anthropology. It was, however, within anthropological theories that a need for differing levels of discourse to support analysis was first encountered. For, within anthropology the notions of emics and etics (one could say codes and metacodes) are clearly outlined. The notion of etics has been employed as a reference term for the various scientific-based, vocabularies which comprise the Cultural Inventory filters and thereby function as the analytical metacodes for the method of cultural analysis.

Emics and etics: metacodes for translation from anthropology

The early developments of American cultural anthropology fostered a break from the nineteenth century 'eurocentric' ethnographic tradition[13] by attempting to "objectively" view cultures in their own terms. Because of this turn in strategy, a half-century accumulation of specific cultural data has made it possible to develop a metalanguage for culture, i.e. generalized and scientifically valid categories for describing culture based on empirically collected evidence. These categories are referred to as etics. The creation of etics as an anthropological discourse, or metacode, has provided an ability to distinguish or view data in two forms; namely, 1. as the specific emic data collected in the field, and 2. as the categorized etic data of anthropological science. "The distinction between emics and etics is analogous to the distinction between phonemics and phonetics;[...]emic refers to the native's viewpoint; etics refers to the scientist's viewpoint."[14] The employment of emic and etic descriptions enables the anthropologist to meaningfully distinguish "...between *culturally specific* knowledge about the human condition and *objectively valid* knowledge pertinent to the domain of anthropological inquiry into that condition."[15]

Etics refers to the anthropological discourse into which collected cultural data is translated through analysis. Etic categories are considered meaningful by the community of scientific observers because they enable abstracted, universal descriptions of cultures and cultural products for the purpose of comparison. And, as Sturtevant concludes:

> the ethnographer's knowledge of etics [i.e. knowledge of the frameworks and universal categories developed by anthropological theories] assists him in discovering the locally-significant features by guiding his initial observations and formulation of hypotheses.[16]

Thus an etic account of cultural products aims at data description approximating 'culture-free' scientific discourse, while emic descriptions are 'culture specific.'[17]

Returning to the question on the tense of the verb in the sentence: "I walk the dog," it is clear that to correctly answer, a student must possess a basic understanding of language and some knowledge of linguistic meta-codes, i.e. vocabulary, to articulate an answer. Without this grammar back*ground* the student can not answer the question, although s/he may be perfectly, albeit unconsciously, adept at using tense correctly in speech.

The understanding of language structure proceeds only as a student learns the terminologies of the linguistic metacode. For, the student can not develop an understanding and awareness of structure without the concepts to describe structure, and without the practice of applying these concepts through sentence analysis. This is the same with culture.

Culture, like grammar, is consistently employed as a mediation mechanism (code). The descriptive and normative propositions of which it is comprised are well learned and employed but most often unconsciously. In most cases, *evidence of their existence* surfaces only after the social actor has experienced a descriptive/normative meaning system break-down resulting in what is commonly referred to as "culture shock." Nonetheless, a conscious awareness of culture as a cognitive system often does not follow a culture shock experience because social actors lack an understanding of how they semiotically employ this system to define their realities; as Edward T. Hall has made clear through comparative example:

> Remember, it is possible to live life with no knowledge of physiology, speak a language well without knowing linguistics or even schoolteachers' grammar, or use a TV set, a telephone, and an automobile without a clue to electronic or mechanical know-how. It is also possible to grow up and mature in a culture with little or no knowledge of the basic laws that make it work... .[18]

In response to Edward T. Hall's question: "...how does one go about learning the underlying structure of culture?"[19] It is proposed that a study of the structure of culture be viewed as analogous a study of the grammar of a language.

To access structural meaning in language study, students break down a sentence by categorizing its words according to grammatical form: i.e. noun, verb, preposition; and/or function: i.e. subject, direct object, verb, etc. When the student cognitively grasps and is able to apply etic terminologies for word forms and functions, this theoretical awareness transfers into an ability to consciously articulate sentences as grammatical structures. Because grammatical analysis is based on a universal linguistic code, students developing linguistic awareness of this code (through knowledge and employment) impart a heightened awareness of construction throughout their total language use. In this way, the practice of structurally analyzing sentences in a foreign language using linguistic codes opens students to the subtleties of syntactic expression in their native language.

A similar cognitive approach to culture is utilized to promote cultural awareness and understanding across the curriculum of foreign language programs. Analyzing foreign cultural phenomena using universal codes from anthropology and sociology to impart understanding of the underlying structure of cultural communication enhances the possibility of cultural reflection on the part of the student, just as learning the structure of a foreign language through the codes of linguistics enhances the possibility of grammatical reflection. The universal etic terminologies to describe culture as cognitive systems are learned by structurally analyzing action sequences in texts via the translation process put forth in the Cultural

Inventory. As the students perform a Cultural Inventory analysis, they translate data using these 'etic' vocabularies. Through this cognitive act of analysis-as-translation, students develop an awareness of cultural products both in terms of their forms and functions. Teaching students to utilize metacodes, or etic terminologies through practice analysis provides students with the back*ground* necessary to analyze the culture content of human interactions. Such practice of analysis-as-translation thus develops into a cultural literacy; for, analyzing and evaluating the meaning systems of the target culture they study enables students to become more aware of the nature and structure of their own shared descriptive and normative meaning systems.

What is a translation process

According to Jakobson, interpretation is synonymous with translation (see figure 4.4). Translation, in turn, constitutes "the essence of semiosis."[20]

Figure 4.4 Interpretation Process in Semiosis

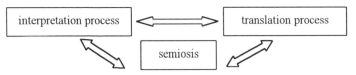

Thus, we can now see semiosis (the action of a sign)[21] as translation. For, "...semiose[22] is a continuous *sign process* that is based on the *interpretation* of one sign through another." A process which "Jakobson described[...] as *translation*."[23] The sign process then, can be seen as a translation process; a view held in semiotic Substitutional Equivalence Theories of Meaning;[24] and, this view provides *the key* for a) determining what constitutes a translation process.

The steps of a translation process

The sign is the tool of semiosis in that it provides, through its act, the event of translation. Once the concepts of semiosis and translation are linked, via Jakobson, it is possible to consider the action of the 'sign' as a translation process (see figure 4.5).

Figure 4.5 Semiosis in the Action of Signs

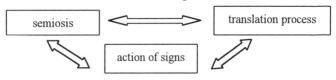

The method of culture analysis presented in the Cultural Inventory was developed from this understanding of the action of a sign as a translation process. The Cultural Inventory method of analysis, therefore, approaches the cultural meanings embodied in human interactions through semiosis.

Applied Semiotics as a method of translation

Interpretation-as-translation is the base pedagogical technique of the Cultural Inventory analysis method; the 'sign as act' for the base structure of a translation process is, in turn, the base structuring principle behind the analytical levels of the Cultural Inventory as a translation tool (see figure 4.6).

Figure 4.6 Action of Signs in the Translation Process

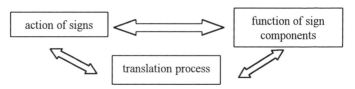

Locating a definition of sign was essential to the foundation structure of the Cultural Inventory method of analysis. A theory of sign was needed that would both define the components of a sign, and provide information on the function of these components. For, in order to replicate the act of a sign (semiosis), it is necessary to understand the elements of a sign and their function in the sign process.

The practice of dividing and classifying the components of signs so as to better understand the manner in which they operate is a central focus of semiotic theories. Since the science of semiotics, in its broadest sense, is the "study or doctrine of signs, sometimes supposed to be a science of signs...,"[25] [which incorporates]... "...theories that explain how signs are related to their meanings and how signs are organized"[26] the field of semiotics was chosen as the source for sign definitions that would provide ideas on how to structure the Cultural Inventory as a translation tool for culture.

Distinguishing between culture and cultural products[27] in the conception of culture enables one to perceive human acts as signs. And, semiotic theories of sign enable the development of a strategy to access culture through human interactions, in the same fashion whereby the meaning of a sign is accessed. We will now outline the basics of our sign definition and then explain how this definition of sign has been used to structure the 'translation-filters' which comprise the Cultural Inventory.

According to the terminology developed by the European linguist Ferdinand Saussure, there are two key elements to a linguistic sign: "...the signifier (a thing, word, or picture) and the signified (the mental picture or meaning indicated by the signifier).[28] In semiotics of the Saussurian tradition the sign model is of a dyadic –or two-part, structure. Although Saussure's dyadic sign definition supplies the theoretical basis for understanding translation as the act of a sign (i.e. a thing stands for some other meaning) it does not include enough elements to demonstrate how this act occurs and therefore proved unproductive for use with the Cultural Inventory. For this reason, a triadic definition of sign was employed.

The American philosopher Charles S. Peirce, a contemporary to Saussure, had also articulated a definition of sign. But, differing from Saussure, Peirce's work both incorporates another element and seeks to describe the associations among these elements:

> I define a sign as anything which is so determined by something else, called its object, and so determines an effect upon a person, which effect I call its interpretant, that the latter is thereby mediated by the former.[29]

Another, of the many definitions supplied by Peirce, indicates how this sign concept moves beyond the dyadic model by incorporating a variable element for context "in some respect" and perspective "to somebody:" :"A sign, or representamen, is something which stands to somebody for something in some respect or capacity."[30] Peirce's concept was chosen for the Cultural Inventory design because the additions, directed toward the conditions of context "in some respect or capacity" and perspective "to somebody," makes his concept of sign a clearer illustration of semiosis and hence more productive for our purpose; namely, to design an analysis structure that would replicate a translation process. In short, the Peircean triadic sign concept makes it possible to more effectively replicate a translation process because it allows a more detailed explanation of the function/action of sign elements within semiosis. The Peircean triadic sign thus provides a model of semiosis as a meaning strategy which John Deely, following Peirce, shows in his distinction between fundamental and formal signs; a distinction that helps clarify the use of the sign as a semiotic process.

Deely explains that a sign is both a fundamental 'thing' and a formal 'process.' When signs are taken to be 'things,' they are being described in a *fundamental* sense, "(as happens, for example, with billboards, or with the red octagons we employ for regulating traffic flow, or with the notices posted along highways, etc.)."[31] For example, if a person points to a red octagon with the letters S T O P painted on it in white and says: "There is a sign." the actual 'thing' (i.e. red octagon) to which that person has pointed is a fundamental sign. However, when signs are taken *semiotically* as a 'process,' they are being described in a *formal* sense. A sign in this sense...

> [...]is never an object simply, for an object *simply represents itself within awareness*, while a [formal] sign[...]*makes something other than itself present in awareness.* Hence an object need not be a [formal] sign in some given respect, and, when it is also a [formal] sign, it is so only in the respect that it stands for some other object.[32]

In the red octagon example, the formal sign is not that to which the person has pointed, but rather, "that for which that to which [the person is] pointing stands."[33]

The formal sign constitutes a (triadic) relationship among three events (perception, association, interpretation): a perception of that to which the person is pointing, namely the stop-sign as thing; an association of the conceptualized command "halt, then proceed" with the perception; and some type of a cognitive interpretation mechanism which, in respect to a context, puts forth the association (see figure 4.7).

Figure 4.7 The Formal Sign Process

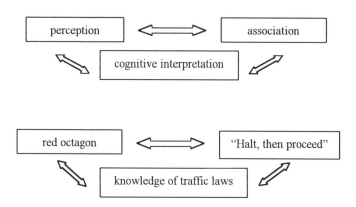

These events can also be listed as (representation, conceptualized meaning, interpretant mechanism): the conceptualized meaning as the command "halt, then proceed," the physical representation of the concept as a red octagon; and, with respect to traffic laws as the interpretant mechanism, the association red-octagon -> "halt, then proceed."

Figure 4.8 The Formal Sign Elements

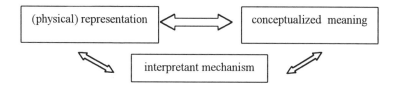

If brought to an empirical outcome, this triadic relationship would surface in the resultant effect: i.e. of stopping the car (see figure 4.9). This "fourth" event (resultant effect) has been added to the example because it is necessary for our purpose of analysis. This fourth event is *not* theoretically part of the triadic sign model as a process. Rather, it is the empirical outcome of the formal sign (see figure 4.10).

Figure 4.9 The Formal Sign and Resultant Effect

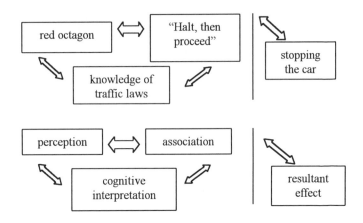

Figure 4.10 Triadic Model of the Formal Sign

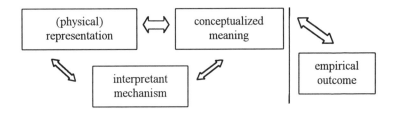

The only way to empirically show that the sign act has occurred is to have evidence via the resultant effect, which then, in turn, becomes a sign that a sign act has occurred. For our analysis purpose; witnessing the function of a sign is dependent on a realization (A) of a translation and its effect (B)...

> A. realization of the translation of 1) the red octagon as representation, or 'representamen' into 2) the command "Halt then proceed" as a conceptualized meaning, or 'object' by means of 3) the traffic laws as the interpertant mechanism; or 'interpretant'...

and...

> B. an effect of this translation materialized in 4) the physical act of stopping the car as an empirical outcome of the sign act outlined in A.[34]

Thus the sign is the process of a cognitive act of translation whereby a representamen comes to stand for an object through an associative element, the interpretant. However, since this translation can only occur within an interpreter, evidence that it has occurred surfaces as an empirical outcome produced by the interpreter. The empirical outcome may, or may not immediately surface in the form of an action through the interpreter (in our case the social actor). If, or when the translation process produces a resultant effect or response, at the moment of response, the interpreter-social actor and resultant effect are one. Because semiotics enables a sign act (translation) to be mapped in this fashion, it permits one to determine what constitutes mediation as the result of "the process of bringing together things that otherwise would be unconnected."[35] In other words, from the perspective of analysis one can work backwards from the empirical outcome and thereby deduce or infer with respect to culture, the core assumption that functioned as the interpretant for the social actor within the process.[36]

Within human interaction [formal] signs perform the function of mediation between a stimulus, or object of direct experience (red octagon) and a response, or resultant effect (stopping the car).

Figure 4.11 Triadic Model of Human Interaction

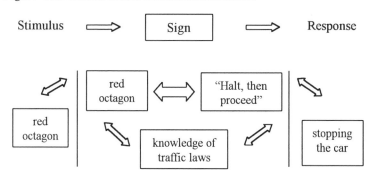

And, within the act of a sign, i.e. in semiosis, the interpretant mechanism (knowledge of traffic laws) performs the function of mediation between a representation (red octagon) and a conceptualized meaning (command: 'Halt then proceed').

Figure 4.12 Semiosis of Human Interaction

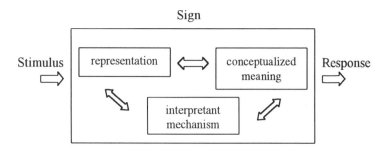

When, in human interaction, the interpretant mechanism of the sign is generated from the social actor's cognitive reservoir of core assumptions (i.e. the social actor's culture) this interaction is cultural; the conceptualized meaning is culturally based, and the response is seen as a cultural product.

> Even at the level of simple or supposedly simple sense perception we are increasingly discovering that the message which comes through the senses is itself mediated through a value system. We do not perceive our sense data raw; they are mediated through a highly learned process of interpretation and acceptance.[...]What this means is that for any individual organism or organization there are no such things as "facts." There are only messages filtered through a changeable value system.[37]

This type of interaction is culturally mediated interaction;[38] it is a prerequisite for the existence of cultural products. Mediated interaction is employed by social actors as the process by which a culturally meaningful association is established between two realities[39] either the real world (nature) and the artificial world (culture); or between two artificial worlds (intra- or cross-cultural encounters). Through the process of semiosis, illustrated by the triadic relationships of the elements of a [formal] sign, "things" and "events" become representations of cultural meanings when mediated by core assumptions in the mind of an interpreter. For, the material objects as representamen will call forth some cultural significance (representamen-object association via an interpretant) and from this significance (conceptualized object) the social actor reacts.

It is important to again stress that in semiosis the Peircean sign model is a *triadic* act of association between a thing/event, its 'new' meaning, and its interpretant, and not a physical thing.

> The sign manifests itself in semiosis not at all as a physical thing, nor even as a peculiar type and variety of object. The sign appears, rather, as the linkage whereby the objects, be they bodily entities or purely objective, come to stand one for another within some particular context or web of experience.[40]

As such, Peirce's definition of sign is aimed at studying the process of semiosis (i.e. the act of association that occurs among sign elements). Since the elements of a sign thus represent semiosis, and since semiosis models the translation process, it seemed plausible to employ sign elements as the components of the Cultural Inventory analysis process. Therefore, the goal has been to structurally design the Cultural Inventory in an attempt to replicate this process of semiosis. For this reason, we will now turn to Peirce's sign elements as they have been interpreted in relation to the Cultural Inventory.

A complete definition of Peirce's triadic sign cited above reads as follows:

> A sign, or *representamen*, is something which stands to somebody for something in some respect or capacity. It addresses somebody, that is, creates in the mind of that person an equivalent sign, or perhaps a more developed sign. That sign which it creates I call the *interpretant* of the first sign. The sign stands for something, its *object*. It stands for that object, not in all respects, but in reference to a sort of idea, which I have sometimes called the *ground* of the representamen.[41]

In order to clarify the elements of Peirce's definition, the abstract redundancy of the root "some" can be substituted with his specific terminology. A sign, then, is a representamen to an interpretant for an object according to some ground. Now, to suit the specific needs of our method, the definition of sign is restated as: a representation (representamen) which activates according to a frame of reference (interpretant-ground) the translation of the representation into some meaning (object).

Robert Marty, in his analysis of the 76 definitions of the sign by Peirce, concludes that

Peircean conceptions of the sign lead us to retain three fundamental elements as theoretical universals resulting from the logical analysis of semiotic phenomena:

-[element 1] the [Representamen R], an object of direct experience ("external" or "internal" object)

-[element 2] the [Object O], present in the semiotic phenomena because it is connected with the sign

-[element 3] the [Interpretant I], present because it is the mental element which ensures this connection.[42]

According to Peirce's triadic sign model, then, a sign is the association of 3 elements. The 3 elements which constitute this relationship or association are 1. the representamen; 2. the object; and 3. the interpretant. The 'interpreter' is, in our case, the actor or mind in which this association is occurring; interpreters are not part of the triadic sign model proper.

The first element listed by Marty should be understood as an object-of-direct-experience (i.e. perceptible stimulus) which performs the role of conveying a meaning beyond itself. "To designate the object of direct experience necessarily at the origin of all semiotic phenomena, Peirce uses the words 'representation,' 'representamen' and especially 'sign'."[43] Deely, in his *Basics of Semiotics*, provides the following guidelines for the function of the first element of a sign:

A representation [or object-of-direct-experience] may be of itself, or it may be of something other than itself. In the former case it constitutes an object [of-direct-experience], but only in the latter case does it constitute a [representamen].[44]

For example, thunder is an object-of-direct-experience; one hears it as sound and sometimes feels the vibrations of the sound in the earth or other structures. But, thunder, the object-of-direct-experience, only functions as the representamen of a sign when it conveys the meaning rain. Thus,

To be a [representamen], it is necessary to represent something other than the self. Being a [representamen] is a form of bondage to another, to the signified, the object [conceptualized meaning / idea] that the [representamen] is not but that the [representamen] nevertheless stands for and represents.[45]

With the introduction of rain one reaches the second of the fundamental Peircean elements, namely, *the Object*.[46] An adjustment of the conventional usage for the word object referring to something embodied in material is necessary here. Peirce uses the term to denote a conceptualized idea precipitated by *the Representamen* of a sign. Thus, when rain is *the Object* of a sign, it is the idea of rain, and not the actual occurrence of rain.[47] The object of the sign can be the idea of anything, in other words it can be the idea of...

> a material 'object of the world with which we have a perceptual acquaintance' [like rain] (§ 2.330) or a merely mental or imaginary entity 'of the nature of a sign or thought' [like Peter Pan] (§ 1.538). It can be a 'single known existing thing' [like Mt. Vesuvius] (§ 2.232) or a class of things [like mothers].[48]

Thus the two elements of a Peircean triadic association so far defined are the representamen (some object-of-direct-experience which stands for an idea beyond itself) and the object (an idea which the perception of the representamen has conveyed into the mind). In the example, thunder becomes the representamen of a triadic association when it ceases to be itself and functions to convey the 'idea of rain'.

The interpretant is the third element of the Peircean sign. This element has been described as the "mental effect," brought about in the consciousness of the interpreter, which causes the association between the object-of-direct-experience (representamen) and the idea evoked (object). In a triadic association, the interpretant functions as the intervening impetus of the representamen-object association; it is the mediation mechanism.

> The idea of the representation itself [representamen] excites in the mind another idea [object] and in order that it may do this it is necessary that *some principle of association between the two ideas* [x] should already be established in that mind.[49]

This makes the interpretant [x] a mediate cause of the representamen-object association and its importance to the process of semiosis is made clear by Marty's example based on *Robinson Crusoe*. "Friday's *footprint in the sand* [the representamen] stands for *a human presence* [the object] only because of the association in Robinson's mind [the interpretant]..."[50]

and "This association can be conceived only in the mind and by the mind to which the two objects are present."[51] One could say that the interpretant provides the perspective from which the representamen is translated into an object:

> An interpretant in general is the [mediation principle] ground on which an object[-of-direct-experience] functions as a sign. Interpretants exist, consequently, at those points in semiosis where objects[-of-direct-experience] are transformed into signs or signs are transformed into other signs.[52]

Prior to conversion into the state of semiosis, the object-of-direct-experience is a potential representamen, in that it has the potential to function as the origin for a triadic association.[53] All objects-of-direct-experience, imagined or otherwise, hold the potential to be activated and or utilized by social actors as cultural representamen, or conduits for descriptive and normative meanings as objects. They become conduits for descriptive and normative meaning when an interpretant (connection) mediates this association. It is through this third sign element that one sees how the representamen comes to stand for an object. And, the triadic sign model is superior to dyadic models because it provides a category for this vital sign element. For, it is the third correlate of the sign which bridges the relationship between the representamen and the object and as such constitutes an essential component to understanding the sign as a translation process:

> ...it is clear that a third element is needed because it is essential in semiotic phenomena to define an element capable of explaining the necessary connection of the two objects that are potentially present to the mind (the perceived [representamen], as such, and the object to which it is connected).[54]

This theoretical model and the function of the interpretant is made clearer through the tangible example of a lamp. For example, think of a lamp not yet turned on. In this instance the lamp has the potential to function as a conduit of electricity. If the switch is turned on the lamp is transformed into a light (see figure 4.13). Until the lamp is turned on, the lamp is only a potential conduit for electricity, a potential light. In the same fashion, a human act has the potential to function as a conduit activating descriptive and normative meaning; as a representamen. If it is activated by an interpretant (the. switch) as a mediation mechanism, the human act now representamen is transformed into an object.

Figure 4.13 Lamp-light Example

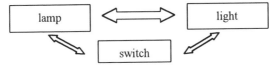

Figure 4.14 Peircean Sign Elements

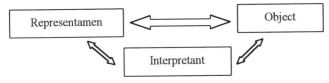

Through the interpretant, as a mediation mechanism, the representamen then becomes something beyond itself. When turned on, the lamp becomes a conduit for electricity manifested into the form of light. In much the same way, a human act as a representamen when activated by an interpretant becomes a conduit for a descriptive or normative proposition manifested in the form of a cultural product (see figure 4.15).

Figure 4.15 Human Act as Cultural Product

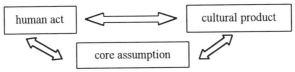

Culture as a cognitive system of descriptive and normative propositions functions for social actors as a prescriptive-code-mediation-mechanism that they use to assign propositional meanings to their environment; from these meanings social actors then respond producing resultant effects of the mediation. Accessing the mediation mechanism involves analyzing the process of semiosis; a triadic association that functions as a culture- meaning-making process for the social actor;[55] the process of association which occurs in the act of a triadic sign. Analyzing human acts or action sequences in literature so as to reach the content of the mediation mechanism, or core assumption, from which such acts or action sequences are produced also involves semiosis. For this reason, semiosis has been employed as the strategy for the method of culture analysis presented in the Cultural Inventory.

The Semiotic Design of the Cultural Inventory

The examination of the structure of a triadic sign showed how semiosis is understood as a three-part association whereby a first element comes to stand for a second element in some respect as determined by a third element (see figure 4.16).

Figure 4.16 Triadic Association

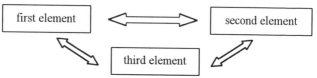

The act of association that occurs through these elements is also a translation.[56]

It is important to address an additional factor in discussing the relationship of triadic sign elements. This factor pertains to the context within which the triadic association occurs and it has been termed 'Ground'. In our application of Peirce's sign definition the term 'ground' has been taken to refer to the condition of context. Again we note Peirce's definition: "A sign, or representamen, is something which stands to somebody for something in some respect or capacity."[57] To return to the thunder-rain example (see figure 4.17 below), the interpretant of this sign would be the interpreter's knowledge of thunder-storms either from prior experience or learning. The interpretant thus generates the representamen-object association; namely 'thunder-idea of rain.'

Figure 4.17 Thunder-rain Example

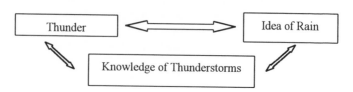

And, the ground, or situation within which the object-of-direct-experience (representamen-Thunder) occurs (i.e. weather outside, dark sky, wind) works to context the representamen-interpretant association.

Figure 4.18 Ground Context with Sign Elements

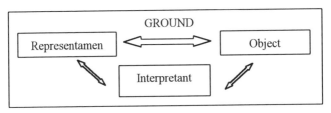

Hence, the ground-context is, for this sign, the environmental situation in which the interpreter first perceives the object-of-direct-experience. Peirce's triadic model of sign is productive for cultural analysis because the multiple sign components enable a replication of the structure of a translation process. For, his triadic sign model not only provides categories for a signifier (representamen) and a signified (object), but also provides categories for the consideration of perspective (interpretant) and context (ground).

The interpretant of a sign has previously been determined as some principle of association between two ideas (the representamen and the object) and "a special aspect or feature of a thing [representamen] which…[serves as]…a proposal, a hypothesis, a means by which the interpretant can reach out toward its object."[58] Thus the ground (as context) alters the interpretant (as association perspective) and object (meaning) of the sign, as David Savan's "thermometer" example indicates:

A thermometer is *a sign of the temperature* of its surroundings. But notice, only if it is so interpreted. I may look at the thermometer only *as a sign that it was made by a particular master craftsman* whose work I am studying, and who designed it to be a beautiful decorative ornament for this patio. Or I may interpret it to be *a sign of the age of this building*, or *of the taste of the person who chose it*. In each of these cases, the ground of the sign will be different. What is significant for deciding the identity of the craftsman who made it, is not the same as the ground of my belief that the age of the thermometer indicated the age of the building.[59]

This is the significance of the Peircian sign model as analytical design structure; for, the concept of 'ground' makes it possible to move textual data through several *analytical filters* –obtaining different cultural data from each. The Cultural Inventory was developed by adapting theoretical frameworks into a series of 'translation-filters.' The various translation-filters of the Cultural Inventory (Situational, Interactional, Feedback, Notional, and Interpersonal) thus became the theoretical *grounds* in which to focus student analysis on different semiotic aspects of cultural communication. By applying Peirce's triadic sign model in this way, the analysis 'object' of the cultural communication varies according to filter similar to what Savan's thermometer example illustrates:

> the object of the sign will vary with the interpretant and ground. In one case it is the master craftsman who is the object, in the other it is the age of the building, and in yet another it is the taste of the person who chose to place this thermometer just here. Thus one thing may be many different signs.[60]

Savan's axiom of Peirce's model; "...the object of the sign will vary with the interpretant and the ground," thus also applies to the Cultural Inventory's analysis design. Each theoretical ground, represented by a different translation-filter, varies the interpretant and hence object of the sign.

Once the triadic sign had been determined as the operative translation structure, the Cultural Inventory was designed to replicate this structure. By using the triadic sign as design principle it was possible to isolate the components of translation and then alter the contents of these components so as to direct the focus of a cultural analysis process. Designing the Cultural Inventory analysis levels from the perspectives of ground and interpretant provided a means to limit the analytical variables; for, by setting translation filters as grounds, it was possible to define the range of interpretants for the student analyst. The analysis process put forth in the Cultural Inventory thus focuses the association of representamen and objects via interpretants within one theoretical ground at a time.

The theoretical design of this analysis technique, based on Peirce's sign, constitutes a triad whereby a third correlate (I, interpretant) is related to the first (R, representamen) via a second (O, object) with respect to a particular context (G, ground). The relationships of these three sign components (diagrammed in figure 4.18 below) is made plain when compared with the more tangible Thunder-rain example given earlier (see figure 4.19).

Figure 4.19 Thunder-rain Example in Ground

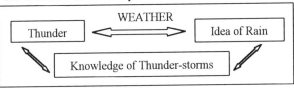

Figure 4.18 Ground Context with Sign Elements

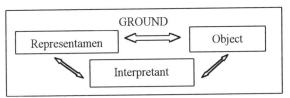

A sign, then, according to its Cultural Inventory application is something (R), from which an interpretant (I), has selected an aspect with respect to a hypotheses (G), which is then used to identify some meaning or significance (O), beyond the thing (R).

(R) textual action sequence
(I) cultural analysis
(G) Cultural Inventory translation-filter
(O) surfaced culture/al data

Figure 4.20 Translation-filter as Ground

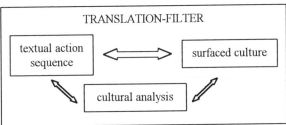

Each translation filter then contains the components of a triadic sign. As the filter-grounds change, the ground-interpretants are altered to associate new 'objects' with the previous representamen. In this way, student's translation analysis is focused, filter by filter, on different aspects of the data, ultimately leading to the deduction of an operative descriptive-normative proposition for both the sequence actor and action sequence.

In viewing the theoretical sign model diagram (see figure 4.21) and comparing it with a diagram of the Situational Filter analysis (see figure 4.22) the underlying triadic-sign-base structure of the Cultural Inventory translation filters is revealed By creating the Cultural Inventory as an analysis tool, with filters and applications designed according to this structure of a formal sign, semiosis is replicated as the process of analysis throughout the Inventory.

Figure 4.21 Peircean Triadic Sign Application

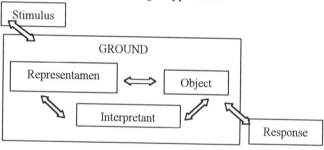

Figure 4.22 Situational-filter Sign

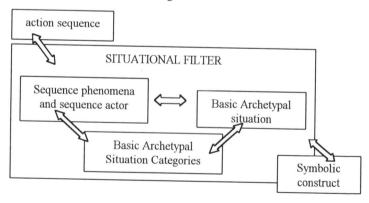

Semiotic theories were employed to structure the Cultural Inventory so that the analysis method and cognitive approach to culture would correspond. For, according to the model based on Spiro's theories, culture, although existing separate from the human actor, can only be witnessed or experienced through human interaction or representations of human action. Because human acts can simultaneously stand for what they are (human acts) and for something else (physically objectified core assumptions), human acts – in reality and in fiction– can be read as cultural phenomena. When read as cultural phenomena, such actions are then perceived as vehicles for the expression of the actor's culture. When analyzed as cultural phenomena, such actions thus function as signs of culture following the traditional definition of sign: (aliquid stat pro aliqo) "something that stands for something else."[61] For the student, human interactions thus become the representamen of 'surfaced culture' because the student analyst, employing the Cultural Inventory, now perceives them from the perspective of, or with respect to cultural analysis. It is, therefore, "surfaced culture" as cultural phenomena that students will learn to read and analyze using the Cultural Inventory.

Notes

[1] D'Andre, Schweder, Douglas, Keesing, etc.
[2] See Spiro's 'Hierarchy of Cognitive Salience' Levels IV and V as noted in Chapter 3 of this study.
[3] As stated in Chapter 3, Melford Spiro's theory, 'Hierarchy of Cognitive Salience,' provided a theoretical base for determining the relationship between material manifestations of culture and 'culture' as a cognitive system in this study.
[4] i.e. behavior, verbalizations and artifacts. Verbalizations include thoughts as mental products, as well as the values and beliefs that are ideational products of culture- the cognitive system. We chose the term verbalizations here because thoughts, values and beliefs are expressed in words. Hence the term verbalization includes both internally and externally manifested verbal products of culture.
[5] Spiro, "Reflections" 38. For our discussion on Spiro's concept of culture and his 'Hierarchy of Cognitive Salience' see Chapter 3 of this study.
[6] Colapietro 141. Colapietro further notes that "this notion [of mediation] is important in Semiotics since signs perform the function of mediation."

[7] Deely, *The Human Use of Signs* 44-45. Deely distinguishes between three modeling systems; the Umwelt as a pre-linguistic primary modeling system; Language as a linguistic secondary modeling system; and Culture as a postlinguistic tertiary modeling system, as he writes: "...the Umwelt as it is structured by linguistically mediated social interaction becomes freed from over-determination by biological heritage, enabling the formation of what I have called the post-linguistic (or "tertiary" modeling system, the semiotic equivalent of what anthropologists hertofore have termed simply culture- a semiotic system postlinguistic in nature but presupposing language both in order to come into being in the first place and in order to be understood in what is proper to it." 45.

[8] We use the prefix here meta- meaning beyond and above to differentiate between language on the one hand, and a specially developed vocabulary/ language designed to talk about language. The entry in Colapietro's *Glossary of Semiotics* defines a 'metalanguage' as: "A language used to talk about another language. The language being talked about is the object language, while the language used to describe, explain, evaluate, etc. the object language is a metalanguage." 143.

[9] According to the *Glossary of Semotics*, there are two basic semiotic understandings for code. The first determines the sense of code as a "key (or set of instructions) for translating a message," 64. For example, "Morse Code is a key for correlating particular clicks and silences to letters of the alphabet," 64. We could call this type of code a translative code. The second determines the sense of code as a "set of rules prescribing how to act or what to do," 64. For example, "Codes as sets of rules[...]provide us the norms to judge whether we are acting appropriately," 64. We could call this code a prescriptive code.

[10] Here, codes would be translative codes, see note 9 this chapter.

[11] Martin Krampen [et al.] *Classics of Semiotics* (New York: Plenum, 1987) 320. Our emphasis.

[12] i.e. a metacode for culture would be a metalanguage "...used to describe, explain, evaluate, etc. ..." culture, see definition of metalanguage in note 8, this chapter.

[13] In their failure to understand culture as a cognitive system nineteenth century conclusions derived from culture studies were tainted due to the inherent biases of the observers. Culturally constituted phenomena of the groups studied were analyzed and evaluated according to the cognitive systems of the observers– in short observers tended to filter raw cultural data through the propositions of their own set of core assumptions. Consequently, early ethnographers judged the cultural manifestations they studied according to their own cultural reference. Most of these early studies are now labeled

eurocentric, but they represent testaments to the importance of employing emics and etics in anthropological discourse.

[14] Lett 62. Colapietro, in his *Glossary of Semiotics*, provides the following definition for the emic/etic distinction: "Adjectives coined by Kenneth L. Pike to designate two different approaches to the study of such things as languages or culture; an emic approach being one that is specifically adapted to one language or culture, while an etic approach is one of general applicability." 97.

[15] Lett 59.

[16] Sturtevant, "Studies in Ethnoscience," in *Culture and Cognition*, ed. James P. Spradley (Prospect Heights: Waveland Press, Inc., 1987) 134.

[17] Sturtevant continues: "Culture-free features of the real world may be called 'etics' (Pike 1954). The label may also be applied to features which are not truly culture-free, but which at least have been derived from the examination of more than one culture...," 133.

[18] Hall, *Beyond Culture* 106.

[19] Hall, *Beyond Culture* 106. Unfortunately Hall only points in the direction of where the answer may begin to be found.

[20] Krampen 244.

[21] Nöth explains: "Peirce (§ 5.472) defined this triadic 'action of the sign,' 'this process in which the sign has a cognitive effect on its interpreter' (§ 5.484), as *semiosis* (or *semeiosis*)." 42.

[22] The spelling "semiose" was used by Charles Peirce, we use the current spelling semiosis.

[23] Krampen 244.

[24] Nöth in his *Handbook of Semiotics* explains: "The semiotic foundation of this principle was made explicit by Peirce, who defines meaning as 'the translation of a sign into another system of signs' (4.127). Jakobson called this 'one of the most felicitous, brilliant ideas which general linguisitcs and semiotics gained from the American thinker' and points out that 'many fruitless discussions about mentalism and anti-mentalism would be avoided if one approached the notion of meaning in terms of translation' (1980:35-36)." 99.

[25] Colapietro 179.

[26] Steven W. Littlejohn, *Theories of Human Communication*, 5th ed. (Belmont: Wadsworth Publishing Company,1996) 64.

[27] Culture- the cognitive system composed of normative and descriptive propositions about reality. Cultural phenomena are the human life-identity acts, whether classified as verbalizations, behaviors, artifacts or a combination of these, which the social actor has imbued with culture.

[28] Terence Hawkes, *Structuralism and Semiotics* (Berkely and Los Angeles: University of California Press, 1977) 126. Quoting Roman Jakobson, Hawkes

writes: "The study of sign systems derives [...]from an initial and very ancient perception that a sign has two aspects: 'an immediately perceptible *signans* and an inferable, apprehensible *signatum*'. This does not essentially differ from the distinction between signifier and signified recorded by Saussure: both elements function as aspects of the 'indissoluble unity' of the sign, and the various relationships between them form the basis of semiotic structures." 126.

[29] John Deely, *Basics of Semiotics* (Bloomington and Indianapolis: Indiana University Press, 1990) 88, citation of Peirce's 'Letter to Lady Welby: December 14-23' in Hardwick, *Semiotics and Significs: The Correspondence between Charles S. Peirce and Victoria Lady Welby*, 1977, pp. 88-89.

[30] Charles Peirce, " v. 1897- C.P. 2-228-Division of signs," in "76 Definitions of the Sign by C.S. Peirce," Robert Marty, 29 June 1999 <http://www.door.net/arisbe/menu/library/rsources/76defs/76defs.htm> 3.

[31] Deely, *Human Use of Signs* 50.

[32] Deely, *Human Use of Signs* 50.

[33] Deely, *Human Use of Signs* 50. Our explanation of the difference between a fundamental and a formal sign is based on Deely.

[34] David Savan, "C.S. Peirce and American Semiotics," *The Peirce Seminar Papers*, vol. 2, ed. Michael Shapiro (Providence: Berg, 1994) 185. Savan explains the dynamic interpretant of a sign as the semiotic effects of a sign: "...dynamic interpretants –plural, since every sign has many– are external to the sign. They are the actual semiotic effects of the sign, the many different ways in which the sign is in fact interpreted. In the example of the Mayan stela, the actual reading, successful and unsuccessful, of the Mayan glyphs are among the dynamic interpretants." 185.

[35] Colapietro 141. See our explanation of 'mediated interaction' in connection with the Interactional Filter in Chapter 6 of this study.

[36] This is the process developed for the Interactional Filter analysis. See chapter 6.

[37] Kenneth E. Boulding, "The Image," *Culture and Cognition*, ed. James P. Spradley (Prospect Heights: Waveland Press, Inc., 1972) 48.

[38] What we have explained here as culturally mediated interaction thus describes the process of how phenomena come to be 'culturally constituted.' For more on mediated interaction see our discussion of the Interactional Filter in Chapter 6 of this study.

[39] Nöth, paraphrasing Mukarovsky in "Nonsigns in mediational and functional theories of action," *Handbook of Semiotics* 82.

[40] Deely, *Basics of Semiotics* 58.

[41] Peirce, "Logic as Semiotic: The Theory of Signs," *Philosophical Writings of Peirce*, ed. Justus Buchler (New York: Dover Publications, Inc., 1959) 99. Peirce continues the definition with a clarification of the term idea, he writes:

"'Idea' is here to be understood in a sort of Platonic sense, very familiar in everyday talk; I mean in that sense in which we say that one man catches another man's idea, in which we say that when a man recalls what he was thinking of at some previous time, he recalls the same idea[...]that is to have a *like* content[...]and is not at each instant of the interval a new idea." 99.

[42] Marty 24-25. Marty has used the term Sign S, but representamen is interchangeable for this term- see definition referenced as note 31 above, in this Chapter. Because we have used the term sign to refer to the triadic relationship we retain the use of the term representamen to refer to the first element of the sign.

[43] Marty, 22. Nöth writes: "Theoretically, Peirce distinguished clearly between the sign, which is the complete tirad, and the representamen which is the first correlate." 42.

[44] Deely, *Basics of Semiotics* 52. We altered Deely's use of the term "Sign" here to [representamen] to maintain consistency and clarity in our explanation.

[45] Deely, *Basics of Semiotics* 35. Deely uses the term "Sign" here for Representamen.

[46] Our use of the term object is based on the findings of Marty's analysis: "To designate the object of the sign, Peirce employs on nearly every occasion the word 'object' accompanied with considerations that render it, explicitly or implicitly, that which is connected to this object of direct experience that is the sign." 22.

[47] Peirce distinguished between dynamical objects and immediate objects. In our example, /rain/ is a dynamical object when it is used to refer to water droplets which are actually falling from the clouds. Thus the actual occurrence of rain, is the dynamical object of our example. As such, a dynamical object is not the object of a triadic relationship. "The object of the sign is called by Peirce the 'immediate object:' it is the concept or idea on which the sign as association is based." Krampen 16.

[48] Nöth, including citations of Peirce's work, 42-43.

[49] Peirce, text notation 6 (1873) in Marty 1.

[50] Marty 23.

[51] Marty 23.

[52] Deely, *Basics of Semiotics* 66, note 26. We have added the terminology here for clarification.

[53] Deely, *Basics of Semiotics* 35. Deely writes: "The sign first of all depends on something other than itself. It is representative but only in a derivative way, in a subordinate capacity. The moment a sign slips out from under this subordination[...]at just that moment does it cease for a while to be a sign. A sign seen standing on its own is not seen as a sign, even though it may remain one virtually. Thus on its own, it is a mere object[...]waiting to become a sign[...]not actually a sign at all."

[54] Marty 23. We have substituted 'representamen' for Marty's use of the term "Sign" in order to maintain consistency in our explanation.

[55] Nöth 42. Peirce defines semiosis as the "process in which the sign has a cognitive effect on its interpreter (§ 5.484)."

[56] See above section 'What is a translation process,' 198-200.

[57] C. S. Peirce, "v. 1887-C.P. 2-228-Division of signs," in Marty 3.

[58] Savan 186-187.

[59] Savan 184.

[60] Savan 184.

[61] Colapietro 18. The entry on "aliquid stat pro aliquo" reads: "Latin expression meaning 'something stands for something else.' The function of one thing standing for another (stare pro) has, from ancient to contemporary times, been taken as the essential characteristic of signs. One influential formulation of this view is found in Augustine's *De Doctrina Christiana*: 'A sign is a thing which, over and above the impressions it makes on the senses, causes something else to come into the mind as a consequence of itself.' One might hear the sound Florence or Firenze and think of a city, or see smoke and think of fire. The power of the sound to convey a conception of the city and the power of sight to suggest the cause of its appearance illustrates what the formula 'aliquid stat pro aliquo' means, for the interpreter of these signs takes something to stand for something else."

Chapter 5

Action Sequence Parameters
and Symbolic Analysis Overview

The Parameters of an Action Sequence

Culture is communicated through texts via the symbolic interaction of characters. The symbolic interaction of characters can be segmented into textual units called action sequences. Each action sequence represents a textual communication of culture and therefore a unit of symbolic interaction. An action sequence thus constitutes the unit of cultural communication chosen for a Cultural Inventory analysis.

To perform a Cultural Inventory analysis, the text of the selected action sequence must be further divided into communicative segments. From the parameters developed to analyze human action as communication, one finds that it is possible to perceive an act in three segments.

> In its most basic form, a social act [or textual action sequence] involves a three-part relationship: an initial gesture from one individual [or perceptive encounter within an individual him/herself], a response to that gesture by another [or interactive encounter within an individual to the perception as a mediated response], and a result of the act [or a response to the perception and interaction as] its meaning...[1]

Employing this three-part functional structure for the analysis of a human act enables one to map a textual action sequence as a communicative encounter composed of three events; namely, a perceptive encounter, an interactive encounter, and a responsive encounter. It is possible to divide the text of an action sequence into three segments using these three events as the parameters. Hence, a textual action sequence as a communication of culture is composed of *an initial segment* depicting a perceptive encounter (i.e. the act takes place in and with regards to a situation usually created out of a need); *a middle segment* depicting a (self)interactive encounter for the sequence actor and from which an act results (i.e. the action is initiated having "been formed or constructed by interpreting the situation. [whereby] the actor selects,[…]and transforms meanings in light of the situation in which he is placed and the direction of his actions);"[2] and *a final segment* depicting a responsive encounter apropos the effectiveness of the act initiated by the sequence actor (i.e. the act is concluded or broken off).[3]

Example Text

The second textual action sequence of the Brother's Grimm fairy tale 'Der Süße Brei' will serve as the text sample for the Cultural Inventory analysis model presented in the definition Chapters 6 and 7 of this study. A text of the complete fairy tale, with translation, is printed below. Although this particular text example is short, it contains three separate action sequences. Each of the three paragraphs that constitute the tale represents one separate action sequence. In the presentation below, the three segments of each action sequence are designated with brackets as 1 [perceptive encounter], 2 [interactive encounter], and 3 [responsive encounter].

Figure 5.1 Action Sequence (1) "Der Süße Brei"

"Der Süße Brei"

1[Es war einmal ein armes frommes Mädchen, das lebte mit seiner Mutter allein, und sie hatten nichts mehr zu essen.] 2 [Da ging das Kind hinaus in den Wald, und begegnete ihm da eine alte Frau, die wußte seinen Jammer schon und schenkte ihm ein Töpfchen, zu dem sollte es sagen: „Töpfchen, koche", so kochte es guten süßen Hirsebrei, und wenn es sagte: „Töpfchen, steh", so hörte es wieder auf zu kochen.] 3 [Das Mädchen brachte den Topf seiner Mutter heim, und nun waren sie ihrer Armut und ihres Hungers ledig und aßen süßen Brei, sooft sie wollten.]¹

"The Sweet Porridge"

1 [ONCE UPON A TIME there was a poor but pious girl who lived alone with her mother and they had nothing more to eat.] 2 [So the girl went out into the forest, where she met an old woman who already knew about her troubles and gave her a small pot, to which the girl was to say: "Little pot, cook," and it would cook a good, sweet millet porridge. And when the girl would say "Little pot, stop!" the pot would stop cooking.] 3 [The girl brought the pot home to her mother, and now they were rid of their poverty and hunger, and they ate sweet porridge as often as they liked.]

Figure 5.2 Action Sequence (2) "Der Süße Brei"

1 [Auf eine Zeit war das Mädchen ausgegangen;] 2 [da sprach die Mutter: „Töpfchen, koche", da kocht es, und sie ißt sich satt; nun will sie, daß das Töpfchen wieder aufhören soll,] 3 [aber sie weiß das Wort nicht. Also kocht es fort, und der Brei steigt über den Rand hinaus und kocht immerzu, die Küche und das ganze Haus voll, und das zweite Haus und dann die Straße, als wollt's die ganze Welt satt machen, und ist die größte Not, und kein Mensch weiß sich da zu helfen.]⁴

1 [One day, when the girl had gone out,] 2 [the mother said, "Little pot, cook," and it began cooking. After she had eaten her fill, she wanted the pot to stop,] 3 [but she didn't know the word. So the pot continued to cook, and the porridge ran over the rim and continued to cook until the kitchen and the whole house were full, and the next house, and then the street, as if it wanted to feed the entire world. The situation was desperate, and no one knew how to help.]

Figure 5.3 Action Sequence (3) "Der Süße Brei"

1 [Endlich, wie nur noch ein einziges Haus übrig ist,] 2 [da kommt das Kind heim und spricht nur: „Töpfchen, steh",] 3 [da steht es und hört auf zu kochen; und wer wieder in die Stadt wollte, der mußte sich durchessen.]⁵

1 [Finally, when only one house was left standing without any porridge in it,] 2 [the girl returned home and simply said, "Little pot, stop!"] 3 [It stopped cooking, and whoever sought to go back into the town had to eat his way through the porridge.]

The second action sequence (see figure 5.2) has been chosen for the Cultural Inventory practice analysis. The remainder of the discussion will focus on the text of this action sequence.

The three segments of an action sequence (2)

Figure 5.2 Action Sequence (2)

> 1 [One day, when the girl had gone out,] 2 [the mother said, "Little pot, cook," and it began cooking. After she had eaten her fill, she wanted the pot to stop,] 3 [but she didn't know the word. So the pot continued to cook, and the porridge ran over the rim and continued to cook until the kitchen and the whole house were full, and the next house, and then the street, as if it wanted to feed the entire world. The situation was desperate, and no one knew how to help.]

The first segment, or perceptive encounter of the sample action sequence begins with the marker "One day...: 1 [*One day*, when the girl had gone out,]. The second segment, or interactive encounter begins at the moment in the text where the mother, as sequence actor, initiates her act: "2 [*the mother said*, "Little pot, cook," and it began cooking. After she had eaten her fill, she wanted the pot to stop, but she didn't know the word]". The final segment constitutes a responsive encounter, here between the sequence actor and action sequence, and begins with text markers indicating that the act initiated by the mother is broken off, rather than concluded:

> 3 [*So the pot continued to cook*, and the porridge ran over the rim and continued to cook until the kitchen and the whole house were full, and the next house, and then the street, as if it wanted to feed the entire world. The situation was desperate, and no one knew how to help.]

The sequence actor of action sequence (2)

The character within the action sequence who incites the interactive encounter is the sequence actor. This character, as the sequence actor, performs as the catalyst for unveiling the core assumption to be confronted in the section of the work to be analyzed. The mother is the designated sequence actor for action sequence (2) of "Der Süße Brei".

The sequence phenomena of action sequence (2)

When sequence phenomena are "culturally constituted" by the sequence actor in an action sequence, such phenomena become activated as dynamic phenomena.[6] Because meanings are thus ascribed to dynamic phenomena through mediated interaction,[7] the dynamic phenomena of an action sequence are understood as "culturally constituted," i.e. phenomena utilized for the communication of culture.

Dynamic phenomena as "objects are of three types –physical (things), social (people), and abstract (ideas)–" and as such "all acquire meaning through symbolic interaction."[8] Potentially anything *material* or *non-material* which has been, or can be imagined (i.e. thoughts), done (i.e. actions), made, or refashioned (i.e. products) through human interaction is included in the category of dynamic phenomena. The pot and the words to control the pot are the designated dynamic phenomena for action sequence (2) of "Der Süße Brei".

The Sequence Creator

Students using the Cultural Inventory will be analyzing the action sequence in a text as a sign of a particular culture communication. From this perspective, the creator of the action sequence (i.e. author) is the communicator and the reader (i.e. student as analyst) is the communicatee. "The user of the signs who effects communication is the communicator and the organism in which the sign-process is aroused by the signs of the communicator is the communicatee."[9] As such, the communicator-author employs an informative usage of the action sequence as a sign of culture.[10] For, the culture to be communicated surfaces through the phases of the action sequence. Therefore, to read an action sequence as a sign of culture(s), the student conducts a symbolic analysis of the action sequence segments, translating the textual data of each segment by employing the first three filters (Situational, Interactional, and Feedback) and first two applications of the Cultural Inventory.[11]

Sign Dimensions in the Cultural Inventory Symbolic Analysis

Signification is defined as "the process by which signs and thus meanings are generated or produced."[12] According to the work of Charles W. Morris, there are three modes, or dimensions of signification for generating meaning.[13] Each of the three modes, or dimensions of signification (designative, prescriptive, and appraisive) has a different function evident in its terminology; namely, to designate, to prescribe, and to appraise or evaluate. Morris' dimensions of signification[14] are used here to explain how the student, applying the first three filters of the Cultural Inventory, will semiotically attend to action sequences as signs of culture. This application of the dimensions of signification is relative to the Cultural Inventory symbolic analysis process and represents an interpretation of the dimensions for this purpose. The following sections of this chapter present a theoretical overview of the signification[15] which will occur for the student as s/he progress through each of the first three analysis filters of the Cultural Inventory.

Situational Filter: designative signification

The student views an action sequence as a designative sign generating meaning pertinent to the situational context in which its culture is communicated: "[…]a sign is designative insofar as it signifies observable properties of the environment or of the actor."[16] Using the Situational Filter to attend to an action sequence as a designative sign enables the student to determine the prominent situational aspects and issues framing the action sequence's cultural communication. The analysis process put forth in this filter thus allows the student to generate meaning pertinent to the situational context of the cultural communication and thereby transforms the action sequence into a designative sign.

Interactional Filter: prescriptive signification

Focusing on the interactive encounter, the student views an action sequence as a prescriptive sign generating meaning pertinent to the belief or value underlying the chosen 'line of behavior' expressed through the interaction: "a sign is prescriptive insofar as it signifies how the object or situation is to be reacted to."[17] Using the Interactional Filter to attend to the action sequence as a prescriptive sign enables the student to deduce the 'sponsor thought' behind a sequence actor's particular act and thereby determine the sequence actor's belief or value. The Interactional Filter analysis permits the student to address *the sequence actor's culture* at its ideational level of manifestation. The action sequence becomes a prescriptive sign of the sequence actor's culture when analyzed through the Interactional Filter; for, it enables the student to generate meaning pertinent to the culture underlying the interaction as mapped out and executed by the sequence actor.

Feedback Filter: appraisive signification

Focusing on the responsive encounter, the student views an action sequence as an appraisive sign generating meaning pertinent to the adequacy of the line of behavior mapped out and executed by the sequence actor to consummate the interaction of the action sequence. "A sign is appraisive insofar as it signifies the consummatory properties of some object or situation"[18] –in other words– "appraisive signs report on the direct experience of consummation or frustration."[19] Using the Feedback Filter to attend to the action sequence as an appraisive sign enables the student to determine the adequacy of the sequence actor's culture, or core assumption, to negotiate the culture, or core assumption, operative for the action sequence. The Feedback Filter analysis permits the student to address *the action sequence's culture* at its ideational level of manifestation. For, the student, in using textual evidence to appraise the interaction and therefore culture of the sequence actor, generates meaning pertinent to the culture underlying the response of the action sequence to the interaction as mapped out and executed by the sequence actor. If the sequence actor's interaction, and hence core assumption is deemed inadequate for negotiating the culture of the action sequence, then the third segment of the action sequence also performs as a prescriptive sign of the action sequence's culture; i.e. as a culture-based, interactive response to the interactive encounter of the sequence actor.

Symbolic Analysis

The symbolic structure of a human act is outlined in the work of G.H. Mead who developed a theory of the human act centered on functions relative to the satisfaction of needs. Mead concluded that "any act consists of three stages –perception, manipulation, and consummation."[20] He termed these phases: orientation, manipulation, and consummation, respectively.[21] In the orientation phase of an act, the sequence actor becomes aware of a sign, i.e. phenomena are brought together into a meaningful context and thereby perceived as objects to meet some need. In the manipulation phase, the sequence actor interprets the sign, i.e. decides how to act and acts. In the consummation phase of an act, the environment responds to the manipulation; the sequence actor's act either satisfies or fails to satisfy the need. "The designative value of signs predominates in the [orientation] stage, the prescriptive value predominates in manipulation, and the appraisive marks the consummation."[22] The following overview of the symbolic analysis performed by student in the first three filters of the Cultural Inventory was generated by combining Mead's symbolic stages of action and Morris' dimensions of signification.[23]

Action sequence orientation and the Situational Filter

Figure 5.4 Translation Filter 1
Situational Filter (1)

BASIC ARCHEPAL SITUAION	PHENOMENON	
	material	non-material
Territorial		
Temporal		
Subsistential		
Exploitational		
Recreational		
Instructional		
Protective		
Associational		
Economic		
Sexual		

The orientation phase of an action sequence is the focus of the symbolic analysis when the analysis objective is to determine the situational aspects in which the action sequence is grounded. The Situational Filter provides this symbolic analysis process. When the

Situational Filter is employed by the student in symbolic analysis, the action sequence functions as a designative sign from which to determine the situational aspects and issues framing the cultural communication depicted in the sequence (see figure 5.4).

Figure 5.4 Translation Filter 1

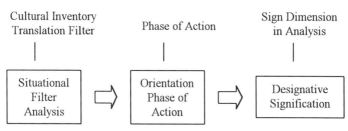

At this first stage in symbolic analysis special focus is placed on the orientation phase of the action sequence; for, the orientation phase of an act is founded on the premise that "action takes place in and with regard to a situation;" for, "whatever be the acting unit[...]any particular action is formed in the light of the situation in which it takes place."[24]

Figure 5.5 Filter 1 Semiotic Design of Symbolic Analysis

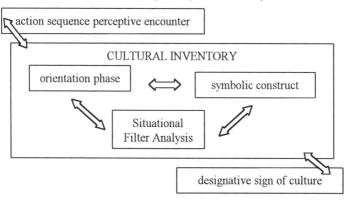

By attending to the orientation phase of the action sequence, the student employs the Situational Filter as an analysis process[25] to determine a situational context for the cultural communication presented in the sequence. This context becomes the base for decoding the culture embedded in the sequence action and is referenced as a symbolic construct. The contextual information gained by interpreting the action sequence as a symbolic construct facilitates the analysis of the following filters. The semiotic design of the analysis process for this section of the Cultural Inventory is presented in figure 5.5.

Action sequence manipulation and the Interactional Filter

Figure 5.6 Translation Filter 2
Interactional Filter (2)

Sequence Phenomena Usage	YES	NO	Supporting Information		Symbolic Embodiment
Incitive Usage				=	Prompt
Systematic Usage				=	Routine
Informative Usage				=	Image
Evaluative Usage				=	Model

The manipulation phase of an action sequence is the focus of symbolic analysis when the analysis objective is to determine the content of the sequence actor's culture. The Interactional Filter provides this symbolic analysis process. When the Interactional Filter is employed by the student in symbolic analysis, the action sequence functions as a prescriptive sign from which to deduce the content of the sequence actor's culture (see figure 5.6).

Figure 5.6 Translation Filter 2

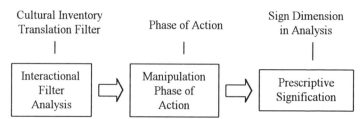

At this second stage in symbolic analysis special focus is placed on the manipulation phase of the action sequence. The manipulation phase of an act is understood here from the premise of self-interaction which concludes that an actor "acts toward his world, interpreting what confronts him and organizing his action on the basis of the interpretation."[26] Analysis emphasis here is on what the sequence actor does, i.e. his/her manipulation of the sequence phenomena, because from an analysis of manipulations culture can be deduced:

> In order to act the individual has to[...]map out a prospective *line of behavior*.[...]he may misinterpret things that he notes[...]he may be faulty in mapping out prospective lines of conduct[...]. Such deficiencies in the construction of his acts do not belie the fact that his acts are still *constructed by him* out of what he takes into account.[27]

In short, because "culturally constituted beliefs serve not only to guide but to instigate action,"[28] the sequence actor will negotiate a plan of manipulation from a sponsor thought based on a belief or value generated out of a core assumption s/he holds about reality. Consequently, because "the human individual confronts a world that he must interpret in order to act,"[29] and because the sequence actor will rely on his/her core assumptions to 'map out the line of conduct' which constitutes his/her act, it is from the manipulation phase of an act, when analyzed symbolically, that one may deduce the content of the sequence actor's culture.

From the perspective of symbolic analysis, the student attends to the action sequence interaction/manipulation phase for the content of the cultural communication. Attending to the manipulation phase of the action sequence, the student employs the Interactional Filter as an analysis process to determine a symbolic usage and embodiment category for the action sequence (Interactional Filter A).[30] Using the Interactional Filter to classify the manipulation phase enables the student to deduce a sponsor thought for the manipulation (Interactional Filter B). The semiotic design of the analysis process for this section of the Cultural Inventory is presented in figure 5.7.

When working in the Interactional Filter, the student attends to the action sequence as a prescriptive sign from which to determine the content of the sequence actor's sponsor thought. From the data gained through the Interactional and Situational Filter analyses, the student formulates a belief or value (see figure 5.11) for the sequence actor.

Figure 5.7 Filter 2 Semiotic Design of Symbolic Analysis

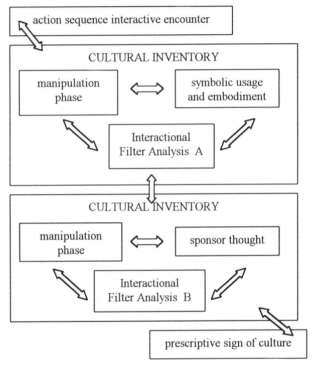

Action sequence consummation phase and the Feedback Filter

Figure 5.8 Translation Filter 3
Feedback Filter (3)

USAGE ADEQUACY MEASUREMENT	YES	NO	Supporting Information
Prompt Persuasive			
Routine Correct			
Image Convincing or Credible			
Model Prescriptively Effective			

The consummation phase of an action sequence is the focus of the symbolic analysis when the analysis objective is to determine the culture operative for the action sequence. The Feedback Filter provides this analysis process. When the Feedback Filter is employed by the student in symbolic analysis, the action sequence functions as an appraisive sign from which to determine the compatibility of the sequence actor's and action sequence's cultures (see figure 5.8).

Figure 5.8 Translation Filter 3

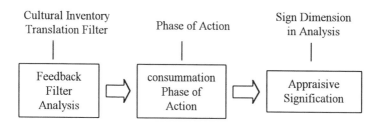

At this final stage in symbolic analysis focus is placed on the consummation phase of the action sequence. The consummation phase of an act depicts either the satisfaction or suppression of the need, interest or inclination which originated the orientation, and incited the manipulation phases.[31] Because a textual action sequence is produced by a communicator-author and used as an informative sign, a consummation phase, for a Cultural Inventory analysis, consists of textual evidence, in the third segment of the action sequence, from which the success or failure of the sequence actor's manipulation can be determined.

From the perspective of symbolic analysis the student attends to the action sequence consummation as an evaluative response to the culture, or 'scheme of interpretation'[32] employed by the sequence actor during his/her manipulation. Attending to the consummation phase of the action sequence, the student employs the Feedback Filter as an analysis process to determine the adequacy of the sequence actor's manipulation, i.e. culture, in negotiating the culture operative for the action sequence. This determination is referenced as a symbolic outcome. From the data gained through the Feedback, Interactional and Situational Filter analyses, the student formulates a belief or value (see figure 5.12) for the action sequence. Using the Feedback Filter to attend to the action sequence as an appraisive sign permits the student to evaluate the culture of the sequence actor relative to the culture of the action sequence. The semiotic design of the analysis process for this section of the Cultural Inventory is depicted in figure 5.9:

Figure5.9 Filter 3 Semiotic Design of Symbolic Analysis

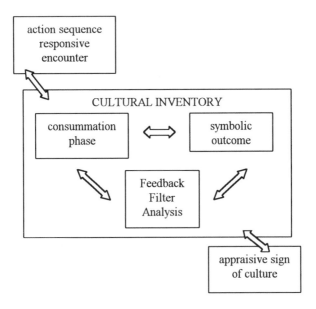

To graphically represent this overview of the symbolic analysis, a synopsis of the three Cultural Inventory filters (Situational, Interactional, and Feedback) the three phases of an action (orientation, manipulation, and consummation) and the three sign dimensions in analysis (designative, prescriptive, and appraisive) is presented in figure 5.10.

Figure 5.10 Symbolic Analysis Translation Filter and Action Phase-Signification Relationship

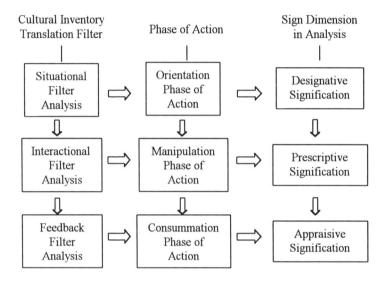

Cultural Inventory Analysis Level 1 Overview of Symbolic Analysis

The statements below represent the foundational axioms for the first four filters and two applications of the Cultural Inventory. These six sections of the Cultural Inventory constitute the symbolic analysis –or analysis of culture within an action sequence. Cultural Inventory Analysis Level 2 consists of Application 3, Synthesis 1 and 2, the Interpersonal Filter, and Evaluation Typologies. The Level 2 Analysis is designed to socially context the results of the symbolic analysis.[33]

Filter 1 axiom: When the dynamic[34]-sequence phenomena of an action sequence are situationally contexted, the action sequence becomes a representamen for a symbolic construct. When interpreted/translated as symbolic constructs for the communication of a core assumption, action sequences serve as designative signs for culture. The semiotic design of the symbolic analysis for this filter within the context of the Cultural Inventory is depicted in figure 5.5 below.

Figure 5.5 Filter 1 Semiotic Design of Symbolic Analysis

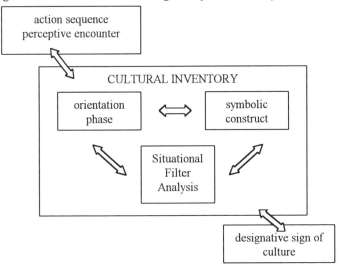

Filter 2 axiom: When sequence phenomena are analyzed according to the purpose of their use by a sequence actor –via the textual evidence found in the manipulation phase of the action sequence as resultant effect of mediation– the sequence actor's manipulation can be translated into a symbolic usage and the action sequence can be translated as a symbolic embodiment (Interactional Filter A). To deduce the interpretant mechanism of the sequence actor's mediation – i.e. the sponsor thought– the manipulation phase of the action sequence is processed by the student as a symbolic embodiment (Interactional Filter B). The action sequence then functions for the student as a prescriptive sign of culture. The semiotic design of the symbolic analysis for this filter within the context of the Cultural Inventory is depicted in figure 5.7 below.

Figure 5.7 Filter 2 Semiotic Design of Symbolic Analysis

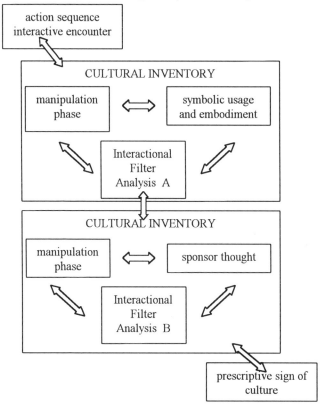

Application 1 axiom: The sponsor thought, deduced from the Interactional Filter analysis and underlying the sequence actor's line of conduct, can be translated into the belief or value operative for the sequence actor.

Figure 5.11 Application 1 Translation

Filter 3 axiom: When the usage adequacy of a symbolic embodiment is assessed using the textual evidence put forth in the consummation phase of an action sequence, a symbolic outcome can be determined for the action sequence. The action sequence then functions for the student as an appraisive sign of culture. The semiotic design of the symbolic analysis for this filter within the context of the Cultural Inventory is depicted in figure 5.9 below.

Figure 5.9 Filter 3 Semiotic Design of Symbolic Analysis

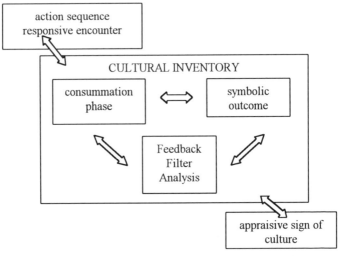

Application 2 axiom: The symbolic outcome of the action sequence, i.e. adequacy of the act of manipulation as determined by the Feedback Filter analysis, is used by the student in reference to the act of manipulation to infer the belief or value operative for the action sequence.

Figure 5.12 Application 2 Translation

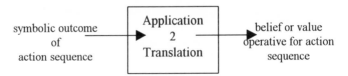

Filter 4 axiom: The beliefs/values of the sequence actor and action sequence generated in Applications 1 and 2, respectively, are classified by the student analyst as descriptive or normative. Categories of Cognitive Orientation are employed to *translate* the belief(s) or value(s) into etic, i.e. cross-culturally comparable, propositions. The semiotic design of the emic-etic translation facilitated by the Notional Filter within the context of the Cultural Inventory is depicted in figure 5.13 below.

Figure 5.13 Filter 4 Semiotic Design of Emic-Etic Translation

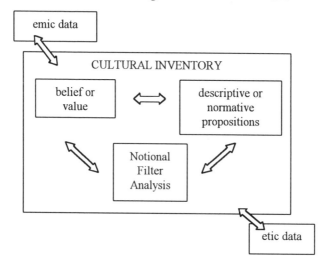

Notes

[1] Littlejohn 161.

[2] Blumer, *Symbolic Interactionism* 5.

[3] Samovar and Porter, *Intercultural Communication* 9-10. See their definitions of 'response' and 'feedback' in 'the ingredients of communication.'

[4] Grimm 366-367.

[5] Grimm 367.

[6] We utilize the term "dynamic" here to illustrate that the phenomena addressed are in a state of flux and/or transition, i.e. the "meaning" and/or significance attributed to these phenomena is in flux.

[7] For details on the process of mediated interaction see Chapter 6.

[8] Littlejohn 163.

[9] Charles W. Morris, *Signs, Language, and Behavior* (New York: G. Braziller, 1955) 118.

[10] For a definition of an informative usage of sign see Interactional Filter analysis Chapter 6.

[11] See Cultural Inventory, filters 1-3 as well as applications 1-2 in Chapter 6.

[12] Colapietro 181.

[13] Charles W. Morris, *Signification and Significance* (Cambridge: Massachusetts Institute of Technology Press, 1964) 15.

[14] Morris, *Signification and Significance* 15. Morris explains that he has discarded the formative mode of signifying and now refers to the modes of signifying as dimensions of signification, see note 16.

[15] Signification is taken to mean "the process by which signs and thus meanings are generated or produced." Colapietro, *Glossary of Semiotics* 181.

[16] Morris, *Signification and Significance* 4.

[17] Morris, *Signification and Significance* 4.

[18] Morris, *Signification and Significance* 4.

[19] Morris, *Signification and Significance* 7.

[20] Littlejohn 66.

[21] Posner, "The Behavioral Foundations of Semiotics," in *Classics of Semiotics* 26-27.

[22] Littlejohn 66.

[23] This section is a theoretical overview, for complete explanations, definitions of the filter elements, and sample analysis see Chapters 6 and 7. The fourth filter (Notional Filter) of the symbolic analysis section of the Cultural Inventory has been excluded from this overview because the analysis process of that filter does not gather raw data from the action sequence, rather, it constitutes a translation of the data compiled from the previous filter analyses.

[24] Blumer, *Symbolic Interactionism* 85.

[25] For details of this analysis process see Situational Filter, Chapter 6.

[26] Blumer, *Symbolic Interactionism* 63.

[27] Blumer, "Sociological Implications of the Thought of George Herbert Mead," in *Symbolic Interactionism* 64. Our emphasis.

[28] Spiro, "Reflections" 38.

[29] Blumer, "The Methodological Position of Symbolic Interactionism," in *Symbolic Interactionism* 15.

[30] For details of this analysis process see Interactional Filter, Chapter 6.

[31] Posner, "The Behavioral Foundations of Semiotics," in *Classics of Semiotics* 27.

[32] Blumer, *Symbolic Interactionism* 67. "Schemes of interpretation are maintained only through their continued confirmation by the defining acts of others.[...] there are innumerable points at which the participants are *re*defining each other's acts."

[33] An overview of the Cultural Inventory analysis Level 2 is presented in Chapter 7.

[34] Dynamic phenomena of an action sequence are those phenomena which come together to constitute the interaction.

Chapter 6

Cultural Inventory Analysis Level 1:
The Symbolic Analysis of the Situational,
Interactional, Feedback and Notional Filters

The Situational Filter Analysis

Figure 6.1 The Situational Filter Analysis

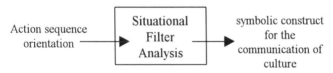

Situational filter

The Situational Filter is the first filter of the Cultural Inventory. It was designed to enable students to categorize an action sequence according to situational context. Through the analysis performed with this filter the student identifies the sequence actor, phenomena and situational issue that constitute the surface expression of the culture communicated in an action sequence. As such, the purpose of the Situational Filter is to help students focus on the situational conditions presented in an action sequence; for, the situational conditions provide the context through which the culture will be communicated. The semiotic function of the Situational Filter within the Cultural Inventory analysis process is depicted below in figure 5.5. The semiotic translation, from action sequence to symbolic construct, facilitated by the Situational Filter is depicted below in figure 6.3.

Figure 5.5 Filter 1 Semiotic Design of the Symbolic Analysis

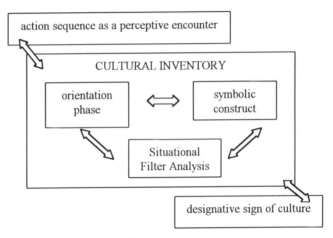

Figure 6.2 The Situational Filter
Situational Filter (1)

BASIC ARCHETYPAL SITUATION	PHENOMENON	
	material	non-material
Territorial		
Temporal		
Subsistential		
Exploitational		
Recreational		
Instructional		
Protective		
Associational		
Economic		
Sexual		

Sequence Actor: _____
Phenomena: _____
B.A.S.: _____

Figure 6.3 Semiotic Design of Situational Filter Analysis

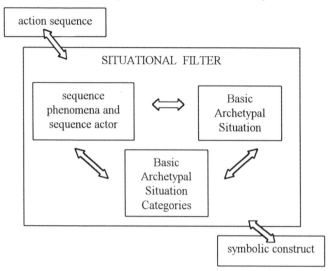

Sequence phenomena- symbolic construct

When a meaning relationship is established between sequence phenomena and a sequence actor through the interaction of the sequence actor, these phenomena become dynamic and, together with the sequence actor, function as the representamen[1] for a basic archetypal situation. This follows closely the point stressed by Blumer regarding the nature of objects for the theory of symbolic interactionism.

> The position of symbolic interactionism is that the 'worlds' that exist for human beings and for their groups are composed of 'objects' and that these objects are the product of symbolic interaction. [...]objects (in the sense of their meaning) must be seen as social creations –as being formed in and arising out of the process of definition and interpretation as this process takes place in the interaction of people.[2]

Therefore, through interaction, sequence phenomena become dynamic; they are activated, or infused with meaning and as such become "culturally-constituted." Using the categories outlined in the Situational Filter, a student establishes a semiotic relationship between sequence actor, sequence phenomena and a Basic Archetypal Situation (see figure 6.3). When this connection occurs, the sequence actor and phenomena become the representamen of a symbolic construct for the communication of culture. The translation of sequence phenomena and actor into a symbolic construct is thus semiotic, i.e. cognitive and designed to attribute additional meanings to the objects, in this case, relating to cultural analysis. As a point of comparison, the Thunder-rain example given in Chapter 3 can be used to illustrate this translation process facilitated by the Situational Filter:

Figure 6.4 Sequence Phenomena-Symbolic Construct Translation

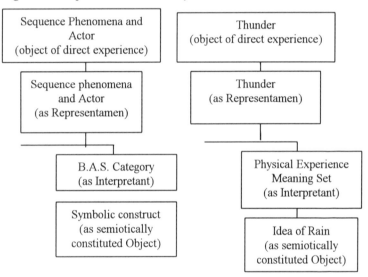

The phenomena and actor of an action sequence become the representamen of a symbolic construct when linked to an archetypal situation. Therefore, the analysis categories of the Situational Filter enable students to classify these phenomena according to set situational parameters, or Basic Archetypal Situations (B.A.S.). By situationally classifying the sequence phenomena and sequence actor, the student has performed a semiotic translation of the action sequence; it is now a symbolic construct. Once translated, the action sequence as symbolic construct is understood as a context for the communication of culture.

As has been the design with all the category sets utilized in each of the five translation-filters of the Cultural Inventory...;

Situational Filter: Basic Archetypal Situation category set;
Interactional Filter: Sequence Phenomena Usage category set;
Feedback Filter: Usage Adequacy Measurement category set;
Notional Filter: Cognitive Orientation category set;
Interpersonal Filter: Interpersonal Relations category set;[3]

...the Basic Archetypal Situation set (B.A.S.) of the Situational Filter provides the etic categories necessary to articulate, and therefore critically perceive an action sequence as the context for a communication of culture.

In the Situational Filter (as Ground), an action sequence, complete with sequence actor and phenomena, is contexted within a B.A.S. and thereby translated into a symbolic construct. The Situational Filter thus helps students articulate the components of an action sequence (Representamen) with regards to a specific B.A.S. category (Interpretant) as a symbolic construct (Object).

Figure 6.5 Triadic Model in Situational Filter

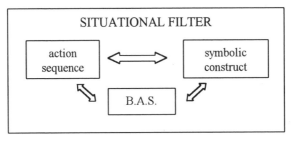

Basic Archetypal Situation categories (B.A.S.)[4]

The ten Basic Archetypal Situation categories which comprise the Situational Filter represent a core group of situational variations utilized by social actors to context dynamic, or 'culturally-constituted' phenomena. These situational variations are universally applicable; for, each B.A.S. category outlines the skeletal parameters of an archetypal human-interaction-sequence. Since these categories can function as reference foci for classifying human cultural interactions, the ten Basic Archetypal Situations (B.A.S.) listed below represent a "topoi" set, or situational repertoire of human interactions in general.

The Basic Archetypal Situations are derived from Hall and Trager's units of "Infra-culture." Infra-culture represent the basis upon which human behavior has been built, the "behavior that preceded culture but later became elaborated by humans into culture as we know it today."[5] In his book, *The Silent Language*, Edward T. Hall outlined his Primary Message System (P.M.S.) Theory; a theory composed of "..ten separate kinds of human activity." From these activity categories, Hall writes of (B.A.S.) or Basic Archetypal Situations in *Beyond Culture*;[6] however, he does not provide specific terminologies or definitions for these Basic Archetypal Situations. The Cultural Inventory definitions listed below have, therefore, been based on readings of Hall's Primary Message System Theory as outlined in *The Silent Language*.[7] Figure 6.6 depicts the Situational Filter as it appears on the Cultural Inventory; a base definition for each B.A.S. follows the diagram:

Figure 6.6 Situational Filter and B.A.S.Definitions
Situational Filter (1)

BASIC ARCHETYPAL SITUATION	PHENOMENON	
	material	non-material
Territorial		
Temporal		
Subsistential		
Exploitational		
Recreational		
Instructional		
Protective		
Associational		
Economic		
Sexual		

territorial: a situation created out of an action sequence which principally reveals how a sequence actor(s) utilizes, defines, and/or otherwise copes with space and spatial relationships.[8]

temporal: a situation created out of an action sequence which principally reveals how a sequence actor(s) conceptualizes and determines time and temporal relationships.[9]

subsistential: a situation created out of an action sequence which principally reveals how a sequence actor(s) addresses the circumstances of, and systematically copes with the factors pertaining to basic physical sustenance, i.e. livelihood in terms of food and/or shelter.[10]

exploitational: a situation created out of an action sequence which principally reveals how a sequence actor(s) employs human-made materials (extensions) to capitalize on, or improve/alter his/her immediate environment and/or meet some need.[11]

recreational: a situation created out of an action sequence which principally reveals how a sequence actor(s) determines and engages in amusing and relaxational activity.[12]

instructional: a situation created out of an action sequence which principally reveals how a sequence actor(s) conceives of the process of learning or the tacit conditions and assumptions in which learning is imbedded, i.e. how s/he learns to learn (pragmatic –i.e. learning through doing; theoretical; by rote, by specialized training, by demonstration or imitation; under approval, under pressure, self- or group paced)[13]

protective: a situation created out of an action sequence which principally reveals how a sequence actor(s) defends against potentially hostile forces both in nature, and within human society.[14]

associational: a situation created out of an action sequence which principally reveals how a group of sequence actors is organized or structured.[15]

economic: a situation created out of an action sequence which principally reveals how a sequence actor(s) addresses the circumstances of, and systematically copes with the factors pertaining to material acquisitions.[16]

sexual: a situation created out of an action sequence which principally reveals how a sequence actor(s) defines or deals with issues regarding the parameters of masculinity and femininity.[17]

"Süße Brei" Action-sequence(2) Situational Filter Analysis

Figure 6.7 Action Sequence (2) Orientation Phase Emphasis

1 [*One day, when the girl had gone out,*] 2 [*the mother said, "Little pot, cook,"* and it began cooking. After she had eaten her fill, she

wanted the pot to stop,] 3 [but she didn't know the word. So the pot continued to cook, and the porridge ran over the rim and continued to cook until the kitchen and the whole house were full, and the next house, and then the street, as if it wanted to feed the entire world. The situation was desperate, and no one knew how to help.]

Using the Situational Filter to focus on the situational issue depicted in the sample action sequence permits the student to determine a sequence actor, phenomena, and Basic Archetypal Situation category .

Figure 6.8 Situational Filter Analysis Phenomena Results

BASIC ARCHETYPAL SITUATION	PHENOMENON	
	material	non-material
Territorial		
Temporal		
Subsistential		
Exploitational	pot	words
Recreational		
Instructional		
Protective		
Associational		
Economic		
Sexual		

Sequence actor

For the text sample, the choice of sequence actor is obvious since the mother is the only actor involved during the orientation and manipulation phases. In other texts, the sequence actor will be the character initiating the manipulation of the action sequence.

Sequence-phenomena

For the text sample, the sequence phenomena are the pot and the magic words used to control the production of porridge "Little pot, cook. Little pot, stop;" as, these are the dynamic phenomena with which the mother, as sequence actor, interacts.

Basic archetypal situation

In considering the ten Basic Archetypal Situation category definitions, the "exploitational" definition appears the most suitable to characterize this sample action sequence. The situation, as created in the orientation phase, reveals the mother employing extensions –in this case, the magic words and the pot– to meet her need for food. The brevity of this particular text sample permits the sequence phenomena to be determined before selecting a Basic Archetypal Situation. For other texts, it may be necessary to use the selected Basic Archetypal Situation category as an aid in determining the sequence phenomena. The results of the Situational Filter Analysis are given in figure 6.9.

Figure 6.9 Situational Filter Analysis Results

Sequence Actor:	mother
Phenomena:	magic words and pot
B.A.S.:	exploitational archetype

Mediated-Interaction: Theory Behind the Interactional Filter

Social actors do not usually respond directly to stimuli, whether behavioral, verbal, or artifactual; rather, they interpret a stimulus before responding. This act of interpretation constitutes cognitive interaction or semiotic mediation.

> One of the most explicit theories of semiotic mediation has been proposed by Vygotsky (1930: 137-38;cf. Rissom 1979:11). Vygotsky distinguishes two elementary forms of human behavior; natural and artificial or instrumental acts. In natural acts, there is a direct associative (conditioned reflex) connection between stimulus A and a response B. In instrumental acts, 'two new connections, A-X and B-X, are established with the help of the psychological [cognitive] tool X.'...such a tool X is a stimulus which functions 'as a means of influencing the mind and behavior' (ibid.:141). In other words, the *mediating* stimulus X is a sign... [18]

Because of an ability to think symbolically, social actors move a stimulus through a thought-translation-process prior to rendering a response. The "psychological tool x" explained as "the mediating stimulus X" referred to above is illustrative of this process. Therefore, when social actors interact with their environments, their interactions are based upon *a notion*, (Stimulus X), *prompted by* the 'stimulus A,' rather than *a direct reaction to* 'stimulus A.' The process can be diagramed in the following fashion:

Figure 6.10 Mediated Interaction

Mediated-interaction occurs rapidly and often escapes conscious, or surface awareness. Nonetheless, most human 'actions' and 'reactions' are indeed mediated as Blumer's explanation of symbolic interaction makes clear.

> The term "symbolic interaction:" refers[…]to the peculiar and distinctive character of interaction as it takes place between human beings. The peculiarity consists in the fact that human beings interpret or "define" each other's actions instead of merely reacting to each other's actions. Their "response" is not made directly to the actions of one another [or objects of the environment] but instead is *based on the meaning* which they attach to such actions [and objects]. Thus, human interaction is mediated by the use of symbols, by interpretation, or by ascertaining the meaning of one another's actions. This mediation is *equivalent to inserting a process of interpretation* between stimulus and response in the case of human behavior.[19]

Thus the term "mediation" describes the semiotic-translation-process which occurs within the social actor while negotiating human acts. The theories of symbolic interactionism are based upon this process,[20] as a merging of both Vygotsky's and Blumer's theories show:

> "In instrumental acts,"[21] "human interaction is mediated by the use of symbols.[…]This mediation is equivalent to inserting a process of interpretation between stimulus and response in the case of human behavior"[22][…]"such a tool X[…]functions 'as a means of influencing the mind and behavior'(ibid.:141). In other words, the *mediating* stimulus [tool] X is a [formal] sign… [23]

A revision of the diagram depicting the semiosis of human interaction[24] can be completed incorporating mediated-interaction, or symbolic interaction as defined by both Vygotsky and Blumer. For, the information gained from semiotic theories now enables the components of the mediation, that is the inserted "process of interpretation" referred to by both Vygotsky and Blumer, to be defined as a formal sign (see 6.11).

Figure 6.11 Formal Sign as Mediation Process

[formal] Sign as the process of interpretation

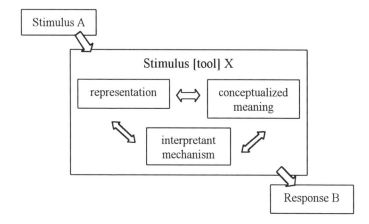

The *notion prompted by* 'stimulus A' is, in fact, the triadic process represented in the box above as 'Stimulus [tool] X'. Consequently, 'Response B' is not a reaction to 'Stimulus A'. Rather, it is the outcome of a mediation generated from a triadic association: 'Stimulus A,' as a 'representation,' has come to stand for a 'conceptualized meaning' as mediated by an 'interpretant mechanism'. The 'Response B' is thus an empirical outcome, or resultant effect, of the mediation that 'Stimulus A,' as an object-of-direct-experience, sparked. The Object of 'Stimulus [tool] X' –here the "conceptualized meaning"– is associated with the 'Stimulus A' as "representation" through the "interpretant mechanism."

When social actors use their core assumptions as the interpretant mechanism, or *basis* from which to "interpret or define each other's actions"[25] and plan their own actions, *culturally*-mediated-interaction takes place.

One of the functions of culture is to provide a highly selective screen between man and the outside world. In its many forms, culture therefore designates what we pay attention to and what we ignore.[26]

Culturally-mediated-interaction can be referred to as symbolic interaction. For,

The view of the human being held in symbolic interactionism[…]is seen[…]in the sense of an organism that engages in social interaction with itself by making indications to itself and responding to such indications.[…]It meets what it notes by engaging in a process of self-indication in which it makes an object of what it notes, gives it a meaning, and uses the meaning as the basis for directing its action. Its behavior with regard to what it notes is not a response called forth by the presentation of what it notes but instead is an action that arises out of the interpretation made through the process of self-indication [mediation].[27]

It stands then, that symbolic interaction produces cultural responses; i.e. responses *prescribed* by the core assumptions of the social actor (see figure 6.12). In Chapter 4 such cultural responses were referred to as empirical outcomes –from the perspective analysis– or resultant effects –from the perspective of function.[28]

Figure 6.12 Culturally-mediated-interaction as Symbolic Interaction

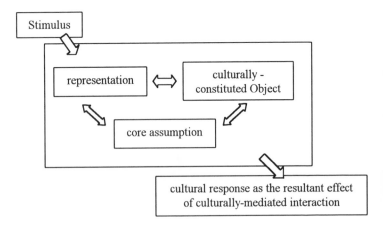

The Interactional Filter helps train students first to focus on the manipulation of sequence phenomena by sequence actors and, secondly to perceive these manipulations as resultant effects of cultural mediated interaction. From the perspective of the Interactional Filter, manipulation phases of action sequences are processed as prescriptive signs of culture.

As linguistic animals, social actors employ mediation (semiosis) to constitute the phenomena around them with meanings. Therefore, social actors do not react, but rather symbolically interact with their environments. It is the same with "real" or with "representational" social actors. For, in both worlds, social actors interact with phenomena (i.e. objects or other social actors) from a 'chosen a line of conduct' based on the core assumptions that direct their perception of reality. The meanings born of these core assumptions and surfaced in the collective form of ideational products –beliefs or values– or in the more individualized form of mental products –sponsor thoughts– are thus utilized by social actors to generate acts and to interpret the acts generated by others. This constitutes mediation as represented in the formal sign diagram (figure. 6.11) and the interpretant mechanism of such mediation is the social actor's reservoir of core assumptions, i.e. his/her culture (see figure 6.13).

The core assumptions which surface as collective beliefs and values, and then surface further as individualized sponsor thoughts abide in the mind of the social actor and not in the physical phenomena.

Figure 6.13 Culture and Interpretant Mechanism in Formal Sign

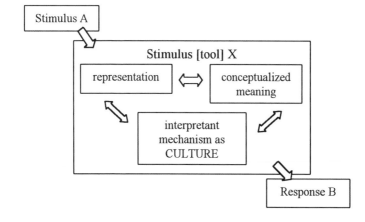

However, core assumptions can be accessed by analyzing a social actor's interaction with phenomena, because through such interactions these phenomena become "culturally-constituted."[29] Hence, dynamic sequence phenomena denote sequence phenomena which have been constituted with culture through the mediated based interaction, i.e. manipulation, of the sequence actor. Manipulation by the sequence actor thus determines the activation status of sequence phenomena as conduits for the expression of culture.

In their discussion of the relationship between social actors' actions and norms (i.e. culture), Holy and Stuchlik address "...the analytical practice of treating pre-set norms [i.e. core assumptions] as ideally isomorphic with actual interactions."[30] Rather than determining actions as proposition-conforming or proposition-binding they suggest that anthropological inquiry proceed from the action first. In other words, "The basic question is not whether the action is norm-conforming or norm-binding, but which norms, ideas and reasons were invoked by the actors for the performance of the action."[31] Such an inquiry analyzes the actions of social actors by attending to their purpose so as to reach the sponsor thoughts from which the actions are generated. For, the sponsor thought behind an action reveals the belief or value operative for the social actor in choosing that particular 'line of action'. From beliefs and values, as the ideational products of culture, core assumptions, or the culture-at-base of social actors, can be deduced. Holy and Stuchlik have thus proposed that anthropological inquiry target the mediation process underlying human actions in order to reach culture.

Because social actors cannot be interviewed within the scope of a Cultural Inventory analysis –CI analysis deals with textual data–, such pragmatic analysis can only be attempted if there is textual evidence of a resultant effect within the action sequence.[32] Therefore, although the conception of culture here is rooted in mentalist approaches (perceiving culture as a cognitive system) this second translation-filter of the Cultural Inventory can only reach culture through the analysis of interaction. The Interactional Filter has, of necessity, been developed from theories in behavioral semiotics for this reason.

> While both mentalism and behaviorism identify meaning as an event within an interpreting organism, behaviorism has emphasized the necessity of external empirical evidence for the discovery of these events.[33]

It is the perspective of a Cultural Inventory analysis that resultant effects as acts-of-manipulation will always be culturally-constituted, i.e. will always have been generated from culture as the interpretant mechanism of the sign: "Stimulus [tool]*X*".

Figure 6.14 Culture as Interpretant Mechanism

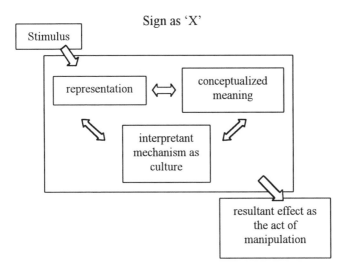

The Interactional Filter Analysis

Figure 6.15 The Interactional Filter Analysis

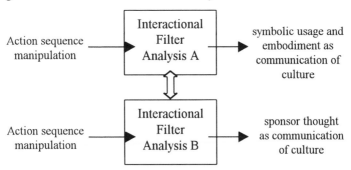

Interactional Filter (2)

Sequence Phenomena Usage	YES	NO	Supporting Information	Symbolic Embodiment
Incitive Usage				Prompt
Systematic Usage				Routine
Informative Usage				Image
Evaluative Usage				Model

S.P.U.:_____

Symbolic Embodiment:_____

Sponsor Thought of the sequence actor:

_____

Axiom: When sequence phenomena are analyzed according to the purpose of their use by a sequence actor –via the textual evidence found in the manipulation phase of the action sequence as resultant effect of mediation– the sequence actor's manipulation can be translated into a symbolic usage and the action sequence can be translated as a symbolic embodiment (Interactional Filter A). To deduce the interpretant mechanism of the sequence actor's mediation – i.e. the sponsor thought– the manipulation phase of the action sequence is processed by the student as a symbolic embodiment (Interactional Filter B). The action sequence then functions for the student as a prescriptive sign of culture.

Interactional Filter

The Interactional Filter is the second filter of the Cultural Inventory. While the first filter focuses on the orientation of the action sequence in order to determine a situational context for the communication of a belief or value, this filter focuses on the manipulation of the sequence actor in order to deduce information pertaining to his/her symbolic interaction. When working with the

Interactional Filter the student focuses on the act of manipulation as the resultant effect of symbolic interaction so as to access the content of the sequence actor's mediation. The student uses the sequence actor's manipulation; for, when the purpose of the sequence actor's manipulation is attended to, the act of manipulation can be categorized as a symbolic embodiment. Interpreting the act of manipulation as a symbolic embodiment further helps the student deduce a sponsor thought pertinent to the sequence actor's symbolic interaction. The semiotic functions of the Interactional Filter within the Cultural Inventory analysis process are depicted below in figure 5.7.

Figure 5.7 Filter 2 Semiotic Design of Symbolic Analysis

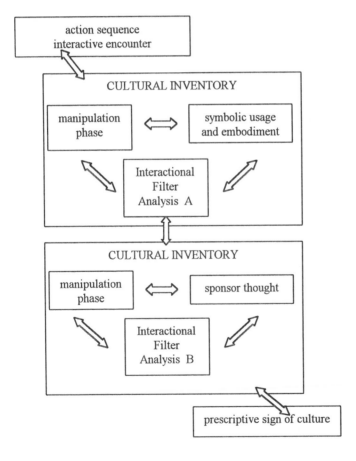

A social actor's beliefs and values generate the sponsor thoughts that are instrumental in deciding how s/he chooses to act. The goal, therefore, of the Interactional Filter analysis is to determine the sponsor thought that directed the sequence actor's *particular line of conduct*. The sponsor thought behind the sequence actor's chosen course of action will provide the content for inferring a belief or value because beliefs and values generate sponsor thoughts.[34] And, the sponsor thoughts are, of course, the generators of the acts. To deduce the sponsor thought behind the sequence actor's chosen course of action one must first determine the sequence actor's purpose or goal for the manipulation, because "the most important factor shaping the actor's decision about the course of his action is[...]the goal which he aims to attain through it."[35]

As the analysis goal for the Interactional Filter is to deduce the sponsor thought behind the act of manipulation (i.e. to deduce "the ideas and reasons [that] were invoked by the actor[...]for the performance of the action") it is necessary for the student analyst first to translate the action sequence into a symbolic embodiment. The process of analysis for this translation filter therefore proceeds in two stages. The first stage involves translating the act of manipulation into a symbolic usage and embodiment (Interactional Filter A). The second stage involves deducing the sponsor thought underlying the act of manipulation (Interactional Filter B). The semiotic translation from action sequence to symbolic embodiment/usage to sponsor thought facilitated by the Interactional Filter is depicted in figure 6.16 below.

Interactional Filter A: Primary Sign Usage

The Interactional Filter analysis has been designed to help students infer the goals of manipulations because, "the goal of the action" is the "bridging concept which [can] relate [beliefs and values] to actions." [36] Focus on the purposeful aspect of the manipulation is key when analyzing interactions for cultural content because it reveals "which norms, ideas, and reasons were invoked by the actors for the performance of the action."[37] The purpose or goal of the manipulation can be determined by attending to the use of the sequence phenomena in the manipulation. Once the student has inferred the sequence actor's goal in the manipulation phase, the act of manipulation can be translated into a symbolic embodiment.

Figure 6.16 Semiotic Design of Interactional Filter Analysis

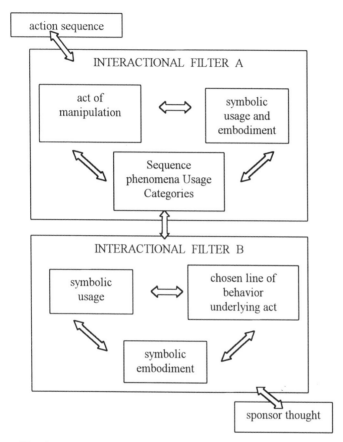

Charles Morris's Primary Sign Usage categories present a semiotic theory designed to analyze behavior, or manipulations, with the purpose of categorizing such interactions according to goals. The "dimensions of sign use focus on the pragmatic aspects of semiosis, [or] the 'question of the purpose for which an organism produces the signs which it or other organisms interpret' (Morris 1946:172)."[38] Determining the employment of the sequence phenomena according to Morris's categories of Primary Sign Usage enables the student to reclassify a manipulation according to purpose.

Depending on the organism's behavioral goals, there is (1) informative usage when the sign is used to inform about something, (2) valuative usage when it is intended to aid in the preferential selection of objects, (3) incitive usage when it incites response-sequences, and (4) systemic usage when it organizes sign-produced behavior into a determinate whole.[39]

When the student thus attends to the purpose behind the manipulation of the sequence phenomena by the sequence actor, the act of manipulation then stands for "something" other than itself; it obtains an additional meaning or significance for the student because determining the goal of the manipulation enables the student to translate the act of manipulation into a symbolic embodiment of culture.

Figure 6.17 Translating the Act of Manipulation

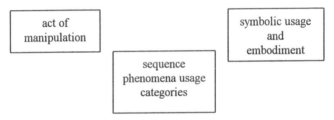

Once a manipulation is classified according to its behavioral purpose, it is then possible to translate the manipulation as a symbolic embodiment from which to deduce "...the ideas and reasons[...]invoked by the [sequence] actors for the performance of the [inter]actions."[40] We have referred to the "ideas and reasons invoked" by sequence actors as their sponsor thoughts.

Sequence phenomena usage categories

To Charles Morris, human acts constitute signs, and his behavioral theory of sign usage is a theory designed to classify human acts as signs according to the purpose or goal behind their production.[41] Hence, in questioning the purpose for which an organism produces the signs which it or other organisms interpret, Morris sought to classify human acts as signs "in terms of their relation to the purposive behavior in which they are produced and which they serve."[42] And, in an attempt to "attain some simple classification which [would] embrace at least the majority of the ways in which signs [i.e. manipulations or human acts] are used"[43] Morris postulated his four Primary Sign Usages.[44] By re-working Morris' categories to classify the manipulation phase of an action sequence it was possible to develop the Interactional and Feedback Filters so as to assist the student first to formulate a sponsor thought for the sequence actor relative to the act of manipulation; and, secondly, to evaluate the adequacy of this sponsor thought in negotiating the manipulation of the action sequence. The categories of Sequence Phenomena Usage, derived from the Primary Sign Usages outlined by Morris, form the theoretical base of the Interactional Filter.

The diagram below depicts the Interactional Filter as it appears in the Cultural Inventory. In the Cultural Inventory, as well as in the definitions listed below, each Sequence phenomena Usage category is presented with its corresponding symbolic embodiment.

Figure 6.18 Interactional Filter
Interactional Filter (2)

Sequence Phenomena Usage	YES	NO	Supporting Information	Symbolic Embodiment
Incitive Usage				Prompt
Systematic Usage				Routine
Informative Usage				Image
Evaluative Usage				Model

S.P.U.:_____
Symbolic Embodiment:_____

Sponsor Thought of the sequence actor:

_____

Incitive usage

An act of manipulation becomes *a prompt* through incitive usage when the sequence actor uses the sequence phenomena/manipulation with the goal to incite a response or instigate his/her own action, or the action of others. As such, the sequence actor's incitive employment of the sequence phenomena enables the student to translate the act of manipulation as a prompt. The incitive usage category is based on Morris' incitive usage of signs:

> In the incitive use of signs, [manipulations as] signs are produced in order to determine how the interpreter of the [manipulation as] sign is to act to something,[…]the aim is to direct behavior into definite channels, and not merely to give information or to determine the preferential status of something or other.[45]

An example of an incitive usage of manipulation could have occurred in the noted action sequence if both the mother and daughter had been at home. In this scenario, the daughter would have begun to speak the magic words, but would have been silenced by the mother holding out her hand in protest. Such an action on the part of the mother would constitute an incitive interaction. Incitive as, in this scenario, the mother's manipulation would have the goal to direct the behavior of the daughter; namely, to stop the daughter from speaking the magic words. As such, the mother's act of manipulation in this scenario could be translated as a prompt to direct the behavior of the daughter.

Systematic usage

An act of manipulation becomes *a routine* through systematic usage when the sequence actor uses the sequence phenomena/manipulation with the goal of performing a sequence of actions or events. As such, the sequence actor's systematic employment of the sequence phenomena enables the student to consider the act of manipulation directed toward the performance of a single element in a routine or as an entire routine. The systematic usage category is based on Morris' category of systemic usage of a sign: "the systemic use of signs is the use of [manipualtions as] signs to systematize (organize) behavior which other signs tend to provoke.[46]

An example of a systematic usage of manipulation is contained in the chosen text example; for, the mother generates the act of manipulation as part of the routine for obtaining food; i.e. controlling the production of the pot with the magic words. This manipulation constitutes a systematic interaction on the part of the mother. Systematic, as the mother's manipulation has as its goal the organizing or controlling of the functions of the pot; namely, the initiation and termination of food production. Her act of manipulation for this action sequence can be translated as a routine with the goal of controlling the production of the pot.

Informative usage

An act of manipulation becomes *an image* through informative usage when the sequence actor uses the sequence phenomena/manipulation to impart information to him/herself, or others. As such, the sequence actor's informative employment of the sequence phenomena enables the student to consider the act of manipulation an image. The informative usage category is related to Morris' informative usage of a sign:

> In the informative use of signs, [manipulations as] signs are produced in order to cause someone to act as if a certain situation has certain characteristics[...]. In the informative use of [manipulations as] signs the producer of a [manipulation as a] sign seeks to cause the interpreter to act as if some present, past, or future situation had such and such characteristics.[47]

An example of an informative usage of manipulation occurs in the first action sequence of "Der Süße Brei." Here, the old woman in the woods employs the pot and the words to show the little girl how to control the production of food. This manipulation constitutes an informative interaction on the part of the old woman. Informative as, in this first action sequence, the old woman's manipulation has the goal of causing the little girl to act as if the pot and words have magical qualities. Therefore, the old woman's act of manipulation can be translated as an image with the goal of informing the little girl about the "special" characteristics of the sequence phenomena.

Evaluative usage

An act of manipulation becomes *a model* through evaluative usage when the sequence actor uses the sequence phenomena/manipulation to influence (positively or negatively) the judgement of him/herself or others. As such, the evaluative employment of sequence phenomena enables the student to consider the act of manipulation a model. The evaluative usage category was developed from Morris' valuative usage of a sign:

> The use of [manipulations as] signs to cause [prejudicial] behavior to certain objects, needs, preferences, responses, or [other manipulations as] signs is to use [manipulations as] signs [e]valuatively[48][...]An individual may use signs [e]valuatively with respect to himself as well as to others.[49]

An example of a evaluative usage of manipulation might have occured if the mother had buried the pot and had forbade her daughter from saying the magic words. This scenario would constitute an evaluative interaction on the part of the mother. Evaluative as, in this scenario, the mother's manipulation would have had the goal of evaluatively influencing the judgement of the daughter regarding the pot, words, and old woman. The mother's act of manipulation could be translated as a model with the goal of prejudicing her daughter against the use of the pot and words.

"Süße Brei" Action sequence(2) Interactional Filter (A) Analysis

Figure 6.19 Action Sequence (2) Manipulation Phase Emphasis

> 1 [One day, when the girl had gone out,] 2 [*the mother said, "Little pot, cook," and it began cooking. After she had eaten her fill, she wanted the pot to stop,*] 3 [but she didn't know the word. So the pot continued to cook, and the porridge ran over the rim and continued to cook until the kitchen and the whole house were full, and the next house, and then the street, as if it wanted to feed the entire world. The situation was desperate, and no one knew how to help.]

In the text example, the sequence actor (mother) uses the sequence phenomena (words and pot) systematically. That is, her act of manipulation depicts an attempt to control the events of the action sequence, namely the production of food from the pot. By determining the usage of the words and pot as systematic, the student analyst translates the manipulation into its corresponding symbolic embodiment; namely, routine.

Figure 6.20 Interactional Filter "Der Süße Brei" Action Sequence (2) Analysis Results

Interactional Filter (2)

Sequence Phenomena Usage	YES	NO	Supporting Information	Symbolic Embodiment
Incitive Usage			`see action` `sequence`	Prompt
Systematic Usage	X		`(2) middle` `segment`	**Routine**
Informative Usage				Image
Evaluative Usage				Model

Figure 6.21 presents a review of the practice analysis including the Situational Filter and the first stage of the Interactional Filter:

Figure 6.21 Situational and Interactional Filter (A) Results

Sequence Actor: _____mother_____
Phenomena: _____magic words and pot_____
B.A.S.: _____exploitational archetype_____

S.P.U.___systematic usage of manipulation_____
Symbolic Embodiment: _____routine_____

Interactional Filter B: Sponsor Thought

The first stage of the Interactional Filter enables the student to work from the act of manipulation back to the goal of the manipulation with the aid of a theory designed to classify human acts as signs according to the purpose behind their production. The main objective of the Interactional Filter is to help the student formulate a sponsor thought for the sequence actor's usage of manipulation; i.e. to articulate the thought that the sequence actor utilized to generate his/her particular act of manipulation. Classifying the goal of the manipulation as either incitive, systematic, informative or evaluative enables the student to interpret the manipulation as the symbolic embodiment of either a prompt, routine, image or model (Interactional Filter A). This enables the student to translate the manipulation into a cultural communication (Interactional Filter B).

The sponsor thought, generated from a belief/value which was generated from a core assumption that had functioned in the sequence actor's mediation –as interpretant mechanism prior to the act of manipulation–, is not explicitly stated. For, the core assumption that had been instrumental in generating the belief or value which then generated the sponsor thought underlying the 'chosen line of behavior' is not located in the sequence phenomena but, rather, in the mind of the sequence actor(s) who holds and, through the manipulation of the phenomena, communicates it.[50] Hence because culture –as a cognitive meaning set– is located in the mind of the sequence actor, the student analyst must infer a sponsor thought from the textual evidence denoting a resultant effect of mediation, i.e. from the manipulation of the sequence phenomena by the sequence actor.

Therefore, once the student has translated the act of manipulation into a symbolic embodiment (Stage A), s/he can infer the sponsor thought that had been generated by the sequence actor during mediation. To infer a sponsor thought for the sequence actor's manipulation, the student must review the act of manipulation from the perspective of the symbolic usage and ask what the sequence actor must have assumed, or thought, in order to have chosen the particular line of conduct.

At this stage of analysis, the symbolic embodiment becomes the interpretant, for it provides the analytical perspective from which to associate the symbolic usage and the chosen line of behavior underlying the act.

Figure 6.22 Translating the Symbolic Usage

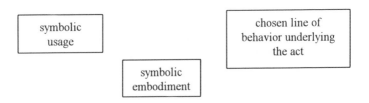

Using the above inputs, the student can process the act of manipulation as a representamen for the sequence actor's sponsor thought underlying his/her chosen line of behavior, as Object. In this manner, the second stage of the Interactional Filter analysis enables the student to deduce the sponsor thought operative for the sequence actor's manipulation within the action sequence, i.e. it enables the student to deduce the "...ideas and [or] reasons [that] were invoked by the actor[...]for the performance of the action."[51]

"Süße Brei" action sequence(2) Interactional Filter (B) Analysis

In the text example, attending to the manner in which the mother used the sequence phenomena, one would thus ask: What did the mother assume about herself in reference to her systematic use of the routine? i.e. What was the sponsor thought that was behind, and relative to her 'chosen line of conduct' in this exploitational situation? The student can infer that the mother, by employing –or attempting to employ– the magic words systematically, believed or assumed that she had the knowledge/ability to operate the pot. In other words, as the text example indicates, the mother understands that there is a procedure to controlling the pot, and that this procedure involves a routine. Her sponsor thought regarding the exploitation of the pot could be articulated as:

Figure 6.23 Interactional Filter (B) Results

> Sponsor Thought of the sequence actor:
>   "I know the words to control the pot"

Figure 6.24 Situational and Interactional Filter (A-B) Results

> Sequence Actor: _____mother_____
> Phenomena: _____magic words and pot_____
> B.A.S.: _____exploitational archetype_____

> S.P.U.___systematic usage of manipulation_____
> Symbolic Embodiment: _____routine_____
> Sponsor Thought: _I know the words to control the pot

To recap, the Interactional Filter is designed to categorize the sequence actor's manipulation according to purpose; for, by determining the goal of the manipulation the student relates the manipulation back to the mediated-interaction and thus may infer the sponsor thought which gave rise to the particular usage. In inferring the sponsor thought for the manipulation, the student must focus only on the act of manipulation. In the text sample this would constitute the sequence actor's thought to engage in the systematic usage –to engage the routine.

Application 1

Figure 6.25 Application 1

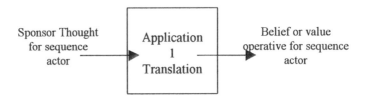

Application 1:

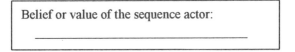

Axiom: The sponsor thought, deduced from the Interactional Filter analysis and underlying the sequence actor's 'line of conduct', can be translated into the belief or value operative for the sequence actor.

Application 1 translation

The Interactional Filter analysis of the manipulation will reveal a sponsor thought generated from a belief or value held by the sequence actor and relative to both the symbolic construct (i.e. exploitational archetype) and symbolic usage/embodiment (i.e. systematic/routine) of the action sequence. The purpose of the Application 1 translation is to formulate a belief or value for the sequence actor based on the sponsor thought resulting from the Interactional Filter analysis.

Sponsor thought-to-belief or value

A sponsor thought, like a belief or value, is a surfaced product of culture. Sponsor thoughts are transformed into material products of culture as behaviors or artifacts; in the text example noted the sponsor thought is translated as a behavior, i.e. the act of manipulation. In Chapter 3 sponsor thoughts were classified as mental products of culture. They are the individualized version of the more general and collectively applicable products classified as "ideational;" namely, beliefs and values. And, as explained, beliefs and values are, in turn, the generated products of core assumptions which constitute the definition of culture-at-base. To illustrate the conception of culture, as defined in Chapter 3, the relationship among sponsor thoughts, beliefs and values, and core assumptions was diagrammed as concentric circles:

Figure 6.26 Concentric Circle Model of Culture

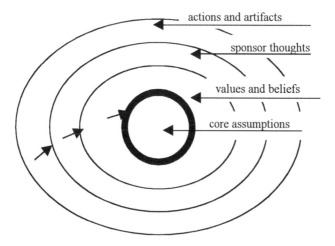

actions and artifacts

sponsor thoughts

values and beliefs

core assumptions

This concentric circle diagram of culture (see figure 6.26) illustrates the levels through which culture surfaces into the consciousness and visible surroundings of social actors. The barrier between the center of the diagram, core assumptions, and the other concentric circles indicates a consciousness barrier for social actors between core assumptions and ideational products. For, rarely are beliefs and values recognized as having been generated from one's core assumptions about reality. In the same fashion, the generative relationship between beliefs/values and sponsor thoughts, represented by the two concentric circles leading out from the center, is rarely cognized for it mostly functions unconsciously.[52]

The diagram of culture in figure 6.26 illustrates how core assumptions are, at root, the generators of beliefs and values, sponsor thoughts, and finally behaviors and artifacts; the levels products, products[2], and products[3] respectively.[53] Hence, it also indicates the translation, or transformation process by which ideational, mental, and material phenomena are constituted with culture. And, this provides the model for translating a sponsor thought into a belief or value. Thus, the interpretant mechanism in culturally mediated interaction contains the levels: culture, products, and products[2]; or, core assumptions, values and beliefs, sponsor thoughts, respectively (see figures 6.27 and 6.28). The ability to perceive these levels of manifestations rests on the student's awareness of the structure and function of culture.

Figure 6.27 Interpretant Mechanism Expanded

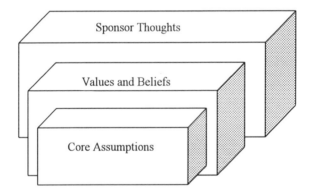

To formulate a belief or value for the sequence actor, the student will translate the sponsor thought from the Interactional Filter into the form of a belief or value following a few guidelines derived from the belief/value concept as used in the work of Melford Spiro. A sponsor thought can be translated into a belief when expressed as descriptive statement, or into a value when expressed as a normative statement "concerning human beings [i.e. self], society [i.e. others], [time, space], and the world that is held to be true."[54] The student formulates a belief or value for the sponsor thought by asking: 'What belief or value pertaining to self, society, time, space, or nature, and related to the Situational and Interactional Filter data, generated the sponsor thought of the sequence actor?'

Figure 6.28 Culturally Mediated Interaction with Expanded Interpretant Mechanism

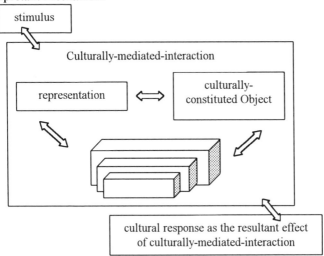

"Süße Brei" Action sequence(2) Application 1 Analysis

In the Situational Filter analysis the example action sequence was determined to represent an exploitational archetype, and in the Interactional Filter analysis the symbolic usage was classified as systematic and the symbolic embodiment as a routine. The sponsor thought for the mother as sequence actor, which reads: "I know the words to control the pot," can be designated as a descriptive statement. In processing the data through Application 1, the sponsor thought can be classified/ translated into the following belief pertaining to self ability:

Figure 6.29 Application 1 Results
Application 1:

Belief or value of the sequence actor:
> The routine for food production requires
> specific words but is simple; I know how
> to perform the routine

The process of the Application 1 translation is depicted in figure 6.30.

Figure 6.30 Theoretical Model of Application 1 Translation

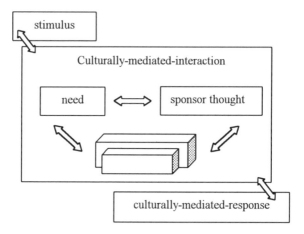

Figure 6.31 "Der Süße Brei" Application 1 Translation

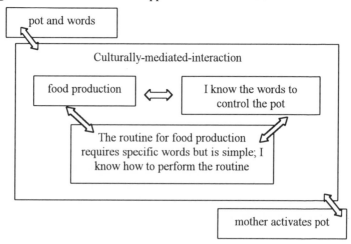

The success or failure of the usage, and hence success or failure of the sequence actor's sponsor thought in negotiating the culture of the action sequence is addressed in the Feedback Filter analysis, Filter 3 of the Cultural Inventory.

Analysis Theory Review

The Situational Filter analysis helps students to focus on textual evidence pertinent to the situational context of the action sequence, i.e. the sequence actor, situational issue, and sequence phenomena. The Situational Filter analysis results provide data for contexting the cultural communication of the action sequence within a basic archetypal situation.

Figure 6.5 Situational Filter
Situational Filter (1)

BASIC ARCHETYPAL SITUATION	PHENOMENON	
	material	non-material
Territorial		
Temporal		
Subsistential		
Exploitational		
Recreational		
Instructional		
Protective		
Associational		
Economic		
Sexual		

Sequence Actor: _____
Phenomena: _____
B.A.S.: _____

The Interactional Filter analysis helps students to focus on textual evidence relating to the interaction of the sequence actor with sequence phenomena. Using this second filter, the student classifies the interaction (actor's manipulation) according to its need fulfilling purpose (symbolic usage). Classifying the act of manipulation according to a symbolic usage enables the student to articulate the act of manipulation as a symbolic embodiment. After completing this process the student can infer a cultural sponsor thought for the sequence actor relative to the situation.

Figure 6.18 Interactional Filter
Interactional Filter (2)

Sequence Phenomena Usage	YES	NO	Supporting Information	Symbolic Embodiment
Incitive Usage				Prompt
Systematic Usage				Routine
Informative Usage				Image
Evaluative Usage				Model

S.P.U.:_____
Symbolic Embodiment:_____

Sponsor Thought of the sequence actor:

_____

Perceiving the act of manipulation as a symbolic embodiment helps the student to infer a sponsor thought for the sequence actor's line of conduct. The inferred sponsor thought is then translated, in Application 1 (see figure 6.25 below), as an expression of the sequence actor's belief or value. The Interactional Filter analysis results thus provide data for inferring the belief or value that is operative for the sequence actor during the manipulation.

Figure 6.25 Application 1
Application 1:

Belief or value of the sequence actor:

_____

The Feedback Filter Analysis

Figure 6.32 The Feedback Filter Analysis

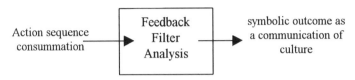

Feedback Filter (3)

USAGE ADEQUACY MEASUREMENT	YES	NO	Supporting Information
Prompt Persuasive			
Routine Correct			
Image Convincing or Credible			
Model Prescriptively Effective			

> U.A.M.: _____
>
> Symbolic Outcome: _____

Axiom: When the usage adequacy of a symbolic embodiment is assessed using the textual evidence put forth in the consummation phase of an action sequence, a symbolic outcome can be determined for the action sequence. The action sequence then functions for the student as an appraisive sign of culture. The semiotic design for the symbolic analysis of this filter is depicted in figure 5.9 below.

The Feedback Filter is designed to help students focus on textual evidence pertaining to the outcome (positive/negative consummation) of the act of manipulation. Using textual evidence from the consummation phase of an action sequence, the student assesses the adequacy of the interaction in its translated form as a symbolic embodiment. Such an assessment enables the student to translate the consummation phase of the action sequence into a symbolic outcome for the action sequence, the goal of the Feedback Filter analysis. After translating the consummation phase into a symbolic outcome, the student infers a belief or value for the action sequence from the results of the Feedback Filter analysis (Application 2), just as s/he inferred a belief or value for the sequence actor in Application 1 from the results of the Interactional Filter analysis.

Figure 5.9 Filter 3 Semiotic Design of Symbolic Analysis

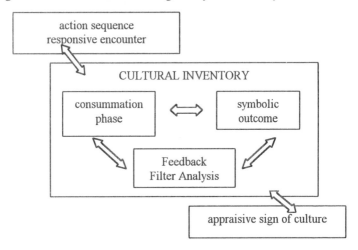

Determining the adequacy of the symbolic usage in this third filter helps the student examine how the action sequence responds, through feedback, to the sequence actor's 'chosen line of conduct' for the manipulation. This analysis filter, in turn, leads to an understanding of how the author, as sequence-creator, employs the sequence actor and phenomena to express a belief or value operative for the action sequence and/or piece in general. The core assumption targeted in the Feedback Filter is that expressed by the action sequence rather than the sequence actor. As such, the analytical results of the Feedback Filter provide data for deducing the belief or value of the action sequence. The semiotic translation facilitated by the Feedback Filter is depicted in figure 6.33.

Feedback Filter

In the Interactional Filter analysis it was shown that the action sequence is translated into a symbolic embodiment by categorizing the act of manipulation according to usage. Viewing the action sequence as a symbolic embodiment enables one to infer a sponsor thought for the sequence actor relative to the act of manipulation. From the inferred sponsor thought, a belief or value operative for the sequence actor is generated (Application 1).

Figure 6.33 Semiotic Design of Feedback Filter Anlaysis

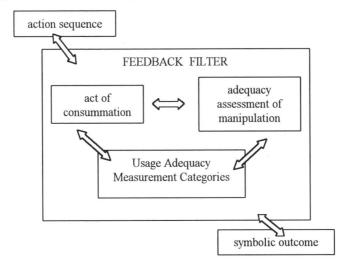

An analysis of the consummation phase of the action sequence, using the Feedback Filter, will enable the student to determine whether the belief or value as expressed through the sequence actor's manipulation is compatible with the belief or value operative for the action sequence/piece in general. In short, the Feedback Filter is designed to reveal whether the 'culture' employed by the sequence actor is adequate for negotiating the overriding 'culture' of the action sequence. For, the consummation phase, when translated into a symbolic outcome, represents the action sequence's culture as response to the sequence actor's manipulation. Thus translated, the consummation phase of the action sequence becomes a symbolic outcome from which to infer a second belief or value. In this manner, the symbolic outcome is used by the student to infer the cultural response of the action sequence and/or piece in general.[55]

The Feedback Filter was designed to determine the culture underlying the outcome of the action sequence by assessing the adequacy of the sequence actor's manipulation.[56] The Usage Adequacy

Measurement categories and the measurement parameters of adequacy on which they are based have been derived from Charles Morris' Sign Adequacy guidelines:

> [A manipulation as symbolic embodiment] is adequate to the degree to which it achieves the purpose for which it is used.[…]To say that [a manipulation as symbolic embodiment] is adequate is to say that *its use reaches a goal in a particular occasion* or that in general *it facilitates the attainment of a certain goal.* An understanding of the kinds of adequacy which [manipulations as symbolic embodiments] have is dependent then upon an understanding of the uses to which [manipulations] are put.[57]

The adequacy measurement of a given symbolic embodiment is both derived from, and dependent on its corresponding usage category as determined in the Interactional Filter analysis. In this respect the Usage Adequacy Measurement categories of the Feedback Filter relate back to their corresponding usage categories; i.e. incitive usage of manipulation is adequate if persuasive; systematic usage of manipulation is adequate if correct; informative usage of manipulation is adequate if convincing; and evaluative usage of manipulation is adequate if prescriptively effective.[58] A comparison of the Interactional and Feedback Filters, see figure 6.34 below, reveals this relationship.

Figure 6.34 Interactional and Feedback Filter Relationship

Interactional Filter (2)

Sequence Phenomena Usage	YES	NO	Supporting Information	Symbolic Embodiment
Incitive Usage				Prompt
Systematic Usage				Routine
Informative Usage				Image
Evaluative Usage				Model

Feedback Filter (3)

USAGE ADEQUACY MEASUREMENT	YES	NO	Supporting Information
Prompt Persuasive			
Routine Correct			
Image Convincing or Credible			
Model Prescriptively Effective			

Usage adequacy measurement

Employing the Feedback Filter, the student determines the adequacy of the manipulation usage from the textual feedback evidence supplied in the consummation phase of the action sequence. Textual feedback evidence is essential to complete a Cultural Inventory analysis of an action sequence. For, feedback evidence is used to evaluate the adequacy of the sequence actor's sponsor thought to negotiate the situation put forth in the action sequence. Hence feedback evidence is used to evaluate the sequence actor's core assumption against the proposition of the action sequence. To evaluate feedback evidence in this manner, the student translates the textual feedback into a symbolic outcome.

The student translates the textual feedback into a symbolic outcome by appraising the adequacy of the consummation relative to the manipulation usage as determined in the Interactional Filter. Following Morris, the four symbolic outcomes listed on the Feedback Filter represent affirmative usage markers; namely, persuasive, correct, convincing, and effective (see Figure 6.35). Textual feedback, in the consummation phase, will reveal the manipulation usage employed by the sequence actor as either adequate, i.e. evince positive consummation relative to its corresponding Usage Adequacy Measurement; or as inadequate, i.e. evince negative consummation relative to its Usage Adequacy Measurement.

When a usage adequacy measurement is matched with its corresponding symbolic embodiment a symbolic outcome is generated. Hence, the symbolic embodiments from the Interactional Filter (prompt, routine, image and model) were combined with the adequacy measurements on the Feedback Filter to generate the symbolic outcomes (prompt persuasive, routine correct, image convincing or credible, model prescriptively effective).

Figure 6.35 The Feedback Filter
Feedback Filter (3)

USAGE ADEQUACY MEASUREMENT	YES	NO	Supporting Information
Prompt Persuasive			
Routine Correct			
Image Convincing or Credible			
Model Prescriptively Effective			

The definitions for the usage measurements presented below represent adequate usage. That is, when a symbolic embodiment has been employed adequately during the act of manipulation one of the affirmative guidelines defined below will correspond to the feedback evidence depicted in the consummation phase of the action sequence. The usage measurements have been cross-listed with their corresponding Sequence Phenomena Usage categories from the Interactional Filter; the corresponding symbolic embodiments (i.e. prompt, routine, image, and model) are included with the usage measurements on the Feedback Filter (see figure 6.35 above).

Persuasive
(incitive usage of manipulation)

If the incitive usage of a symbolic embodiment by the sequence actor is adequate within the action sequence, then the purpose of the act of manipulation, as prompt, has been fulfilled within the consummation phase of the action sequence. That is, the manipulation functions and/or is used persuasively by the sequence actor "to direct behavior into definite channels".[59] Hence, if textual evidence in the consummation phase of the action sequence indicates that the incitive usage of a manipulation as prompt has been persuasive in directing, or seeming to direct, the course of action, then the usage of the manipulation as a prompt has been affirmed, and therefore determined adequate.

Returning to the example of incitive usage for an act of manipulation,[60] the following scenario was generated:

> with the mother and daughter both at home, the daughter would have begun to speak the magic words, but would have been silenced by the mother holding out her hand in protest (incitive usage).

If the text were to present the following consummation: "Having thus stopped her daughter from speaking, the mother said, "Little pot, cook," and the pot began to cook..." there would be textual feedback evidence –namely; "Having thus stopped her daughter from speaking, the mother said..."– of a positive consummation for the mother's incitive usage of manipulation. Within this scenario, the purpose of the act of manipulation, as prompt, would have been fulfilled; since, the prompt would have been persuasive in directing the behavior of the daughter. A symbolic outcome for this example would thus read: prompt persuasive because the incitive usage of the act of manipulation is adequate.

Correct
(systematic usage of manipulation)

If the systematic usage of the symbolic embodiment by the sequence actor is adequate within the action sequence, then the purpose of the act of manipulation, as routine or as a routine element, has been fulfilled within the consummation phase of the action sequence. That is, the manipulation functions and/or is used correctly by the sequence actor with reference to an established pattern within the action sequence, or work in general.[61] Hence, if textual evidence in the consummation phase of the action sequence indicates that the systematic usage of a manipulation as routine, or routine element, has been correct with regard to the pattern required by the action sequence, then the usage of the manipulation as routine has been affirmed, and is therefore adequate.

An example of systematic usage for an act of manipulation was cited in the sample text "Der Süße Brei":[62] "...the mother said, "Little pot, cook," and it began cooking. After she had eaten her fill, she wanted the pot to stop..." (systematic usage). The consummation phase of this sample text continues:

> 3 [but she didn't know the word. So the pot continued to cook, and the porridge ran over the rim and continued to cook until the kitchen and the whole house were full, and the next house, and then the street, as if it wanted to feed the entire world. The situation was desperate, and no one knew how to help.]

In this action sequence there is textual feedback evidence –"she didn't know the word.[...]the pot continued to cook,[...]the situation was desperate, and no one knew how to help"– of negative consummation for the mother's systematic usage of manipulation. From the feedback evidence it can be concluded that the purpose of the act of manipulation, as routine 'to control the pot', has not been fulfilled. The routine, as performed by the mother, is incorrect since the established pattern for controlling the pot is left incomplete. A symbolic outcome for this example thus reads: routine incorrect because the systematic usage of the act of manipulation is inadequate.

Convincing or credible
(informative usage of manipulation)

If the informative usage of the symbolic embodiment by the sequence actor is adequate within the action sequence, then the purpose of the act of manipulation, as image, has been fulfilled within the consummation phase of the action sequence. That is, the act of manipulation functions and/or is used informatively by the sequence actor "when its production causes its interpreter to act as if something has certain characteristics." An elaboration on the adequacy guideline for informative usage explains that:

> The convincingness of [images] is ultimately determined by seeing whether their production by one organism causes other organisms to respond to something as having the characteristics which the producer of the [image] intends to convey.[63]

Hence, if textual evidence in the consummation phase of the action sequence indicates that the informative usage of a manipulation as image has been convincing, or credible, to other sequence participants, then the usage of the manipulation as image has been affirmed, and is therefore adequate.

The first action sequence of "Der Süße Brei" was cited as providing an example of informative usage, by the old woman, for an act of manipulation.[64] The manipulation phase of this first action sequence reads:

> 2 [So the girl went out into the forest, where she met an old woman who already knew about her troubles and gave her a small pot, to which *the girl was to say*: "Little pot, cook," and it would cook a good, sweet millet porridge. And when the girl would say "Little pot, stop!" the pot would stop cooking.](informative usage)

For this first action sequence, the consummation phase continues: "3 [The girl brought the pot home to her mother, and now they were rid of their poverty and hunger, and they ate sweet porridge as often as they liked.]" Here, there is textual feedback evidence –namely; "they were rid of their poverty and hunger,[…]they ate sweet porridge as often as they liked"– of a positive consummation for the old woman's informative usage of the manipulation. From the feedback evidence it can be concluded that the purpose of the act of manipulation, as image, has been fulfilled; for, the image put forth by the old woman is convincing and credible because it has caused the little girl and the mother, its interpreters, to respond as if the pot and words have the magical characteristics that the old woman intended to convey. A symbolic outcome for this example thus reads: image convincing and credible because the informative usage of the act of manipulation is adequate.

Prescriptively effective
(evaluative usage of manipulation)

If the evaluative usage of the symbolic embodiment by the sequence actor is adequate within the action sequence, then the purpose of the act of manipulation, as model, has been fulfilled within the consummation phase of the action sequence. That is, the manipulation functions and/or is used prescriptively by the sequence actor to induce "...some organism to accord to something, or other, a desired preferential [i.e. prejudicial] behavior."[65] Hence, if textual evidence in the consummation phase of the action sequence indicates that the evaluative usage of the manipulation as model has been effective in prescribing a prejudicial status to some-thing, or other, for the sequence participants, then the usage of the manipulation as model has been affirmed, and is therefore adequate.

Returning to the example of evaluative usage for an act of manipulation,[66] the following scenario was generated:

> when the daughter arrives home, she shows her mother the pot and tells her of the encounter with the old woman in the woods. Upon hearing the story, the mother buries the pot, forbids the daughter from saying the magic words, and begins praying. (evaluative usage)

If the text were to present the following consummation: "That night when her mother was sleeping, the little girl exhumed the pot, spoke the magic words, and ate her fill." there would be textual feedback evidence –namely; "the little girl exhumed the pot, spoke the magic words, and ate her fill"– of a negative consummation for the mother's evaluative usage of manipulation. Within this scenario, the purpose of the act of manipulation, as model, would not have been fulfilled; for, the model behavior as exhibited by the mother was not prescriptively effective. The little girl was neither dissuaded from using the pot and words, nor persuaded to pray. A symbolic outcome for this example would thus read: model prescriptively ineffective because the evaluative usage of the act of manipulation is inadequate.

"Der Süße Brei" Action Sequence (2) Feedback Filter Analysis

The Interactional Filter analysis of "Süße Brei"(2) concluded a systematic usage determination for the act of manipulation by the mother thus rendering the manipulation a routine. To determine the adequacy of the systematic usage/routine based on the textual feedback in the consummation phase, it is necessary to consider the textual feedback in light of the adequacy measurement developed to correspond with systematic usage To be assessed as adequate, the mother's systematic usage of the manipulation –as routine– must be fulfilled. That is, the action sequence's consummation phase must provide textual evidence of correct usage regarding the routine.

Figure 6.36 Action Sequence (2): Consummation Phase Emphasis

1 [One day, when the girl had gone out,] 2 [the mother said, "Little pot, cook," and it began cooking. After she had eaten her fill, *she wanted the pot to stop,*] 3 [*but she didn't know the word. So the pot continued to cook, and the porridge ran over the rim and continued to cook until the kitchen and the whole house were full, and the next house, and then the street, as if it wanted to feed the entire world. The situation was desperate, and no one knew how to help.*]

Using categories to translate the manipulations into symbolic embodiments streamlines the adequacy assessment. Thus having interpreted the act of manipulation as a routine in the Interactional Filter helps the student to clearly determine the adequacy of its usage with the Feedback Filter. In the "Süße Brei"(2) example, the adequacy question reads: "Is the mother's usage of the manipulation as routine met with positive or negative consummation according to the textual feedback of the action sequence?" Here adequacy assessment is negative; for, the text of the consummation phase:"...she didn't know the word."; "the pot continued to cook"; and "The situation was desperate, and nobody knew what to do."(see figure 6.36) provides evidence that the mother's act of manipulation as routine is incorrect.

The narrative of the consummation phase provides evidence of inadequate systematic usage as the description of the devastation of the town by porridge illustrates. Thus the consummation phase feedback for "Süße Brei"(2) indicates that the routine is incorrect. Textual evidence from the consummation phase is used to support (see figure 6.37) the negative determination for this Usage Adequacy Measurement.

Figure 6.37 Feedback Filter "Der Süße Brei" Action Sequence (2) Analysis Results

Feedback Filter (3)

USAGE ADEQUACY MEASUREMENT	YES	NO	Supporting Information
Prompt Persuasive			
Routine Correct		X	**resulted in a desperate situation in which "no one knew how to help"**
Image Convincing or Credible			
Model Prescriptively Effective			

A review of the example analysis for the first three filters is given in figure 6.38 below.

Figure 6.38 Situational, Interactional, Feedback Filter Results

Sequence Actor: _____mother_____
Phenomena: _____magic words and pot_____
B.A.S.: _____exploitational archetype_____

S.P.U.___systematic usage of manipulation_____
Symbolic Embodiment: _____routine_____
Sponsor Thought: _I know the words to control the pot

U.A.M.: _____inadequate consummation_____
Symbolic Outcome: ___incorrect usage of routine__

Situational Filter (1)

BASIC ARCHETYPAL SITUATION	PHENOMENON	
	material	non-material
Territorial		
Temporal		
Subsistential		
Exploitational	pot	words
Recreational		
Instructional		
Protective		
Associational		
Economic		
Sexual		

Sequence Actor: _____mother_____
Phenomena: _____magic words and pot_____
B.A.S.: _____exploitational archetype_____

Interactional Filter (2)

Sequence Phenomena Usage	YES	NO	Supporting Information	Symbolic Embodiment
Incitive Usage			`see action`	Prompt
Systematic Usage	X		`sequence`	**Routine**
Informative Usage			`(2) middle`	Image
Evaluative Usage			`segment`	Model

> S.P.U.___ systematic usage of manipulation_____
> Symbolic Embodiment: _____routine_____
> Sponsor Thought: _I know the words to control the pot

Application 1:

> Belief or value of the sequence actor:
> > The routine for food production requires
> > specific words but is simple; I know how
> > to perform the routine

Feedback Filter (3)

USAGE ADEQUACY MEASUREMENT	YES	NO	Supporting Information
Prompt Persuasive			
Routine Correct		X	**resulted in a desperate situation**
Image Convincing or Credible			**in which "no one knew how to help"**
Model Prescriptively Effective			

> U.A.M.: _____inadequate consummation_____
> Symbolic Outcome: ___incorrect usage of routine__

Propositions, Core Assumptions, Values and Beliefs

From an etic perspective, culture as a meaning system is a shared body of propositions. These propositions provide the descriptive and normative foundation for the ideational products of culture –the values and beliefs of social actors. When these propositions are referenced from the subjective perspective of the social actor they are referred to as that actor's core assumptions. Through the analysis of texts, students using the Cultural Inventory will acquire an understanding of how to approach and analyze culture from both an etic and emic perspective. In the former perspective of analysis, culture is objectively described as descriptive and normative propositions, while in the latter it is subjectively referenced as one's core assumptions. The analytical distinction between culture as a cognitive system composed of propositions and the ideational products of such cognitive systems will now be revisited to clarify the terms propositions, core assumptions, and values and beliefs as they are employed in the next three sections of the Cultural Inventory (Application 2, Notional Filter, and Application 3)

Developing an understanding for the various consciousness levels at which culture manifests and is internalized is key to understanding cultural communication. Terminologies designed to articulate these levels have been employed in the Cultural Inventory to aid in the development of this understanding. Hence, the use of various concepts –namely values/beliefs, core assumptions, and descriptive-normative propositions– is necessary to highlight the emic/etic perspective difference in the description and analysis of culture:

Figure 6.39 Emic / Etic Perspective Terminologies

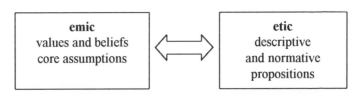

The use of three terminologies also reveals the base level at which culture is manifested, and/or becomes influential for a given social actor. In Chapter 3, 'descriptive and normative propositions' were defined as etic terms used to describe the components of a core assumption set. Hence, a cognitive conception of culture is etically described as an intellectual formation containing two types of propositions; namely, descriptive and normative. When this intellectual formation is described emically, the two types of propositions are collapsed into one category and referenced as "core assumptions".

Figure 6.40 Etic/Emic Culture at Base

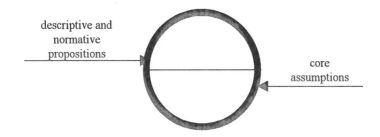

descriptive and normative propositions

core assumptions

Dividing the concentric circle diagram of culture used in Chapter 3 into two sections permits a representation of the difference between the etic and emic terminologies employed to describe culture, as well as those employed to describe the forms in which culture surfaces through the social actor (see figure 3.14 below). The terminologies on the top half of the diagram are etic, those on the bottom half emic. In learning the etic/emic distinctions for articulating culture, students become aware of culture from both an analytical and a native perspective. This dual awareness eventually leads to a proficiency in distinguishing between analytical and native perspectives when discussing culture, as students employ the respective terms throughout the Cultural Inventory analysis process. By thus employing these concepts in their respective contexts, students become critically aware of the levels at which culture as descriptive-normative propositions becomes salient. And so through the use of these terminologies students learn to designate the 'saliency' of culture.

Propositions, core assumptions, and beliefs/values are, therefore, not taken as synonyms because highlighting their distinctions enables one to note differences in two areas; first, to note a difference in the various levels at which culture is operative for the sequence/social actor. That is, to what extent a proposition becomes the influential aspect (or interpretant mechanism) of the actor's mediated-interaction.

And, secondly, one is able to note a difference in the level of conscious awareness an actor has that his/her line of conduct is guided by a proposition. Determining the saliency of a proposition is tantamount to determining these two factors; namely, influence and conscious awareness. To speak about the saliency of a descriptive-normative proposition in relation to a sequence actor, is to reference that actor's awareness level of the proposition as the interpretant mechanism for his/her mediated-interaction [67]

Figure 3.15 Etic/Emic Concentric Circle Model of Culture

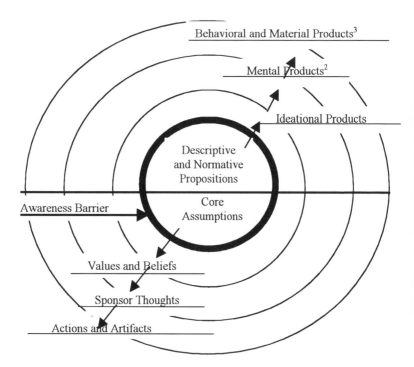

Melford Spiro developed a theory which orders propositions held by social actors into five varying degrees of internalization.[68] At each descending stage on the 'Hierarchy,' the cognitive saliency, or degree of a proposition's internalization, increases until at level 5 it is assumed by the social actor to be self-generated, rather than culture-generated. These "assumed-self-generated" propositions about reality are what was termed above as the social actor's core assumptions. Using Spiro's five stage 'Hierarchy of Cognitive Salience' as a guideline, and attending to the anthropological perspective of emic/etic analytical distinctions, the following three definitions of propositions, core assumptions, and values/beliefs were formulated for employment within the Cultural Inventory analysis.

Descriptive-normative propositions

Following Spiro, the term proposition references tenets, descriptive or normative, pertinent to the reality of a social actor and accepted or supposed true relative to the perspective of that social actor. Because of the objective perspective necessary to describe the content of one's own culture-at-base in proposition format, the term is usually employed to describe the culture of another. Hence, when the term proposition is chosen to describe culture-at-base, the culture being described has not been internalized as an operative fact. This understanding of proposition has been developed from Spiro's description of the first and second stages of "Cognitive Salience":

> (1) [students] learn about the propositions; [...]they acquire an "acquaintance" with them; (2) [students] not only learn about the propositions, but they also understand their traditional meanings as they are interpreted in authoritative texts for example, or by recognized specialists;[69]

Following the analytical and pedagogical purposes of the Cultural Inventory, the theoretical, i.e. propositional, nature of culture is emphasized when culture is referenced as propositions. For, a proposition denotes a statement accepted or supposed true within a theoretical framework.[70] When the term proposition is used to describe culture-at-base, this use constitutes an etic description of culture.

Students who employ the Cultural Inventory to evaluate culture as propositions develop an awareness of the fluid and ideologically influential nature of culture in general. Learning to reference culture as propositionaly based thus promotes an analytical perspective that encourages a conscious awareness of culture's heuristic nature, including the heuristic nature of one's own culture. This conscious awareness disrupts the ideological influence of one's own tenets and hinders those tenets from becoming *unconsciously internalized* core assumptions. Therefore, describing the content of culture-at-base in the format of descriptive or normative propositions advances a discernment of the propositional nature of culture.

Values/beliefs

The terms "values and beliefs" are used in Cultural Inventory analysis to denote shared descriptive and normative propositions that are internalized within the social actor and are therefore perceived by him/her as personally-generated beliefs and values. This concept of beliefs and values was developed from Spiro's description of propositions at the fourth level on the 'Hierarchy of Cognitive Salience:'[71]

> (4) at the fourth level of cognitive salience, cultural propositions are not only held to be true, but they inform the behavioral environment of social actors, serving to structure their perceptual worlds and, consequently, to guide their actions. When cultural propositions are acquired at this level we may say that they are genuine beliefs, rather than cultural clichés.[72]

With the change in terminology from descriptive and normative propositions to beliefs and values, one moves from the etic terms used to designate culture-at-base, to the emic beliefs and values that represent the collectively manifested ideational products of culture operative for the sequence actor (see figure 3.15 above).

Core assumption

A core assumption is the emic equivalent of an etic descriptive or normative proposition; it is culture-at-base emically described. The concept "core assumptions" thus references the emic source of the values/beliefs of the sequence actor. As operative facts, these core assumptions influence the sequence actor's interaction, and his/her perception of the action of others. Distinguishing between the terms value/belief and core assumption reveals the extent of the internalization process of culture and thereby reveals the extent to which the sequence actor is unconsciously influenced by the propositions of a given socio-cultural reality.

Thus a core assumption is a thought about the world which the sequence actor both holds as an unexamined, unconscious truth, and utilizes as an action-guiding-generating-and-interpreting principle for the beliefs and values which define his/her reality. For, an assumption denotes "a statement accepted or supposed true without proof or demonstration."[73] The understanding of core assumptions in the Cultural Inventory is also clear in Schein's usage of "basic assumptions:"

> Basic assumptions, in this sense, are similar to what Argyris has identified as 'theories-in-use' the implicit assumptions that actually guide behavior, that tell group members how to perceive, think about, and feel about things. (Argyris, 1976; Argryis and Schön, 1974).[74]

Core assumptions, like the values and beliefs which they generate "possess emotional and motivational, as well as cognitive, salience."[75] Spiro's explanation of the doctrine of infant damnation as a core assumption provides a cogent example of the cognitive, emotional, and motivational salience of core assumptions:

> The doctrine of infant damnation, a ...[descriptive]... proposition that is part of the theological system of certain Christian denominations, must be explained,[...]by the history of Christian theology. The moment, however, that some Christian actor says, "By God, it's true!" it is internalized as a personal belief..., one who acquires the religious doctrine of infant damnation as a personal belief at this level of cognitive salience not only incorporates it as part of his (theological) belief system but also internalizes it as part of his motivational system [core assumptions]: It arouses strong affect (anxiety), which, in turn, motivates him to action (the baptism of his children) whose purpose is to save them from damnation.[76]

It is clear that at this final level of cognitive salience, a core assumption is an operative fact to the social actor; a guiding principle for interpreting her/his reality. The concept of core assumption employed in the Cultural Inventory has been developed from Spiro's description of the fifth level on the 'Hierarchy of Cognitive Salience:'

> (5) As genuine [core assumptions] [descriptive and normative propositions] not only guide, but they also serve to instigate action; they possess motivational as well as cognitive properties. Thus, one who has acquired, for example, the doctrine of hell at this –the fifth– level of cognitive salience, not only incorporates this doctrine as part of his cosmography, but he also internalizes it as part of his motivational

system [core assumptions]; it arouses strong affect (anxiety) which, in turn, motivates him to action whose purpose is the avoidance of hell.[77]

As operative facts and guiding principles, core assumptions reference culture-at-base from an emic perspective. Core assumptions are distilled of their emotional and motivational salience when articulated as, or translated into descriptive and normative propositions. Translating core assumptions into descriptive-normative propositions thus references culture-at-base from an etic perspective.

Application 2

Figure 6.41 Application 2 Translation

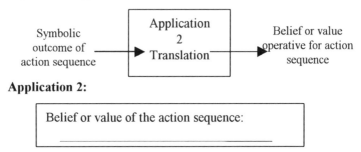

Application 2:

> Belief or value of the action sequence:
>
> _____

Axiom: The symbolic outcome of the action sequence, i.e. adequacy of the act of manipulation as determined by the Feedback Filter analysis, is used by the student in reference to the act of manipulation to infer the belief or value operative for the action sequence.

Deducing a belief or value

Interactional Filter A was designed to enable students to classify an act of manipulation according to purpose, so that the sponsor thought underlying the sequence actor's interaction may be inferred (Interactional Filter B). Using textual evidence presented in the consummation phase, the Feedback Filter was designed to enable students to assess the adequacy of the manipulation in fulfilling its purpose within the sequence, and consequently the adequacy of the sequence actor's sponsor thought relative to the action sequence's operative proposition. At the completion of the Feedback Filter, the student will have determined whether the manipulation, as symbolic embodiment, was successful by measuring the feedback: according to the standards set down in the filter; namely: persuasive, correct, convincing or credible, prescriptively effective. This determination establishes a symbolic outcome for the action sequence. From this symbolic outcome, a belief or value is inferred for the action sequence.

The symbolic outcome is used to formulate a belief/value for the action sequence just as the sponsor thought underlying the symbolic embodiment was used to formulate a belief/value for the sequence actor. The belief/value necessary to successfully negotiate the culture of the action sequence may, or may not concur with the belief/value employed by the sequence actor. If the symbolic outcome is adequate, then the belief/value operative in the action sequence will be compatible with the belief/value employed by the sequence actor. That is, if the usage of the act of manipulation is found to be adequate, then the sequence actor's sponsor thought and value/belief inferred in Application 1 *is* adequate to negotiate the culture of the action sequence. In such a case, the student would use the belief/ value generated for Application 1 to articulate, in Application 2, a concurring belief or value for the action sequence. Here, the beliefs/values generated for Applications 1 and 2 will correspond since the action sequence's feedback affirms the sequence actor's manipulation.

Conversely, if the usage of the act of manipulation is found to be inadequate, then the sequence actor's sponsor thought and value/belief is correspondingly inadequate and at variance with the culture of the action sequence. In this instance, the student would use the belief/value generated for Application 1 to articulate, in Application 2, an opposing belief or value for the action sequence. Here, the beliefs/values generated for Application 1 and 2 will conflict since the action sequence's feedback negates the sequence actor's manipulation.

In the text example, the belief formulated for the mother in Application 1 reads:

Figure 6.29 Application 1 Results
Application 1:

> Belief or value of the sequence actor:
> <u>The routine for food production requires</u>
> <u>specific words but is simple; I know how</u>
> <u>to perform the routine</u>

If the Feedback Filter analysis had resulted in an adequate measurement, i.e. if the measurement had shown "routine correct", then a belief/value necessary to successfully negotiate action sequence (2) of "Der Süße Brei" would concur with the belief stated above in figure 6.29. In such a case, the belief of the action sequence stated in Application 2 would read:

Figure 6.42 Action Sequence (2) Belief Evincing Adequate Usage of the Act of Manipulation

Application 2:

> Belief or value of the action sequence:
> _The routine for food production requires specific_
> _words but is simple; anyone can perform the routine_

"Der Süße Brei" Action Sequence (2) Application 2 Analysis

In the text example, the belief of the sequence actor as articulated in Application 1 is based on the textual evidence of the manipulation phase and results of the Interactional Filter analysis:

Figure 6.29 Application 1 Results

Application 1:

> Belief or value of the sequence actor:
> _The routine for food production requires_
> _specific words but is simple; I know how_
> _to perform the routine_

However, the Feedback Filter analysis of textual evidence from the consummation phase resulted in an inadequate assessment for the act of manipulation.

Figure 6.37 Feedback Filter "Der Süße Brei" Action Sequence (2) Analysis Results

Feedback Filter (3)

USAGE ADEQUACY MEASUREMENT	YES	NO	Supporting Information
Prompt Persuasive			
Routine Correct		X	**resulted in a**
Image Convincing or Credible			**desperate situation** **in which "no one** **knew how to help"**
Model Prescriptively Effective			

U.A.M.: _____ inadequate consummation _____

Symbolic Outcome: ___ incorrect usage of routine ___

The results of the Feedback Filter analysis indicate that the belief utilized by the mother to negotiate her manipulation is inadequate and at variance with the belief/value operative for the action sequence. Consequently, a normative statement, *opposing* the belief stated in Application 1, is articulated as the value for "Der Süße Brei" action sequence (2):

Figure 6.43 Action Sequence (2) Value Evincing Inadequate Usage of the Act of Manipulation

Application 2:

Belief or value of the action sequence:
     The routine for food production requires specific words;
     only those who have been taught the words can perform
     the routine and those who have not been taught the
     words should not attempt the routine

When the student examines whether the belief or value manifested by the action sequence is in agreement with the belief or value underlying the sponsor thought of the sequence actor, s/he has begun to critically address the culture communicated through the action sequence. In action sequences where the symbolic outcome evinces a negative consummation of the manipulation, the sequence actor's culture data conflicts with that of the action sequence. The Inventory data gathered thus far in practice analysis on "Der Süße Brei" action sequence (2) depicts such a conflict.

Analysis Theory Review

The Situational Filter analysis helps students to focus on textual evidence pertinent to the situational context of the action sequence, i.e. the sequence actor, situational issue, and sequence phenomena. The results of the Situational Filter analysis provide data for contexting the cultural communication of the action sequence within a basic archetypal situation.

Figure 6.5 Situational Filter

Situational Filter (1)

BASIC ARCHETYPAL SITUATION	PHENOMENON	
	material	non-material
Territorial		
Temporal		
Subsistential		
Exploitational		
Recreational		
Instructional		
Protective		
Associational		
Economic		
Sexual		

Sequence Actor: _____
Phenomena: _____
B.A.S.: _____

The Situational Filter was designed to provide data for situationally contexting the beliefs and values that have been generated through the Interactional and Feedback Filter analyses.

The Interactional Filter analysis focuses on the act of manipulation. Using this second filter, the student classifies the act of manipulation according to purpose and thereby translates it into a symbolic embodiment from which to infer the cultural sponsor thought underlying the act.

Figure 6.18 Interactional Filter
Interactional Filter (2)

Sequence Phenomena Usage	YES	NO	Supporting Information	Symbolic Embodiment
Incitive Usage				Prompt
Systematic Usage				Routine
Informative Usage				Image
Evaluative Usage				Model

S.P.U.:_____
Symbolic Embodiment:_____

Sponsor Thought of the sequence actor:

_____

The sponsor thought is then translated, Application 1, into an expression of the sequence actor's belief or value.

Figure 6.25 Application 1
Application 1:

Belief or value of the sequence actor:

_____

The Feedback Filter focuses on the outcome (i.e. positive or negative consummation for the act of manipulation) of the action sequence. Using textual evidence from the consummation phase of the action sequence to determine the adequacy of the manipulation, as symbolic embodiment, the student translates the final phase of the action sequence into a symbolic outcome.

Figure 6.35 The Feedback Filter
Feedback Filter (3)

USAGE ADEQUACY MEASUREMENT	YES	NO	Supporting Information
Prompt Persuasive			
Routine Correct			
Image Convincing or Credible			
Model Prescriptively Effective			

U.A.M.: _____

Symbolic Outcome: _____

Viewing the consummation phase of the action sequence as a symbolic outcome enables the student to assess the belief/value of the sequence actor and from this assessment generate an operative belief/value for the action sequence. Accordingly, the analytical results of the Feedback Filter provide data for inferring the operative belief or value of the action sequence which is then stated in Application 2.

Figure 6.44 Application 2
Application 2:

Belief or value of the action sequence:

_____

The Notional Filter Analysis

Figure 6.45 The Notional Filter Analysis

| Belief or value for action sequence and sequence actor | → | Notional Filter Analysis | → | Descriptive or normative proposition for action sequence and sequence actor |

Axiom: The beliefs/values of the sequence actor and action sequence generated in Applications 1 and 2, respectively, are classified by the student analyst as descriptive or normative. Categories of Cognitive Orientation are employed to *translate* the belief(s) or value(s) into etic, i.e. cross-culturally comparable, propositions. The semiotic design of the emic-etic translation facilitated by the Notional Filter within the context of the Cultural Inventory is depicted in figure 5.13 below.

Figure 6.46 The Notional Filter
Notional Filter (4)

COGNITIVE ORIENTATION	**PROPOSITION TYPE**	
	descriptive	normative
Time		
Human Nature		
Nature		
Society		
Space		

Descriptive-normative proposition of the sequence actor:
_____

Descriptive-normative proposition of the action sequence:
_____

Notional Filter

The Notional Filter is the fourth filter of the Cultural Inventory. Using the work of Melford Spiro and other cognitive anthropologists, such as Tinsley and Woloshin, Kerney, Schein, and Boulding,[78] Notional Filter categories were developed that enable the student to translate the beliefs or values of Applications Stages 1 and 2 into

Figure 5.13 Filter 4 Semiotic Design of Emic-Etic Translation

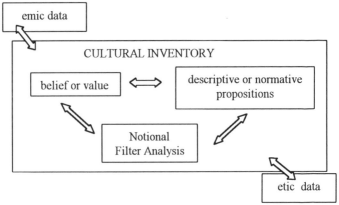

corresponding descriptive or normative propositions suited for the comparative etic discourse of anthropology. The translation-analysis facilitated by the Notional Filter is depicted in figure 6.47below.

Figure 6.47 Semiotic Design of Notional Filter Translation

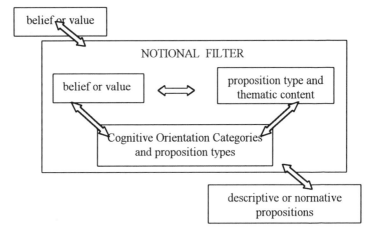

Propositions

Beliefs and values are generated from core assumptions. The term core assumption references an element of culture-at-base from an emic or non-analytical perspective. The employment of the term core assumptions to reference culture-at-base does not present enough classification categories for notional analysis. Therefore, for the purpose of notional analysis, culture-at-base is described as composed of propositions rather than assumptions. When this emic-to-etic code switch is employed, students can begin to address culture data in its propositional form. Such perception permits further classification of culture data into two categories; namely descriptive or normative. As noted in the above section *Propositions, core assumptions, values and beliefs*, the term 'proposition' is used to describe an etic articulation of a core assumption. "Descriptive and normative propositions", therefore, are terminologies employed to etically classify core assumptions. The Notional Filter analysis has been designed to enable students to re-articulate values/beliefs as propositions so as to achieve an analytical description of the culture data manifested in the action sequence.

To translate a belief or value into a proposition one must re-articulate the belief/value using etic terminologies. All beliefs and values are capable of being articulated in propositional form.[79] The goal of the Notional Filter analysis, then, is to translate the beliefs/values determined for both the sequence actor and the action sequence into their respective propositional formulations.

Figure 6.46 The Notional Filter
Notional Filter (4)

COGNITIVE ORIENTATION	PROPOSITION TYPE	
	descriptive	normative
Time		
Human Nature		
Nature		
Society		
Space		

Core assumption to descriptive propositions

Core assumptions unconsciously employed by social actors to represent and interpret the expositive aspects of their realities surface ideationally in these social actors as beliefs. As core assumptions these tenets perform descriptive functions relating the social actor's reality and are therefore referred to etically as descriptive propositions.

Accordingly, most propositions articulated from beliefs are classified as descriptive in type. For example, a social actor holding the belief that sailing into the western horizon entails death discloses a core assumption that represents/describes the world as a flat plane extending to infinity. The proposition into which this belief can be translated is, therefore, descriptive in type. Or, another social actor holding the belief that there is not enough time to accomplish tasks discloses a core assumption that interprets/describes time as fixed and measurable. The proposition into which this belief can be translated is also descriptive in type.

Core assumptions to normative propositions

Core assumptions unconsciously employed by social actors to set standards for, and judge the manifestations and behavioral aspects of their realities surface ideationally in these social actors as values. As core assumptions these tenets perform evaluative functions relating the social actor's reality and are therefore referred to etically as normative propositions. Accordingly, most propositions articulated from values are classified as normative in type. For example, a social actor holding a value that stealing is wrong discloses a core assumption that distinguishes ownership rights and hence the necessity to judge the act of theft. The proposition into which this value can be translated is, therefore, normative in type. Or, another social actor holding the value that people should kill in defense only discloses a core assumption that people kill and hence the necessity to set standards for the act of murder. The proposition into which this value can be translated is also normative in type.

Descriptive propositions are thus indicative while normative propositions are prescriptive. Although descriptive propositions relate more to describing realities and normative propositions relate more to judging realities,[80] as core assumptions both equally function to construct "objective" realities and their validity is not subject to empirical fact. Their validity rather is based on the assumptions of the social actors who hold and employ them:

> What this means is that for any individual organism or organization there are no such things as "facts". There are only messages filtered through a changeable value system.[81]

When core assumptions are articulated as propositional formulations, these propositions constitute an etic description of culture.

Five cognitive orientations for core assumptions

The nominal conception of culture presented in Chapter 3 defines culture-at-base as a cognitive, core assumption set employed by social actors to imbue their interactions with meaning. By re-articulating the ideational products of this core assumption set, i.e. by re-articulating the beliefs and values, the core assumptions can be etically categorized, as propositions: descriptive or normative depending. Using values or beliefs therefore helps to discern whether a core assumption will translate into either a descriptive or a normative proposition.

Both descriptive and normative propositions can be further classified according to thematic content. For, values and beliefs –as well as their generative core assumptions– can be grouped into five thematic subsets based on five orientations through which humans process perceptual information. Common to all human groups, the categories represented by these five cognitive orientations are "universal.".[82]

> There are five universal problems of cultural orientation which are common to all human groups: 1) Human Nature, 2) Social Relations, 3) Man and Nature, 4) Time, and 5) Space. The behavioral patterns of every culture are consistent, in general, with the *fundamental* [core] *assumptions* postulated by that cultural group for these five problem areas, and these assumptions, in turn, determine the major *themes* [beliefs] or *values* [values] of the culture. [83]

Cognitive orientation definitions

The definitions for the five categories of Cognitive Orientation were derived from categories developed by various theorists; Boulding's space, time, personal relations, nature and emotion segmentations for his 'Image' Theory;[84] Tinsley and Woloshin's human nature, social relations, man and nature, time, and space categorizations of 'fundamental assumptions' in their comparison of German and American culture;[85] Kearney's self, nature and society, time, and space orientation universals for his 'Worldview' Framework;[86] and Schein's time, space, human nature, and human relationships 'shared assumptions' categories for describing 'Organizational Culture.'[87]

Figure 6.48 The Notional Filter and Cognitive Orientation Definitions

Notional Filter (4)

COGNITIVE ORIENTATION	PROPOSITION TYPE	
	descriptive	normative
Time		
Human Nature		
Nature		
Society		
Space		

Time:

The 'time' orientation category encompasses propositions dealing with perceptions of human temporal existence. For example, existence within the context of a linear and/or a cyclical historical reality, i.e. how time is defined; various perceptions of time passage, i.e. how time is measured; the conceptualization of past, present and future in relation to the self; and, the importance of time.

Human Nature:

The 'human nature' orientation category encompasses propositions dealing with perceptions of human nature. For example, explanations of motives relative to human interaction, i.e. is human nature evil, good, or neutral; conceptualizations of interpersonal behavior; and the extent of the belief in an ability to predict, mold, and/or alter human behavior.

Nature:

The 'nature' orientation category encompasses propositions dealing with perceptions of the natural environment. For example, rationalizations of the relationship between humankind and the natural environment; perceptions of environmental chaos, order and/or control; and the extent of a belief in an ability to exploit the natural environment.

Society:

The 'society' orientation category encompasses propositions dealing with perceptions of human associations. For example, an actor's understanding of self in relation to others; the actor's reality of belonging and/or not belonging, i.e. is life cooperative or competitive; and the conceptualization of roles, groups, or ideas of nationhood, i.e. how conflict should be resolved.

Space:

The 'space' orientation category encompasses propositions dealing with perceptions of physical placement. For example, the actor's understanding of physical space as fixed, situational, temporary or egocentric, i.e. the role of space in defining aspects of relationships such as degrees of intimacy or definitions of privacy; and the extent of an actor's ability to delineate private and public space; i.e. how space is allocated and owned.

Generating descriptive or normative propositions

Figure 6.46 The Notional Filter

Notional Filter (4)

COGNITIVE ORIENTATION	PROPOSITION TYPE	
	descriptive	normative
Time		
Human Nature		
Nature		
Society		
Space		

To perform the Notional Filter analysis/translation, the student classifies the beliefs/values generated in Applications 1 and 2 into their corresponding proposition type and cognitive orientation category on the Notional Filter. The analytical categories –proposition types (descriptive/normative) and cognitive orientation themes (time, human, nature, nature, society, and space)– of the Notional Filter are used to articulate the belief or value held by the sequence actor as an etic-proposition, as well as to articulate an etic proposition for the belief or value operative in the action sequence. The Notional Filter analysis results thus produce an etic description of the culture communicated in the action sequence. The propositions that are generated through the Notional Filter analysis can be used for comparative purposes.[88]

Returning to the proposition type examples noted above, the core assumption which represented the world as a flat plane extending into infinity, and which was categorized as a descriptive proposition, can be classified thematically as oriented to space. An emic-etic translation of this core assumption and attendant belief, using the Notional Filter, is given in figure 6.49.

Figure 6.49 Notional Filter Example 1

Belief: sailing into western horizon entails death
Assumption: world is flat plane extending into infinity

COGNITIVE ORIENTATION	PROPOSITION TYPE	
	descriptive	normative
Time		
Human Nature		
Nature		
Society		
Space	X	

Proposition: descriptive; thematically oriented to spatial assumptions and particularly assumptions about unknown space.

For the second descriptive example, the core assumption which interpreted time as fixed and measurable, and which was categorized as a descriptive proposition, can be classified thematically as oriented to time. A Notional Filter translation of this core assumption and attendant belief is given in figure 6.50.

Figure 6.50 Notional Filter Example 2

Belief: there is not enough time to accomplish tasks
Assumption: time is fixed and measurable

COGNITIVE ORIENTATION	PROPOSITION TYPE	
	descriptive	normative
Time	X	
Human Nature		
Nature		
Society		
Space		

Proposition: descriptive; thematically oriented to temporal
assumptions and particularly assumptions about time passage.

Returning to the normative examples, the value: 'stealing is wrong,'
discloses a core assumption that human nature will violate private
ownership, and can therefore be classified thematically as oriented to
human nature. A Notional Filter translation of this core assumption
and attendant value is given in figure 6.51.

Figure 6.51 Notional Filter Example 3

Value: stealing is wrong
Assumption: people will steal things

COGNITIVE ORIENTATION	PROPOSITION TYPE	
	descriptive	normative
Time		
Human Nature		X
Nature		
Society		
Space		

Proposition: normative, thematically oriented to assumptions
about human nature and particularly the need to enforce regulations
that protect individual property.

For the second normative example, the value: 'humans should kill in
defense only,' discloses a core assumption that people will kill and can
therefore be classified thematically as oriented to human nature. A
Notional Filter translation of this core assumption and attendant value
is given in figure 6.52.

Figure 6.52 Notional Filter Example 4

Value: humans should kill in defense only
Assumption: people will attempt to kill each other

COGNITIVE ORIENTATION	PROPOSITION TYPE	
	descriptive	normative
Time		
Human Nature		
Nature		
Society		X
Space		

Proposition: normative; thematically oriented to assumptions about society and particularly the need to protect physical life.

"Der Süße Brei" action sequence (2) Notional Filter practice analysis

Returning to the Application 1 box of the sample Cultural Inventory analysis, the mother's sponsor thought indicates a belief rather than a value, see figure 6.29 below:

Figure 6.29 Application 1 Results
Application 1:

> Belief or value of the sequence actor:
>   The routine for food production requires
>   specific words but is simple; I know how
>   to perform the routine

For, the mother, as sequence actor, has acted on the belief that the routine for food production is not complicated and that she has the knowledge necessary to perform the routine. The sequence actor holding this belief thus discloses a core assumption that estimates her own skill to exploit the pot as capable and sufficient based on knowledge gained informally, i.e. through observing the girl and not through specific training by the old woman. This belief will be translated into a descriptive proposition.

  sequence actor:
  a *descriptive* proposition.

The sequence actor's core assumption which understands skills as learnable through observation and which has been categorized as a descriptive proposition, can be classified thematically as oriented to human nature. A Notional Filter translation of the sequence actor's core assumption and attendant belief is given in figure 6.53:

Figure 6.53 Notional Filter "Der Süße Brei" Action Sequence (2) Sequence Actor Analysis

> *Belief*: the routine for food production requires specific words but is simple, I know how to perform the routine.
> *Assumption*: skills can be acquired informally through observation learning

COGNITIVE ORIENTATION	PROPOSITION TYPE	
	descriptive	normative
Time		
Human Nature	X	
Nature		
Society		
Space		

> *Proposition*: descriptive; thematically oriented to assumptions about human nature and particularly the reliance on human ingenuity and the possibility to informally acquire knowledge and skills.

Returning to the Application 2 box of the sample Cultural Inventory analysis, the symbolic outcome of the Feedback Filter indicates a value rather than a belief to represent the action sequence, see figure 6.43 below.

Figure 6.43 Action Sequence (2) Belief Evincing Inadequate Usage of the Act of Manipulation
Application 2:

> Belief or value of the action sequence:
> <u>The routine for food production requires specific words; only those who have been taught the words can perform the routine and those who have not been taught the words should not attempt the routine</u>

The consummation phase of the action sequence communicates a value concerning the pot exploitation; namely, that those who have not been taught the words to exploit the pot cannot, and should not attempt to perform the routine. The action sequence in presenting this value thus discloses a core assumption regarding the acquisition of knowledge and skills; namely, the necessity of standards through formal instruction. This value will be translated into a normative proposition.

action sequence:

a *normative* proposition

The action sequence's core assumption which sets a formal learning standard for knowledge/skill acquisition and which has been categorized as normative proposition, can be classified thematically as oriented to human nature. A Notional Filter translation of the action sequence's core assumption and attendant value is given in figure 6.54.

Figure 6.54 Notional Filter "Der Süße Brei" Action Sequence (2) Action Sequence Analysis

Value: the routine for food production requires specific words; only those who have been taught the words can perform the routine and those who have not been taught the words should not attempt the routine
Assumption: knowledge and skills to exploit environment can only be acquired through formal instruction

COGNITIVE ORIENTATION	PROPOSITION TYPE	
	descriptive	normative
Time		
Human Nature		X
Nature		
Society		
Space		

Proposition: normative; thematically oriented to assumptions about human nature and particularly the limits of human ingenuity and the importance of specialized training for acquiring knowledge and skills.

The results of the Notional Filter analysis for "Der Süße Brei" action sequence (2) are given in figure 6.55.

Figure 6.55 Notional Filter "Der Süße Brei" Action Sequence (2) Analysis Results

Sequence Actor Proposition:

COGNITIVE ORIENTATION	PROPOSITION TYPE	
	descriptive	normative
Time		
Human Nature	X	
Nature		
Society		
Space		

> **Descriptive proposition of the sequence actor:**
> Thematically oriented to assumptions about human nature and particularly the reliance on human ingenuity and the possibility to informally acquire knowledge and skills.

Action Sequence proposition:

COGNITIVE ORIENTATION	PROPOSITION TYPE	
	descriptive	normative
Time		
Human Nature		X
Nature		
Society		
Space		

> **Normative proposition of the action sequence:**
> Thematically oriented to assumptions about human nature and particularly the limits of human ingenuity and the importance of specialized training for acquiring knowledge and skills.

A review of the sample analysis to this point is given in figure 6.56 below.

Figure 6.56 Situational, Interactional, Feedback, Notional Filter Results

Sequence Actor: _____ mother _____
Phenomena: _____ magic words and pot ____
B.A.S.: _____ exploitational archetype _____

S. P. U. ____ systematic usage of manipulation _____
Symbolic Embodiment: _____ routine _____
Sponsor Thought: _I know the words to control the pot

Sequence Actor Belief:
          The routine for food production requires
          specific words but is simple; I know how
          to perform the routine

U.A.M.: ____ inadequate consummation _____
Symbolic Outcome: ___ incorrect usage of routine __

Action Sequence Value:
          The routine for food production requires specific words;
          only those who have been taught the words can perform
          the routine and those who have not been taught the
          words should not attempt the routine

Descriptive Proposition of the sequence actor:
Thematically oriented to assumptions about human nature and
particularly the reliance on human ingenuity and the possibility
to informally acquire knowledge and skills.

Normative Proposition of the action sequence:
Thematically oriented to assumptions about human nature and
particularly the limits of human ingenuity and the importance of
specialized training for acquiring knowledge and skills.

Situational Filter (1)

BASIC ARCHEPAL SITUAION	PHENOMENON	
	material	non-material
Territorial		
Temporal		
Subsistential		
Exploitational	**pot**	**words**
Recreational		
Instructional		
Protective		
Associational		
Economic		
Sexual		

Sequence Actor: _____mother_____

Phenomena: ____magic words and pot____

B.A.S.: _____exploitational archetype_____

Interactional Filter (2)

Sequence Phenomena Usage	YES	NO	Supporting Information	Symbolic Embodiment
Incitive Usage			see action sequence **(2) middle segment**	Prompt
Systematic Usage	**X**			**Routine**
Informative Usage				Image
Evaluative Usage				Model

S. P. U. ____systematic usage of manipulation____

Symbolic Embodiment: _____routine_____

Sponsor Thought: _I know the words to control the pot_

Application 1:

> Belief or value of the sequence actor:
> The routine for food production requires specific words but is simple; I know how to perform the routine

Feedback Filter (3)

USAGE ADEQUACY MEASUREMENT	YES	NO	Supporting Information
Prompt Persuasive			
Routine Correct		X	**resulted in a desperate situation in which "no one knew how to help"**
Image Convincing or Credible			
Model Prescriptively Effective			

> U.A.M.: _____ inadequate consummation _____
> Symbolic Outcome: ___ incorrect usage of routine__

Application 2:

> Belief or value of the action sequence:
> The routine for food production requires specific words; only those who have been taught the words can perform the routine and those who have not been taught the words should not attempt the routine

Notional Filter (4)

COGNITIVE ORIENTATION	PROPOSITION TYPE	
	descriptive	normative
Time		
Human Nature	**mother**	**sequence**
Nature		
Society		
Space		

> **Descriptive Proposition of the sequence actor**:
> Thematically oriented to assumptions about human nature and particularly the reliance on human ingenuity and the possibility to informally acquire knowledge and skills.
>
> **Normative Proposition of the action sequence**:
> Thematically oriented to assumptions about human nature and particularly the limits of human ingenuity and the importance of specialized training for acquiring knowledge and skills.

Notes

[1] Representamen is one of the components which constitute the triadic sign. The Representamen is essentially a sign vehicle. See Chapter 4.

[2] Blumer, "Symbolic Interactionsim," *Culture and Cognition*, ed. James P. Spradley (Prospect Heights: Waveland Press, Inc., 1972) 74-75.

[3] For full category definitions of each filter see respective filter explanations in this and the following chapters. The Basic Archetypal Situation category set can be abbreviated as B.A.S; the Sequence Phenomena Usage category set can be abbreviated as S.P.U.; the Usage Adequacy Measurement category set can be abbreviated as U.A.M; the Cognitive Orientation category set can be abbreviated as C.O.; and the Interpersonal Relations category set can be abbreviated as I.R.

[4] According to our application the Basic Archetypal Situations do not represent "culture;" rather, they provide a lens through which to observe culture as it surfaces in material form.

[5] Edward T. Hall, *The Silent Language* (New York: Doubleday, 1990) 36.

[6] Hall, *Beyond Culture* 135.

[7] Hall, *Silent Language* 44-57.

[8] This definition is derived from Hall's explanation of "Territoriality," *Silent Language* 44-45.

[9] This definition is derived from Hall's explanation of "Temporality," *Silent Language* 45.

[10] This definition is derived from Hall's explanation of "Subsistence," *Silent Language* 40-41.

[11] This definition is derived from Hall's explanation of "Exploitation," *Silent Language* 55-57.

[12] This definition is derived from Hall's explanation of "Play," *Silent Language* 50-52.

[13] This definition is derived from Hall's explanation of "Learning and Acquisition," *Silent Language* 45-50.

[14] This definition is derived from Hall's explanation of "Defense," *Silent Language* 52-55.

[15] This definition is derived from Hall's explanation of "Association," *Silent Language* 38-40.

[16] This definition is derived from Hall's explanation of "Subsistence," _Silent Language* 40-41.

[17] This definition is derived from Hall's explanation of "Bisexuality," *Silent Language* 41-44.

[18] Nöth, quoting the theory of Vygotsky 82.

[19] Blumer, "Society as Symbolic Interaction," in *Symbolic Interactionism* 78-79. Our emphasis.

[20] Ruth A. Wallace and Alison Wolf, "Symbolic Interactionism" in *Contemporary Sociological Theory: Continuing the Classical Tradition* (Englewood Cliffs: Prentice-Hall, Inc., 1986) 187-231.

[21] Nöth, quoting theory of Vygotsky 82.

[22] Blumer, "Society as Symbolic Interactionism," in *Symbolic Interactionism* 79.

[23] Nöth, quoting the theory of Vygotsky 82.

[24] See Chapter 4 figure 4.12.

[25] Blumer, "Society as Symbolic Interaction," in *Symbolic Interactionism* 79.

[26] Hall, *Beyond Culture* 85.

[27] Blumer, "Symbolic Interactionism," in *Culture and Cognition* 77.

[28] See Chapter 4 of this study. Inherent in the understanding of the term "response" is a sense of overtness, i.e. that some observable trace of the culturally-mediated-interaction is present. If, instead, we use the term resultant effect there is no predisposition to expect an immediate empirical result of the culturally-mediated-interaction. Moreover, the term resultant effect allows students to consider actions, thoughts, and artifacts as cultural responses.

[29] Spiro, "Representations" 162. Spiro writes that these propositions "...are encoded in those [interactions with] public and visible...[phenomena]...but since the latter neither posses nor announce their meanings, they must be found in the minds of social actors."

[30] Ladislav Holy and Milan Stuchlik, *Actions, norms and representations: Foundations of Anthropological Inquiry* (New York: Cambridge University Press, 1983) 110.

[31] Holy and Stuchlik 82.

[32] The absence of textual evidence for a resultant effect does not indicate the absence of a resultant effect. It simply makes our Cultural Inventory analysis of such impossible as currently conceived.

[33] Nöth 100-101.

[34] See 'the manipulation phase and Interactional Filter' in the discussion on the 'parameters of an action sequence' Chapter 5.

[35] Holy and Stuchlik 87.

[36] Holy and Stuchlik 83. Their whole quote reads: "there is a need to stipulate some mediating motivational mechanism through which norms [beliefs and values] can be brought to bear on actions. [...]we need to employ some bridging concept which would relate norms [beliefs and values] to actions. We consider as such bridging concept the goal of the action." We have substituted their term norms for our term [beliefs and values] in the text above.

[37] Holy and Stuchlik 82.

[38] Nöth 55.

[39] Nöth 55.

[40] Holy and Stuchlik 82.

[41] Morris, *Signs, Language, and Behavior* 92-106.

[42] Morris, *Signs, Language, and Behavior* 92.

[43] Morris suggests, in *Sign, Language, and Behavior*, that his four usages provide a general primary, perhaps even universal, classification system under which secondary uses and further consequences of a sign's existence can be subsumed. He writes: "The classification of the uses of signs is made difficult by the fact that almost every need which an organism [sequence actor] has may utilize signs as means to its attainment. Signs may serve as a means to gain money, social prestige, power over others; to deceive, inform, or entertain; to reassure, comfort, or excite; to record, describe, or predict; to satisfy some needs and to arouse others; to solve problems objectively and to gain a partial satisfaction for a conflict which the organism is not able to solve completely; to enlist the aid of others and to strengthen one's own independence; to 'express' oneself and to conceal oneself. And so on without end." 93.

[44] Morris, *Signs, Language, and Behavior* 94.

[45] Morris, *Signs, Language and Behavior* 102. An individual may use signs to, according to Morris, "…incite a particular response in himself or others to objects or signs, to call out submission in some one else, or to get the reply to a question which bothers him, or to provoke co-operative or disruptive behavior in the members of some community." 95.

[46] Morris, *Signs, Language, and Behavior* 104.

[47] Morris, *Signs, Language, and Behavior* 97.

[48] Morris, *Signs, Language, and Behavior* 99.

[49] Morris, *Signs, Language, and Behavior* 101. We have replaced Morris' term "preferential" with our term prejudicial, as the term prejudicial implies both positive or negative influence.

[50] Spiro, "Reflections" 163.

[51] Holy and Stuchlik 82.

[52] The relationship we see among beliefs, values and sponsor thoughts parallels, to some extent, the relationship among beliefs, values and attitudes described in the work of Milton Rokeach described in Littlejohn, *Theories in Human Communication*, 143-145.

[53] To review these aspects of our conception of culture see the discussion on "form" in chapter 3 of this study.

[54] Spiro, "Representations" 162-163.

[55] It should be noted that the action sequence represents the world in which the sequence actor is operating. As such it will be representative of a particular socio-cultural reality complete with its own descriptive and normative propositions. Hence, the goal for analysis through the Feedback Filter is to articulate the two potentially different beliefs/values present in the action sequence. The final goal of the Cultural Inventory analysis is to assign a respective socio-cultural reality both to the action sequence, as representative of the work in general, and to the sequence actor

[56] In short, students are assessing the adequacy of the sequence actor's mediation.

[57] Morris, *Signs, Language, and Behavior* 93. Our emphasis.

[58] For complete definitions of the Adequacy Measurements see Usage Adequacy Measurement in this section.

[59] Morris, *Signs, Language, and Behavior* 102.

[60] See incitive usage definition above

[61] Regarding the adequacy of systemic usage Morris writes, "...Insofar as signs are systemically adequate they are called[...]correct." Morris, *Signs, Language, and Behavior* 105. For this category, only Morris' terms have been borrowed. The use of the term systematic manipulation and correct adequacy measurement in the Cultural Inventory differs greatly from Morris' theory where these terms are used in reference to formators. In Morris' theory: "Formators are language signs having only contextual functions, such as conjunctions, quantifiers, other function words and punctuation marks." Nöth 55.

[62] See systematic usage definition above.

[63] Morris, *Signs, Language, and Behavior* 99.

[64] See informative usage definition above.

[65] Morris, *Signs, Language, and Behavior* 101.

[66] See evaluative usage definition above.

[67] See figures 6.10-13.

[68] See the discussion on Spiro's 'Hierarchy of Cognitive Salience' Chapter 3.

[69] Spiro, "Representations" 163-164. For clarity, the term propositions has been substituted for "doctrines" and students for "the actors" which occurs in the original.

[70] See Chapter 3. The issue here is that reflecting on one's own core assumptions as propositions undermines the ideological process of assumptions as reality and reveals their 'constructive' function.

[71] Excluded is Spiro's level (3) at which: "The actors not only understand the traditional meanings of the propositions, but understanding them, they *believe* that the propositions[...]are true, correct, or right. That actors hold a proposition to be true does not in itself, however, indicate that it importantly effects the manner in which they conduct their lives." Spiro, "Representations" 164. However, the cultural cliché/genuine belief distinction inherent in the distinction between levels (3) and (4) makes it possible to distinguish between two types of cultural beliefs. Namely, an espoused cultural value/belief which would correspond to level (3): actors hold the value/belief to be true (i.e. one

should not lie) but it does not effect how they conduct their lives; and, a genuine cultural value/belief which would correspond to level (4): the belief guides the social actor's actions (i.e. belief in the sacredness of all animal life and the conscious practice of Vegetarianism). A distinction between core and espoused values is also mentioned by Edgar Schein in reference to organizational culture: "...if values[...]are not based on prior learning, they may also reflect only what Argyris and Schön (1978) have called espoused values, which predict well enough what people will *say* in a variety of situations but which may be out of line with that which they will actually *do* in situations where those values should, in fact, be operating." Schein 20-21.

[72] Spiro, "Representations" 164. Earlier in the same article Spiro expands his definition of beliefs which we have also incorporated in our term cultural beliefs, his expansion reads: "By 'belief' I will mean any proposition concerning human beings, society, and the world that is held to be true." 162-163.

[73] *American Heritage Dictionary* entry for "assumption," 80.

[74] Schein 22.

[75] Spiro, "Reflections" 38.

[76] Spiro, "Reflections" 38.

[77] Spiro, "Representations" 164.

[78] See Cognitive orientation definitions.

[79] We hold this view from Spiro who writes that although cultural information is not always stated in propositional form "they are susceptible of statement in that form." "Reflections" 32.

[80] Many cognitive theorists have articulated this distinction in propositions; i.e. Boulding's images of fact and images of value in "The Image", *Culture and Cognition*; Holy and Stuchlik's representations and norms in *Actions, norms and representations*.

[81] Boulding 48.

[82] Tinsley and Woloshin 126.

[83] Royal L. Tinsley and David J. Woloshin, "Approaching German Culture" *Die Unterrichtspraxis* (Spring 1974): 126. Our emphasis.

[84] Boulding 41.

[85] Tinsley and Woloshin 125-136.

[86] Kearney 106.

[87] Schein 95-96.

[88] It is possible to end the cultural analysis at the Notional Filter. As such, the student would accumulate cultural propositions for various works. Ending the analysis at the Notional Filter, however, discards the interpretative dimension of the second level of Cultural Inventory which has been designed to context the propositions relative to their corresponding socio-cultural realities.

Chapter 7

Cultural Inventory Analysis Level 2:
Socially Contexting the Symbolic Analysis

Overview of Analysis Level 2

The data gathered from the Cultural Inventory's symbolic analysis filters (Filters 1-4 and Applications 1-2) is utilized on this second level of analysis to examine the social context(s) within which the sequence actor operates. Depending on the symbolic analysis results, specifically whether the action sequence is found to depict concurring or opposing propositions, two different socio-cultural realities may be determined for the sequence actor; namely, the reality *from which* s/he negotiates the act of manipulation and the reality *in which* s/he finds her/himself at the close of the action sequence. For example, if there is a conflict or aberration in the action sequence, as with "Der Süße Brei" sample, the reality from which the sequence actor acts and that which the action sequence presents him/her in will differ. The level 2 analysis sections of the Cultural Inventory thus focus on determining both a pre- and post manipulation phase socio-cultural reality for the sequence actor based on, and relative to the results of the Level 1 Cultural Inventory symbolic analysis.

To accommodate the possibility of two separate socio-cultural realities, the filters and stages of the Level 2 Analysis on the Cultural Inventory address the social-contexting analysis from two perspectives; first, a pre-manipulation perspective referred to as 'pre-usage outcome' (or pre-outcome) representing the reality from which sequence actor negotiates the act of manipulation and, secondly, a post manipulation perspective referred to as 'post-usage outcome' (or post-outcome) representing the reality in which the sequence actor finds him/herself at the close of the action sequence should his/her initial reality be negated by the consummation phase of the action sequence.

The analysis structure for this second level on the Cultural Inventory was inspired from Mary Douglas' 'Grid-Group Theory' which "...is intended to have the sort of general applicability necessary for analyzing the relationship of the social and symbolic orders."[1] The analysis process for this second level of the Cultural Inventory thus represents a typology method as an adaptation of Douglas' 'Grid-Group Theory'.[2] To conduct a Level 2 analysis the student completes analyses set forth in the Application 3, Interpersonal Filter and Syntheses 1-2 analyses, in order to determine both Grid and Group dimensions for the sequence actor (see figures 7.1 and 7.2).

Figure 7.1 Application 3 and Synthesis 1
Application 3:

Is the sequence actor proposition **restrictive** ?	**Pre**-Usage Outcome	
	Yes	No

Is the action sequence proposition **restrictive** ?	**Post**-Usage Outcome	
	Yes	No

Synthesis 1:

> **Grid Determination (pre-outcome)**: _____
> **Grid Determination (post-outcome)**: _____
> [+ grid] = Proposition restrictive for actor(s)
> [– grid] = Proposition not restrictive for actor(s)

Figure 7.2 Interpersonal Filter and Synthesis 2
Interpersonal Filter (5)

INTERPERSONAL RELATIONS	Pre-Usage Outcome	Post-Usage Outcome
Ranked Member inclusion into ranked network		
Non-ranked Member inclusion into non-ranked network		
Involuntary Non-member involuntary exclusion from network		
Voluntary Non-member voluntary exclusion from network		

Synthesis 2:

> **Group Determination (pre-outcome)**_____
> **Group Determination (post-outcome)**: _____
>   [+ group] = Member (ranked and non-ranked)
>   [– group] = Non-member (involuntary and voluntary)

These Grid and Group dimensions are then used to position the sequence actor within a cell, 1-2-3-or-4, of the evaluation typology (see figure 7.3). It will be demonstrated in this chapter how the student, by completing this second level of analysis (containing Application 3, Synthesis 1 and 2, Interpersonal Filter, and Evaluation Typology), is able to determine both social contexts for the symbolic analysis data[3] and socio-cultural realities for the sequence actor.

Figure 7.3 Evaluation Typology
Evaluation Typology:

	Pre-Usage Outcome	
	+ Grid	– Grid
+ Group	1	2
– Group	3	4

	Post-Usage Outcome	
	+ Grid	– Grid
+ Group	1	2
– Group	3	4

> **Typology Determination (pre-outcome):** _____
> **Typology Determination (post-outcome):** _____

Application 3

Figure 7.4 Application 3 Questions

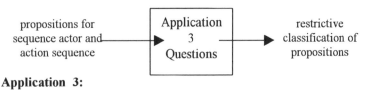

Application 3:

Is the sequence actor proposition **restrictive** ?	**Pre**-Usage Outcome	
	Yes	**No**

Is the action sequence proposition **restrictive** ?	**Post**-Usage Outcome	
	Yes	**No**

Like the Notional Filter, the conclusions drawn from Application 3 focus on the propositions of the sequence actor and action sequence. The questions posed in Application 3 address how free the sequence actor is to interact with regards to his/her own proposition (pre-usage outcome), and with regards to the proposition operative for the action sequence (post-usage outcome). The 'grid' aspect of 'Grid-Group Theory' has been employed as a baseline for determining an answer to the Application 3 questions.

The grid dimension of Mary Douglas' 'Grid-Group Theory' was developed to "define the behavioral options" of the social actor "within personal interactions;"[4] as such grid

> indicates the degree to which an individual's life is circumscribed by externally imposed [propositions]. The more binding and extensive the scope of the [propositions], the less of life that is open to individual negotiation. [For example] A highly regulated (high grid) social context is signified by an explicit set of institutionalized classifications [i.e. a set of propositions thematically related to society] that keep individuals apart and regulate their interactions.[5]

The concept of 'restrictive' is derived from Douglas' 'grid' determination.

Restrictive-yes:

A determination of 'yes' for the restrictiveness of a proposition indicates that the proposition is binding; it restricts the interaction options of the sequence actor. The more restrictive or binding a proposition is for the sequence actor's reality, either pre-or post usage outcome, the fewer the options for this actor to independently negotiate an act of manipulation. Such a proposition thus binds the choices of sequence actor's behavior to the specific conditions set forth by it. And, such a proposition is restrictive for the sequence actor because it functions to limit his/her choices for action.

Restrictive-no

A determination of 'no' for the restrictiveness of the proposition indicates that the proposition is not binding; it does not restrict the interaction options of the sequence actor.

Pre-Usage-Outcome Sequence Actor's Proposition

The pre-usage outcome Application 3 question addresses the restrictiveness of the sequence actor's proposition relative to the act of manipulation in the action sequence. Pre-usage outcome is thus a temporal determination for the proposition *operative for the sequence actor* and its impact on the sponsor thought underlying the act of manipulation. To answer this question, the student determines whether the proposition held by the sequence actor binds, i.e. restricts, his/her behavioral options to negotiate the action sequence. As such, the student must ask whether the content of the sequence actor's proposition (see Notional Filter analysis results) serves to restrict his/her interaction options; yes or no. The pre-outcome answer to the first Application 3 question thus pertains to the content of the sequence actor's assumption regarding the chosen line of conduct necessary to negotiate the action sequence; hence "pre-usage outcome" (i.e. at the outset of the act of manipulation, prior to the analysis results of the Feedback Filter and therefore focused on the pre-usage outcome cultural reality of the sequence actor).

"Der Süße Brei" Action-sequence(2) Application 3-Question 1 Analysis

For "Der Süße Brei" sample, one considers the descriptive proposition of the sequence actor as determined in the Notional Filter analysis (see figure 6.53) and asks: Is this proposition restrictive for the mother prior to and during the act of manipulation in the action sequence, i.e. does this proposition in any way restrict the interaction options of the mother?

Figure 6.53 Notional Filter "Der Süße Brei"
Action Sequence (2) Sequence Actor Analysis

Belief: the routine for food production requires specific words but is simple, I know how to perform the routine.
Assumption: skills can be acquired informally through observation learning

COGNITIVE ORIENTATION	PROPOSITION TYPE	
	descriptive	normative
Time		
Human Nature	X	
Nature		
Society		
Space		

Proposition: descriptive; thematically oriented to assumptions about human nature and particularly the reliance on human ingenuity and the possibility to informally acquire knowledge and skills.

The pre-outcome Application 3 answer for "Der Süße Brei" sample is no (see figure 7.5). For, if the descriptive proposition employed by the mother had evinced content that would restrict her successful performance of the routine, she would not have attempted the act of manipulation.

Figure 7.5 Pre-Usage Outcome Application 3 Question 1 Results

Is the sequence actor proposition **restrictive** ?	**Pre**-Usage **Outcome**	
	Yes	No

Post-Usage-Outcome Action Sequence's Proposition

The post-usage outcome Application 3 question addresses the restrictiveness of the action sequence's proposition for the sequence actor relative to the act of consummation in the action sequence. Post-usage outcome is thus a temporal determination for the proposition operative *in the action sequence* and its impact on the sequence actor post-manipulation. To answer this question the student determines whether the proposition of the action sequence binds, i.e. restricts, the behavioral options of the sequence actor to negotiate the action sequence. As such, the student must ask whether the content of the action sequence's proposition (see Notional Filter analysis results) serves to restrict the interaction options of the sequence actor; yes or no. In determining an answer for the second Application 3 question, the student may look back from a post-consummation phase perspective; hence "post-usage outcome" (i.e. from the conclusion of the action sequence, considering the analysis results of the Feedback Filter and therefore focused on the post-usage outcome cultural reality of the sequence actor).

"Der Süße Brei" Action Sequence(2) Application 3-Question 2 Analysis

For "Der Süße Brei" sample, one considers the normative proposition of the action sequence as determined by the Notional Filter analysis (see figure 6.54) and asks: Is this proposition restrictive for the mother at the completion of the action sequence, i.e. does the proposition in any way restrict the interaction options of the mother?

Figure 6.54 Notional Filter "Der Süße Brei"
Action Sequence (2) Action Sequence Analysis

> *Value*: the routine for food production requires specific words; only those who have been taught the words can perform the routine and those who have not been taught the words should not attempt the routine

> *Assumption*: knowledge and skills to exploit environment can only be acquired through formal instruction

COGNITIVE ORIENTATION	PROPOSITION TYPE	
	descriptive	normative
Time		
Human Nature		X
Nature		
Society		
Space		

Proposition: normative; thematically oriented to assumptions about human nature and particularly the limits of human ingenuity and the importance of specialized training for acquiring knowledge and skills.

The post-outcome Application 3 answer for "Der Süße Brei" sample is yes, the proposition is restrictive since non-adherence to the action sequence's proposition creates a disastrous situation that threatens the survival of the whole town.

Figure 7.6 Post-Usage Outcome Application 3 Question 2 Results

Is the action sequence proposition **restrictive** ?	**Post**-Usage **Outcome**	
	Yes	**No**

When restrictive propositions are an element of the cultural reality in which the actor operates –from choice or necessity–, such propositions can be binding for the actor, even if they are not derived from the core assumptions of the actor. As in "Der Süße Brei" sample, the action sequence's proposition proved restrictive for the mother although it was not derived from her core assumptions. The key, therefore, to recognizing a restrictive proposition lies in determining whether its content intends to "restrict" the manipulation options of the sequence actor. The determination of restrictiveness for both the sequence actor's and action sequence's propositions is thus based on the content of the propositions as determined by the Notional Filter analysis.

It is important to make both a pre- and post-usage outcome restrictiveness assessment; for, the assessments often pertain to different propositions exhibiting opposing restrictive determinations.

For example, in "Der Süße Brei" sample, the mother holds a non-restrictive proposition regarding learning prior to the act of manipulation. However, her non-restrictive proposition (pre-outcome reality) is negated by the restrictive proposition of the action sequence in the consummation phase. For "Der Süße Brei" sample, adherence to the action sequence's restrictive proposition becomes obligatory for the sequence actor since non-adherence threatens survival. Therefore, from the consummation, the mother is forced to operate within the reality of the action sequence's restrictive proposition. Thus, while a non-restrictive proposition directed the mother's per-outcome reality, a restrictive proposition controls her post-outcome reality. For the sample, therefore, the action sequence's proposition alters the cultural reality of the sequence actor post-outcome.

Synthesis 1

Figure 7.7 Synthesis 1 Translation

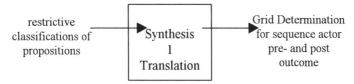

Synthesis 1:

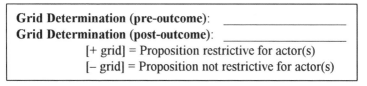

Grid determination

Both the 'grid determination' and the 'group determination', to be addressed in connection with the Interpersonal Filter analysis, have been borrowed from Mary Douglas' Grid-Group Typology as outlined in *In the Active Voice* (1982). Douglas' typology was created from two dimensions, namely grid and group. The grid dimension has been employed as a measurement of restrictiveness   (Application 3) in determining whether the culture of the sequence actor and the culture of the action sequence function to restrict the interaction choices of the sequence actor pre- and post-usage outcome, respectively. Thus, for Synthesis 1, a '(+) Grid' determination indicates that the proposition was found to be restrictive in Application 3; while, a'(–) Grid' determination indicates that the proposition was found to be non-restrictive in Application 3. To perform Synthesis 1, the student chooses a (+) or (–) Grid for the culture realities based on the pre- and post-usage outcome restrictive determinations in Application 3. As such, the completion of Synthesis 1 constitutes a translation of the data from the 'Application 3' analysis into the first category of the 'Grid-Group Typology'

"Der Süße Brei" Action-sequence (2) Synthesis 1 Analysis

For "Der Süße Brei" sample, the pre-outcome proposition was determined as non-restrictive (see figure 7.5). As a non-restrictive proposition it receives a (–) grid determination in Synthesis 1. The post-outcome proposition was determined as restrictive (see figure 7.6). As a restrictive proposition it receives a (+) grid determination in Synthesis 1. The Synthesis 1 results are given in figure 7.8. The significance of these results will be further explained in connection with the Evaluation Typology later in this chapter.

Figure 7.5 Pre-Usage Outcome Application 3 Question 1 Results

Is the sequence actor proposition **restrictive** ?	Pre-Usage Outcome	
	Yes	No

Figure 7.6 Post-Usage Outcome Application 3 Question 2 Results

Is the action sequence proposition **restrictive** ?	Post-Usage Outcome	
	Yes	No

Figure 7.8 Synthesis 1 Grid Determinations

Grid Determination (pre-outcome):	– grid
Grid Determination (post-outcome):	+ grid

[+ grid] = Proposition restrictive for actor(s)
[– grid] = Proposition not restrictive for actor(s)

The Interpersonal Filter Analysis

Figure 7.9 The Interpersonal Filter Analysis

Interpersonal Filter (5)

INTERPERSONAL RELATIONS	Pre-Usage Outcome	Post-Usage Outcome
Ranked Member inclusion into ranked network		
Non-ranked Member inclusion into non-ranked network		
Involuntary Non-member involuntary exclusion from network		
Voluntary Non-member voluntary exclusion from network		

The Interpersonal Filter is the final filter of the Cultural Inventory. It enables the student to conduct an analysis of the action sequence's interpersonal relations; i.e. the social formation of the action sequence and the social status of the sequence actor within this social formation. The categories which comprise this filter allow the student to determine the social structure of the sequence actor's interpersonal reality, as it is depicted in the action sequence both before and after the act of manipulation, hence pre- and post-usage-outcome.

It is necessary to determine the interpersonal relations operative in the action sequence both pre- and post-outcome; for, the sequence-feedback of the consummation phase can reveal alternative interpersonal relations which change the sequence-actor's and other sequence-participants' (including the audience's) understanding of the social formation depicted within the action sequence.

Interpersonal Relations

Group

The 'Group' dimension of Mary Douglas' 'Grid-Group Theory' is used as a baseline for determining the social formation of the action sequence within a Cultural Inventory analysis. In "Grid-Group Theory' the 'Group' dimension addresses the "dimension of social incorporation"[6] whereby 'group' relates to "the choice of interpersonal contacts,"[7] and is defined

> in terms of the claims it makes over its constituent members, the boundary it draws around them, the things it confers on them [i.e.] to use its name and other protections, and the levies and constraints it applies.[8]

Text network

The use of the term network, pertains to the nucleus, or decisive center of the group indicated in the text analyzed. In terms of the propositions acquired through the symbolic analysis of the action sequence, the network constitutes the segment of the text's group that is both knowledgeable of, and has internalized the operative proposition for the action sequence. The network, therefore, is the segment of the text's group that has access to obtaining the information and/or the means necessary to successfully negotiate the culture of the action sequence. For "Der Süße Brei" sample analysis, considering the whole text reveals that the old woman and the little girl constitute the network actors for the group, as both have the means and information necessary to correctly perform the routine.

The categories of interpersonal relations on the Cultural Inventory, as applied in the Interpersonal Filter analysis, represent four different patterns of social identity based on the network status of the sequence actor. These four social identities are, in turn, defined according to the sequence actor's membership, and if membership then role in the network of the text.

The group-actors included in the network may not be *in* the action sequence chosen for analysis. Determining which group-actors constitute the network of a text is of issue for determining a network within a text, but it is not the focus of the Interpersonal Filter analysis. Rather, the focus of the Interpersonal Filter analysis is to determine the *network status* of the sequence actor, first from the perspective of the sequence actor him/herself (the pre-usage outcome determination); and, secondly to determine the network status of the sequence actor from the perspective of the action sequence (the post-usage outcome determination).

Interpersonal Filter

Defined below are each of the four possible network categories that comprise the Interpersonal Filter. These four categories have been created from both determinations in the sequence actor's network membership (i.e. network member, or non-member) and distinctions in network structure of the group (i.e. ranked, or non-ranked).

Figure 7.10 The Interpersonal Filter
Interpersonal Filter (5)

INTERPERSONAL RELATIONS	Pre-Usage Outcome	Post-Usage Outcome
Ranked Member inclusion into ranked network		
Non-ranked Member inclusion into non-ranked network		
Involuntary Non-member involuntary exclusion from network		
Voluntary Non-member voluntary exclusion from network		

Ranked network member

This interpersonal relations category represents the network status of a sequence actor who is already considered a network member. For this category of interpersonal relation, network status is ranked, or arranged according to some type of classification system. A group, or social formation organized as a ranked network presents a group environment

in which everyone knows his place, but in which that place may vary over time.[...]Examples of this type of social organization include bureaucracies that base their roles on seniority (an ascribed basis) rather than merit (an achieved basis);[...]individual choices and opportunities are reserved for persons according to their categories in the system.[9]

As a ranked network member, the sequence-actor's access to information, i.e. his/her network status, will be commensurate with his/her rank relative to the classification system depicted or implied in the text. Classification systems delineating differences in network status based on age, friendship, assets, strength, intelligence, beauty, marital status, or ancestry are representative of a few of the systems by which networks have been ranked. The classifications themselves are arbitrary and varied. They serve merely to establish some type of system for measuring differences among network members. Examples of variously ranked network members would include any member in the military; a government worker with a level of classified clearance; a professor at the university; or a teacher in a school.

In "Der Süße Brei" text sample there is evidence of a ranked network structure for the network within the text group. The two members of the network, the old woman and the little girl, exhibit a ranked master-pupil relation in the first action sequence (see figure 5.1) and the little girl holds the qualification of 'fromm' (is obedient and follows the rules). Receiving the training and thus possessing the skill to perform the routine is a classification which separates the ranked network members of this text group (old woman and little girl) from the other text group members (mother and town inhabitants) who, through involuntary exclusion, are not network members.

Non-ranked network member

This interpersonal relations category represents the status of a sequence actor who is already considered a network member. A group or social formation organized as a non-ranked network presents

> a social context in which the external group boundary is typically the dominant consideration. All other aspects of interpersonal relations are ambiguous and open to negotiation[...].[10]

Here all network members have equal access to information and equal status within the network of the text group. The only classificatory system employed is a determination of network member or non-member; there is no other classification system for ranking, hence the term non-ranked network. Examples of members in a non-ranked network would include a member in a commune; a member in one of the first Christian communities that endured persecution; or a member in an activist group like those attempting to save old growth forests.

In "Der Süße Brei" text sample (see figures 5.1-3), there is no evidence of a non-ranked network structure for the text group. Such a formation would depict all text group members as equally trained to perform the routine; mother and/or other town inhabitants included. However, as stated above, the network within the text depicts a ranked master-pupil relation between the old woman and the little girl.

Involuntary non-member: non-member through involuntary exclusion

This interpersonal relations category represents the status of a sequence actor who is considered an involuntary network non-member. A text group, or social formation composed of involuntary network non-members presents

> an environment in which the way a person may behave is strongly regulated according to their socially assigned classifications. [These non-members][...]are classified out of the decision-making-process [hence, involuntary non-members of network.][...]In this environment, persons in favorable categories are protected by their classifications from many of the effects of misfortune. [But][...]favorable categories are harder to find here than unfavorable ones[11].

As an involuntary network non-member, the sequence actor is not part of the network for reasons either known, or unknown to the actor but beyond his/her control to alter, hence the term involuntary. However, although a non-member of the network, the sequence actor remains subject to the network's propositions. Examples of group members holding involuntary network non-membership status include the precarious existence of slaves who are subject to the dictates of their masters yet have no recourse to challenge their status; the political position of women prior to suffrage; or the victim of a candid camera joke.

In "Der Süße Brei" text sample, there is post-usage outcome evidence of involuntary non-member network status for the sequence actor and other sequence participants (i.e. the town people who did not know how to help). None of these text group members possess the knowledge/skill to perform the routine correctly, hence they are not network members. And, additional evidence of the mother's *involuntary* non-network member status is found through the failed consummation of her manipulation; for, it is only after the failure of her act of manipulation that she recognizes herself as a network non-member. If she had known of the action sequence proposition – limiting control of the pot to those who had training– and if she had complied with this proposition her network-status would still be that of an involuntary network non-member as she does not have the training to control the pot and therefore cannot be considered a network member.

Voluntary non member: non-member through voluntary exclusion

This interpersonal relations category represents the status of a sequence actor who is considered a voluntary network non-member. A text group or social formation composed of voluntary network non-members presents an environment that can not be described as a text group in any permanent or sustainable sense; for, this social formation

> allows the maximum options for negotiating [the culture of the action sequence]. [In such a text group][...]no one cares about the past or about anyone's ancestry. Each person is responsible for himself and for whomsoever else he chooses.[12]

There are no applicable group boundaries and, consequently, no particular network for the voluntary non-member. These actors tend to 'buck the system'. The sequence actor who holds the status of a voluntary network non-member is not part of the network through choice; i.e. s/he voluntarily excludes him/herself from the network. As a matter of independent choice, the sequence actor is not subject to the propositions of the network. Examples of group actors holding voluntary non-member network status include a draft-dodger; a political exile; a "small scale entrepreneur in new energy technologies;"[13] or a frontiersman.[14]

"Der Süße Brei" Action Sequence (2) Interpersonal Filter Analysis

Pre-usage outcome social identity

When determining an interpersonal relations category for the sequence actor, the student first considers the network status of the sequence actor pre-usage outcome, i.e. the social identity of the mother from her own perspective. To complete this section of the Interpersonal Filter, the student must consider the analysis results of the Situational and Interactional Filters, as well as the belief/value operative for the sequence actor noted in Application 1 and the his/her proposition as articulated in the Notional Filter analysis (see figure 7.11).

Figure 7.11 Pre-Usage Outcome Symbolic Analysis Results
Situational Filter (1)

BASIC ARCHEPAL SITUAION	PHENOMENON	
	material	non-material
Territorial		
Temporal		
Subsistential		
Exploitational	**pot**	**words**
Recreational		
Instructional		
Protective		
Associational		
Economic		
Sexual		

Sequence Actor: _____mother_____
Phenomena: ____magic words and pot____
B.A.S.: _____exploitational archetype_____

Interactional Filter (2)

Sequence Phenomena Usage	YES	NO	Supporting Information	Symbolic Embodiment
Incitive Usage			see action sequence **(2) middle segment**	Prompt
Systematic Usage	**X**			**Routine**
Informative Usage				Image
Evaluative Usage				Model

S.P.U.___ systematic usage of manipulation_____
Symbolic Embodiment:_____routine_____
Sponsor Thought: _I know the words to control the pot

Application 1:

Belief or value of the sequence actor:
　　　　The routine for food production requires
　　　　specific words but is simple; I know how
　　　　to perform the routine

Notional Filter (4)

COGNITIVE ORIENTATION	PROPOSITION TYPE	
	descriptive	normative
Time		
Human Nature	**mother**	
Nature		
Society		
Space		

Descriptive proposition of the sequence actor:
Thematically oriented to assumptions about human nature and particularly the reliance on human ingenuity and the possibility to informally acquire knowledge and skills.

A review of the Situational, Interactional, and Notional Filters and Application 1 analysis results indicates that the mother considers herself a member of a non-ranked network. First, she considers herself a *member* of the network; for, her choice of interaction shows that she believes she has the knowledge/skill to perform the routine successfully. Secondly, she considers herself a *non-ranked* member; for, her act of manipulation indicates that she does not perceive any formal classifications (i.e. specialized training or particular attributes such as "fromm") to be associated with the ability to perform the routine correctly. Consequently, the Interpersonal Filter pre-outcome determination for the mother in "Der Süße Brei" sample is 'non-ranked member' (see figure 7.12).

Figure 7.12 "Der Süße Brei" Action Sequence (2)
Interpersonal Filter Pre-Usage Outcome Analysis Results

Interpersonal Filter (5)

INTERPERSONAL RELATIONS	Pre-Usage Outcome	Post-Usage Outcome
Ranked Member inclusion into ranked network		
Non-ranked Member inclusion into non-ranked network	**Mother**	
Involuntary Non-member involuntary exclusion from network		
Voluntary Non-member voluntary exclusion from network		

Post-usage outcome social identity

To determine a post-outcome interpersonal relations category for the mother, the student now examines data pertinent to the conclusion of the action sequence, especially considering the analysis results of the Feedback Filter. The interpersonal relation category chosen here focuses on the post-outcome cultural reality of the sequence actor, and thus the social identity of the mother from the perspective of the action sequence. To complete this section of the Interpersonal Filter, the student must consider the analysis results of all previous filters and stages: namely, the Situational, Interactional, Feedback, and Notional Filters, as well as the belief/value operative for the sequence actor and for the action sequence noted in Applications 1 and 2.

A review of the Situational, Interactional, Feedback, and Notional Filters, as well as the Application 1 and 2 analysis results (see figure 7.13) indicates that the mother holds the social identity of an involuntary network non-member according to the perspective of the action sequence. First, she represents a *non-member* of the network as she has not been taught the words to perform the routine correctly. And, secondly, her non-membership is *involuntary* since prior to, and during the act of manipulation she believes she holds the knowledge/skill to perform the routine correctly.

Figure 7.13 Pre-and Post-Usage Outcome Symbolic Analysis Results

Situational Filter (1)

BASIC ARCHEPAL SITUAION	PHENOMENON	
	material	non-material
Territorial		
Temporal		
Subsistential		
Exploitational	**pot**	**words**
Recreational		
Instructional		
Protective		
Associational		
Economic		
Sexual		

Sequence Actor: _____mother_____
Phenomena: _____magic words and pot_____
B.A.S.: _____exploitational archetype_____

Interactional Filter (2)

Sequence Phenomena Usage	YES	NO	Supporting Information	Symbolic Embodiment
Incitive Usage			see action sequence	Prompt
Systematic Usage	X		(2) middle segment	**Routine**
Informative Usage				Image
Evaluative Usage				Model

S.P.U. _____systematic usage of manipulation_____
Symbolic Embodiment: _____routine_____
Sponsor Thought: _I know the words to control the pot_

Application 1:

> Belief or value of the sequence actor:
> The routine for food production requires
> specific words but is simple; I know how
> to perform the routine

Feedback Filter (3)

USAGE ADEQUACY MEASUREMENT	YES	NO	Supporting Information
Prompt Persuasive			
Routine Correct		X	resulted in a desperate situation in which "no one knew how to help"
Image Convincing or Credible			
Model Prescriptively Effective			

> U.A.M.: _____ inadequate consummation _____
> Symbolic Outcome: ____ incorrect usage of routine __

Application 2:

> Belief or value of the action sequence:
> The routine for food production requires specific words;
> only those who have been taught the words can perform
> the routine and those who have not been taught the
> words should not attempt the routine

Notional Filter (4)

COGNITIVE ORIENTATION	PROPOSITION TYPE	
	descriptive	normative
Time		
Human Nature	**mother**	**sequence**
Nature		
Society		
Space		

> **Descriptive Proposition of the sequence actor**:
> <u>Thematically oriented to assumptions about human nature and particularly the reliance on human ingenuity and the possibility to informally acquire knowledge and skills.</u>
>
> **Normative Proposition of the action sequence**:
> <u>Thematically oriented to assumptions about human nature and particularly the limits of human ingenuity and the importance of specialized training for acquiring knowledge and skills.</u>

Consequently, the Interpersonal Filter post-outcome determination for the mother in "Der Süße Brei" sample is 'involuntary non-member' (see figure 7.14).

Figure 7.14 "Der Süße Brei" Action Sequence (2) Interpersonal Filter Pre- and Post-Usage Outcome Analysis Results

Interpersonal Filter (5)

INTERPERSONAL RELATIONS	Pre-Usage Outcome	Post-Usage Outcome
Ranked Member inclusion into ranked network		
Non-ranked Member inclusion into non-ranked network	**Mother**	
Involuntary Non-member involuntary exclusion from network		**Mother**
Voluntary Non-member voluntary exclusion from network		

Synthesis 2

Figure 7.15 Synthesis 2 Translation

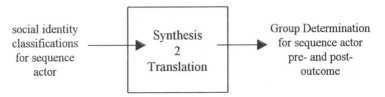

social identity classifications for sequence actor ⟶ Synthesis 2 Translation ⟶ Group Determination for sequence actor pre- and post-outcome

Synthesis 2:

> **Group Determination (pre-outcome)**_____
> **Group Determination (post-outcome)**: _____
> [+ group] = Member (ranked and non-ranked)
> [– group] = Non-member (involuntary and voluntary)

Group determination

"Group" is the second of the two dimensions which constitute Douglas' 'Grid-Group Typology'. Douglas developed the Group assessment as a factor for determining the extent to which a social actor's life is absorbed in and sustained by a group. Within the Cultural Inventory analysis, Group has been employed as a baseline for determining the social identity of a sequence actor from the perspective of the sequence actor (pre-outcome) and from the perspective of the action sequence (post-outcome). The four interpersonal relations categories that comprise the Interpersonal Filter enable the student to context the sequence actor both within a social identity relative to his/her perceived network status (pre-outcome social identity) and within a social identity relative to the network operative in the action sequence (post-outcome social identity). Of the four network scenarios for interpersonal relations defined in the Interpersonal Filter, two are based on network membership, ranked and non-ranked; and, two are based on network non-membership, voluntary and involuntary (see Interpersonal Filter definitions).

For Synthesis 2, a '(+) Group' determination can be assigned to the sequence actor if, as a result of the Interpersonal Filter analysis, s/he is found to represent the social identity of a network member, either ranked or non-ranked. A '(–) Group' determination can be assigned to the sequence actor if, as a result of the Interpersonal Filter analysis, s/he is found to represent the social identity of a network non-member, either through involuntary or voluntary exclusion. The student chooses a (+) or (–) group determination for the sequence actor based on the pre- and post-outcome interpersonal relations determinations indicated in the Interpersonal Filter analysis results. As such, the performance of Synthesis 2 constitutes a translation of the Interpersonal Filter data into the second category of the 'Grid-Group Typology'

"Der Süße Brei" Action-sequence (2) Synthesis 2 Analysis

For "Der Süße Brei" sample, the pre-outcome social identity of the mother was determined as 'non-ranked member' (see figure 7.14 below). As a 'non-ranked member,' the mother receives a (+) group determination in Synthesis 2. The post-outcome social identity of the mother was determined as 'involuntary non-member' (see figure 7.14 below). As an 'involuntary non-member,' the mother receives a (–) group determination in Synthesis 2. These Synthesis 2 results are depicted below in figure 7.16.

Figure 7.14 "Der Süße Brei" Action Sequence (2)
Interpersonal Filter Pre- and Post-Usage Outcome Analysis Results

Interpersonal Filter (5)

INTERPERSONAL RELATIONS	Pre-Usage Outcome	Post-Usage Outcome
Ranked Member inclusion into ranked network		
Non-ranked Member inclusion into non-ranked network	**Mother**	
Involuntary Non-member involuntary exclusion from network		**Mother**
Voluntary Non-member voluntary exclusion from network		

Figure 7.16 Synthesis 2 Group Determinations

Group Determination (pre-outcome)_____ + group_____	
Group Determination (post-outcome): _____ – group_____	
[+ group] = Member (ranked and non-ranked)	
[– group] = Non-member (involuntary and voluntary)	

Evaluation Typology

Figure 7.17 The Evaluation Typology Analysis

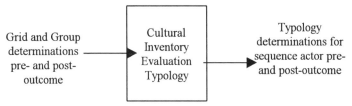

Evaluation Typology:

	Pre-Usage Outcome	
	+ Grid	– Grid
+ Group	1	2
– Group	3	4

	Post-Usage Outcome	
	+ Grid	– Grid
+ Group	1	2
– Group	3	4

Typology Determination (pre-outcome): _____

Typology Determination (post-outcome): _____

Determining a position for the sequence actor within a cell on both the pre- and post-usage outcome typologies is the goal for this final evaluation stage on the Cultural Inventory. Based on this typology positioning, a pre- and post-usage-outcome socio-cultural reality for the sequence actor is selected. By following the Application 3 and Synthesis 1 analysis procedures, the student decides dimensions of grid for the propositions of both the sequence actor and action sequence (see figure 7.1 below).

Figure 7.1 Application 3 and Synthesis 1
Application 3:

Is the sequence actor proposition **restrictive** ?	**Pre**-Usage Outcome	
	Yes	No

Is the action sequence proposition **restrictive** ?	**Post**-Usage Outcome	
	Yes	No

Synthesis 1:

> **Grid Determination (pre-outcome)**: _____
> **Grid Determination (post-outcome)**: _____
> [+ grid] = Proposition restrictive for actor(s)
> [– grid] = Proposition not restrictive for actor(s)

And, by following the Interpersonal Filter and Synthesis 2 analysis procedures, the student decides pre- and post-usage dimensions of group for the social identity of the sequence actor (see figure 7.2 below).

Figure 7.2 Interpersonal Filter and Synthesis 2
Interpersonal Filter (5)

INTERPERSONAL RELATIONS	Pre-Usage Outcome	Post-Usage Outcome
Ranked Member inclusion into ranked network		
Non-ranked Member inclusion into non-ranked network		
Involuntary Non-member involuntary exclusion from network		
Voluntary Non-member voluntary exclusion from network		

Synthesis 2:

> **Group Determination (pre-outcome)** _____
> **Group Determination (post-outcome)**: _____
> [+ group] = Member (ranked and non-ranked)
> [– group] = Non-member (involuntary and voluntary)

This final analysis/evaluation stage of the Cultural Inventory enables the student to combine the results of the symbolic analysis as translated through Synthesis 1 into grid coordinates (see figure 7.18) with the results of the social context analysis as translated through Synthesis 2 into group coordinates (see figure 7.19) and using these two coordinates of grid and group thus link the culture data of the Cultural Inventory Level 1 analysis with the social relation data of the Cultural Inventory Level 2 analysis.

Figure 7.18 Synthesis 1 Grid Coordinates
Synthesis 1:

Grid Determination (pre-outcome): _____
Grid Determination (post-outcome): _____
[+ grid] = Proposition restrictive for actor(s)
[– grid] = Proposition not restrictive for actor(s)

	Pre-Usage Outcome				Post-Usage Outcome	
	+ Grid	**– Grid**			**+ Grid**	**– Grid**
+ Group	1	2		+ Group	1	2
– Group	3	4		– Group	3	4

Figure 7.19 Synthesis 2 Group Coordinates
Synthesis 2:

Group Determination (pre-outcome)_____
Group Determination (post-outcome): _____
[+ group] = Member (ranked and non-ranked)
[– group] = Non-member (involuntary and voluntary)

	Pre-Usage Outcome				Post-Usage Outcome	
	+ Grid	**– Grid**			**+ Grid**	**– Grid**
+ Group	1	2		**+ Group**	1	2
– Group	3	4		**– Group**	3	4

Mary Douglas' 'Grid-Group Typology'[15] is the framework developed to allow this type of analysis combination and consequent evaluation; as, it provides a method of linking cultural biases with social relations.

> The fundamental purpose of grid/group analysis is to provide a framework within which a cultural analyst may consistently relate differences in organizational structures to the strength of the values that sustain them.[...]The two-dimensional diagram [of Grid and Group] thus presents a set of limits within which the individual can move around, or within which social organizations may develop and change.[16]

The Evaluation Typology analysis stage of the Cultural Inventory duplicates Douglas' typology technique. To employ this typology technique, the student plots the grid determinations from Synthesis 1 and the group determinations from Synthesis 2, pre-and post-outcome respectively. Accordingly, in plotting grid and group on the typology, the student positions the sequence actor in a cell temporally relative to the act of manipulation within the action sequence, i.e. pre- or post-usage-outcome. The pre-usage-outcome typology cells pertain to the cultural reality of sequence actor prior to the manipulation. The post-usage-outcome typology cells pertain to the cultural reality of the sequence actor as depicted from the reality of the action sequence.

To select a pre-usage-outcome typology cell for the sequence actor, the student applies the (pre-outcome) grid and group determinations from Synthesis 1 and 2 as pre-usage-outcome typology coordinates (see figure 7.20).

Figure 7.20 Pre-Usage-Outcome Grid/Group Coordinates and Typology

Synthesis 1:

Grid Determination (pre-outcome):   – grid

Synthesis 2:

Group Determination (pre-outcome)   – group

	Pre-Usage **Outcome**	
	+ Grid	– Grid
+ Group	1	2
– Group	3	(4)

The pre-usage-outcome typology result, (1,2,3 or 4), is then used to designate the socio-cultural cell of the sequence actor both prior to and during the act of manipulation. In the figure 7.20 example, the coordinates '– grid' and '– group' denote a #4 socio-cultural cell for the sequence actor.

To select a post-usage-outcome typology cell for the sequence actor, the student applies the (post-outcome) grid and group determinations from Synthesis 1 and 2 as post-usage-outcome typology coordinates (see figure 7.21).

Figure 7.21 Post-Usage-Outcome Grid/Group Coordinates and Typology

Synthesis 1:

Grid Determination (post-outcome): _____+ grid_____

Synthesis 2:

Group Determination (post-outcome) _____+ group_____

	Post-Usage Outcome	
	+ Grid	– Grid
+ Group	1	2
– Group	3	4

The post-usage-outcome typology result, (1,2,3 or 4), is then used to designate the socio-cultural cell of the sequence actor from the perspective of the action sequence, hence following the consummation of the action sequence. In the figure 7.21 example, the coordinates '+ grid' and '+ group' denote a #1 socio-cultural cell for the sequence actor.

"Der Süße Brei" Action-sequence (2) Evaluation Typology Analysis

For "Der Süße Brei" sample the Application 3 Question-1 received a determination of 'no' for the restrictiveness of the mother's proposition. This result was then translated into a '– grid' determination for the pre-outcome Synthesis 1 (see figures 7.5 and.7.22 below)

Figure 7.5 Pre-Usage Outcome Application 3 Question 1 Results

Is the sequence actor proposition **restrictive** ?	**Pre-**Usage Outcome	
	Yes	No

Figure 7.22 Synthesis 1 "Der Süße Brei" Action Sequence (2) Pre-Outcome Grid Determination

Grid Determination (pre-outcome):	— grid
[+ grid] = Proposition restrictive for actor(s)	
[− grid] = Proposition not restrictive for actor(s)	

At the Interpersonal Filter analysis, the mother's pre-usage social identity was classified as a 'non-ranked member' (see figure 7.12 below).

Figure 7.12 "Der Süße Brei" Action Sequence (2) Interpersonal Filter Pre-Usage Outcome Analysis Results

Interpersonal Filter (5)

INTERPERSONAL RELATIONS	Pre-Usage Outcome	Post-Usage Outcome
Ranked Member inclusion into ranked network		
Non-ranked Member inclusion into non-ranked network	**Mother**	
Involuntary Non-member involuntary exclusion from network		
Voluntary Non-member voluntary exclusion from network		

This result was then translated into a '+ group' determination for the pre-outcome Synthesis 2 (see figure 7.23 below)

Figure 7.23 Synthesis 2 "Der Süße Brei" Action Sequence (2) Pre-Outcome Group Determination

Group Determination (pre-outcome)	+ group
[+ group] = Member (ranked and non-ranked)	
[− group] = Non-member (involuntary and voluntary)	

When the pre-outcome grid and group determinations for "Der Süße Brei" sample noted above are applied in the Evaluation Typology, the coordinates '– grid' and '+ group' denote a #2 socio-cultural cell for the mother (see figure 7.24).

Figure 7.24 "Der Süße Brei" Action Sequence (2) Pre-Usage-Outcome Grid/Group Coordinates and Typology

Synthesis 1

Grid Determination (pre-outcome):	_____ – grid_____

Synthesis 2

Group Determination (pre-outcome)_____ + group_____

	Pre-Usage **Outcome**	
	+ Grid	– Grid
+ Group	1	②
– Group	3	4

For "Der Süße Brei" sample the Application 3 Question-2 received a determination of 'yes' for the restrictiveness of the action sequence's proposition (see figure 7.9 below). This result was then translated into a '+ grid' determination for the post-outcome Synthesis 1 (see figure 7.25 below).

Figure 7.6 Post-Usage Outcome Application 3 Question 2 Results

Is the action sequence proposition **restrictive** ?	**Post**-Usage **Outcome**	
	Yes	**No**

Figure 7.25 Synthesis 1 "Der Süße Brei" Action Sequence (2) Post-Outcome Grid Determination

Grid Determination (post-outcome): _____ + grid_____
[+ grid] = Proposition restrictive for actor(s)
[– grid] = Proposition not restrictive for actor(s)

At the Interpersonal Filter analysis, the mother's post-usage social identity was classified an 'involuntary non-member'(see figure 7.26 below).

Figure 7.26 "Der Süße Brei" Action Sequence (2) Interpersonal Filter Post-Usage Outcome Analysis Results

Interpersonal Filter (5)

INTERPERSONAL RELATIONS	Pre-Usage Outcome	Post-Usage Outcome
Ranked Member inclusion into ranked network		
Non-ranked Member inclusion into non-ranked network		
Involuntary Non-member involuntary exclusion from network		**Mother**
Voluntary Non-member voluntary exclusion from network		

This result was translated into a '– group' determination for the post-outcome Synthesis 2 (see figure 7.27 below).

Figure 7.27 Synthesis 2 "Der Süße Brei" Action Sequence (2) Post-Outcome Group Determination

Group Determination (post-outcome)_____ – group_____
[+ group] = Member (ranked and non-ranked)
[– group] = Non-member (involuntary and voluntary)

When the post-outcome grid and group determinations for "Der Süße Brei" sample are applied in the Evaluation Typology, the coordinates '+ grid' and '– group' denote a #3 socio-cultural cell for the mother (see figure 7.28).

Figure 7.28 "Der Süße Brei" Action Sequence (2) Post-Usage-Outcome Grid/Group Coordinates and Typology

Synthesis 1:

Grid Determination (post-outcome): _____ + grid _____

Synthesis 2:

Group Determination (post-outcome) _____ – group _____

	Post-Usage Outcome	
	+ Grid	– Grid
+ Group	1	2
– Group	③	4

The Evaluation Typology designations for the mother as sequence actor in "Der Süße Brei" sample analysis are presented in figure 7.29.

Figure 7.29 "Der Süße Brei" Action Sequence (2)
Evaluation Typology Results

Evaluation Typology:

	Pre-Usage Outcome	
	+ Grid	– Grid
+ Group	1	②
– Group	3	4

	Post-Usage Outcome	
	+ Grid	– Grid
+ Group	1	2
– Group	③	4

Typology Determination (pre-outcome): _____ # 2 _____
Typology Determination (post-outcome): _____ # 3 _____

From Typology Cells to Socio-cultural Realities

As was shown in the explanation of the Evaluation Typology, the Grid/Group analysis technique is used to locate the sequence actor, and his/her proposition, within a particular cell of the typology. In cases where the symbolic outcome of the action sequence denotes an inadequate act of manipulation, like in "Der Süße Brei" sample, the *post*-outcome typology is used to *re*locate the sequence actor in cell that reflects his/her socio-cultural identity relative to the proposition and social formation operative for the action sequence.

A completion of both levels on the Cultural Inventory is necessary because the Level 2 analysis (including Application 3, Synthesis 1-2, Interpersonal Filter, and Evaluation Typology) provides a process whereby the cognitive-symbolic Level 1 analysis results (Situational, Interactional, Feedback, and Notional Filters, and Applications 1-2) are related to the social structure depicted in the action sequence. In this the complete Cultural Inventory represents an analysis process addressing both the cognitive-intellectual core and social-formational aspects of culture.

The Cultural Inventory analysis is completed once the Evaluation Typology cells that have been assigned to the sequence actor are translated into their respective socio-cultural reality. To effect this translation the student links the cell category (1,2,3, or 4) to one of four socio-cultural reality definitions derived from the "ways of life" vignettes developed in Thompson, Ellis, and Wildavsky's 'Theory of Socio-Cultural Viability.'

Socio-cultural Reality Definitions

Figure 7.30 Evaluation Typology Cell Translation

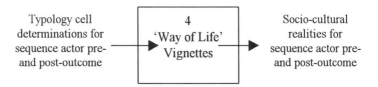

The socio-cultural reality categories listed below were developed for the Cultural Inventory using Thompson, Ellis and Wildavsky's 'way of life' vignettes. As employed in Thompson, Ellis, and Wildavsky's 'Theory of Socio-cultural Viability', the vignettes represent 'fleshed out' descriptions of the four cell quadrants (A,B,C,D) extent in Douglas's 'Grid-group Typology.' We developed the Cultural Inventory baseline definitions for the four socio-cultural reality categories by combining Thompson, Ellis and Wildavsky's 'way of life' vignettes and the five themes constituting the Cognitive Orientation categories on the Notional Filter. The socio-cultural reality categories –hierarchical, egalitarian, fatalist, and individualist– and attendant definitions correspond to Evaluation Typology cells 1 through 4. Using the definitions listed below, the student translates the typology cell number assigned to the sequence actor into its respective socio-cultural reality.

#1 Hierarchical socio-cultural reality

Figure 7.31 + Grid; + Group Evaluation Typology Cell

	Pre-Usage Outcome			Post-Usage Outcome	
	+ Grid	– Grid		+ Grid	– Grid
+ Group	1		+ Group	1	
– Group			– Group		

Time: Now is the best of times for the hierarchist. S/he looks to the past to justify the present; forward progression, or even the speculation of forward progression, is unnecessary. The future within the hierarchical perception is predictable as long as the status quo is maintained. However, any variation in the status quo spells historical disaster for the hierarchist. Time stands still for the hierarchist. *Human Nature*: S/he interprets human nature as naturally evil, but maintains that human nature can be molded to the good by good institutions. *Nature*: S/he perceives nature as a bountiful cornucopia as long as the exploitation of the environment is controlled by strict institutional limits. From the hierarchist-perspective, nature is forgiving of excesses, but also vulnerable to occasional catastrophe. Thus, the experts of the managing institutions must regulate against unusual and extreme occurrences of exploitation. Expertise management generates predictability and certainty. *Society*: The hierarchist-life is absorbed in and sustained by group membership. Like the fatalist, s/he exists in a social context which is organized by sets of institutional classifications. From hierarchist-perspective, society is designed to keep individuals apart by regulating their interactions. *Space*: Space is fixed, predetermined. S/he perceives space as interchangeably public and private depending on the needs as determined by the experts, or those in charge. And, the recognized experts are always in charge of the space. The hierarchist-perception of space depends on status; all space belongs to the Queen/King.

#2 Egalitarian socio-cultural reality

Figure 7.32 – Grid; + Group Evaluation Typology Cell

	Pre-Usage Outcome			Post-Usage Outcome	
	+ Grid	– Grid		+ Grid	– Grid
+ Group		2	**+ Group**		2
– Group			– Group		

Time: In the present the egalitarian confronts, and if necessary destroys past illusions. S/he wants to break with the past in order to insure an improved future. The future within the egalitarian-perception stands in opposition to the past. For the egalitarian, a positive future is imminent only when past faults are exposed, confronted and rectified. The egalitarian fights with the past. *Human Nature*: S/he interprets human nature as naturally good; however, s/he maintains that human nature is highly susceptible to, and hence corrupted by institutional influences. *Nature*: S/he perceives nature as fragile and unforgiving; the least jolt may trigger total collapse. Thus, the egalitarian contends that sanctions be established on institutions to stop their inevitable over-exploitation of nature. Only in this manner can environmental catastrophe be prevented. *Society*: The egalitarian-life is absorbed in, and sustained by group membership; however, s/he exists in a loosely-to-unregulated social context (society) which is not organized by sets of institutional classifications. From an egalitarian-perspective, society is not designed to keep individuals apart, nor is it designed to regulate their interactions. *Space*: For the egalitarian, space is situational; that is, everything within the group is public, equally shared space. There is little-to-no concept of private space for the egalitarian. What is not public space for his/her group is public space for another group. An egalitarian-perception of space is determined by membership.

#3 Fatalist socio-cultural reality

Figure 7.33 + Grid; – Group Evaluation Typology Cell

	Pre-Usage Outcome			Post-Usage Outcome	
	+ Grid	– Grid		**+ Grid**	– Grid
+ Group			+ Group		
– Group	3		**– Group**	3	

Time: The fatalist lacks the ability to predict the future because his/her conception of an historical past centers on a fate driven wheel of random events. Without a patterned past there is no predictable future for the fatalist. Time and events hinge on being either in the right place at the right time, or the wrong place at the wrong time-usually the latter. The fatalist merely attempts to cope with the random now; s/he is at the mercy of time. *Human Nature*: The fatalist interprets human nature as unpredictable. Thus s/he perceives, and consequently understands human nature as essentially random in character, sometimes good and sometimes evil. *Nature*: The fatalist perceives nature as a lottery controlled cornucopia. "Life is and remains a lottery. It is luck and not learning that from time to time brings resources his/her way."[17] In this random world s/he must cope with the erratic events of nature. *Society*: The fatalist has a low sense of group membership; however, s/he exists in a highly regulated society, or social context, which is organized by sets of institutional classifications. From his/her perspective society is designed to keep individuals apart by regulating their interactions. *Space*: For the fatalist, all space, both private and public, is temporary space since s/he lacks the ability and resources to control either public or private space. The fatalist's spatial location depends on luck; therefore, s/he is at the mercy of space, s/he simply adjusts.

#4 Individualist socio-cultural reality

Figure 7.34 – Grid; – Group Evaluation Typology Cell

	Pre-Usage Outcome			Post-Usage Outcome	
	+ Grid	**– Grid**		+ Grid	**– Grid**
+ Group			+ Group		
– Group		4	**– Group**		4

Time: The individualist-perception of time is predominately linear. S/he is future oriented, only glancing backward in order to more successfully predict the future. In this way, s/he rests in the security that the future is under her/his control. The individualist has time on her/his side. *Human Nature*: The individualist interprets human nature as predominately self-seeking. From the individualist-perspective, try as it may, society or institutions cannot modify human nature. *Nature*: S/he perceives nature as a skill-controlled cornucopia. Those with the best skills to exploit can exploit most effectively. For the individualist, the world of nature is neither perverse, capricious or fragile. There is a global equilibrium; the world is forgiving and self-healing. Therefore, from the individualist-perspective, trial and error in the exploitation of nature is both encouraged and justified. *Society*: S/he has a low sense of group membership. Like the egalitarian, s/he exists in a loosely-to-unregulated social context which is not organized by sets of institutional classifications. From the individualist perspective, society is not designed to keep individuals apart, nor is it designed to regulate their interactions. *Space*: For the individualist, space is predominately egocentric and thus predominately private. When s/he opts to enter a 'public' space s/he does so as an autonomous entity –as an individual. At all times s/he determines and controls her/his own space.

Narrative Write-up of Analysis

Returning to the anthropological study model of four phases outlined in the introduction:

> Phase 1: theoretical approach and analysis technique
> Phase 2: determination of data-field
> Phase 3: data collection and analysis
> Phase 4: interpretation and evaluations

one finds that the 'Phase 1: theoretical approach and analysis technique' has been provided in Chapters 2 through 7 of this study. For the 'Phase 2: determination of data field', a data field as one particular text: "Der Süße Brei," was determined in Chapter 5. The practice analysis conducted in Chapters 6 and 7 on "Der Süße Brei" action sequence 2 illustrate how 'Phase 3: data collection and analysis' proceeds using the Cultural Inventory. Finally, the narrative write-up of the Cultural Inventory analysis results for "Der Süße Brei" action sequence 2 will provide an example of the student generated 'Phase 4: interpretation and evaluations'.

For the analysis write-up, the student should be discouraged from recounting the events of the action sequence in terms of surface behavior only, as such an account would merely constitute a summary of the action sequence's *textual narrative*. Rather, the student should be encouraged to re-articulate the events of the action sequence employing the etic terminologies gained through the Cultural Inventory analysis. By exposing the text's underlying ideologies through re-articulation, the results of a Cultural Inventory analysis will enable students to discuss action sequences as a cultural communications. As such, the student's write-up should seek to reveal the *cultural narrative* presented by the analysis of the textual evidence.

Symbolic analysis

The symbolic analysis process put forth in Level 1 of the Cultural Inventory provides the steps for translating the textual interactions of sequence actors as cultural interactions. On the level of the text's cultural narrative, the sequence actor will negotiate an interaction based on a proposition compatible with a particular socio-cultural reality. For, a sequence actor stipulates the action sequence(world) as one way and will interact according to this sponsor thought. The sponsor thought underlying this interaction is generated from his/her culture, –core assumption reservoir– and manifests as a emic belief or value relative to the particular archetypal situation depicted in the textual narrative. The proposition *of the sequence actor* will either be supported or negated by the proposition *of the action sequence*.

It is possible to conclude the Cultural Inventory analysis process at the first level with the articulation of propositions. Such a conclusion constitutes only a symbolic analysis and will result in the translation of a textual narrative conflict into a cultural narrative of opposing propositions. To reveal the socio-cultural realities manifested through the opposing propositions of the cultural narrative, the Cultural Inventory continues with an additional analysis level providing steps for the student to analyze textual data in order to socially context the sequence actor. This second level of analysis achieves an additional translation of the textual narrative into the underlying cultural narrative; for, its completion reveals the socio-cultural realities manifested through the sequence actor.

Social context analysis

Progressing through the write-up, once the student has articulated the negotiation/conflict of the action sequence in the symbolic form of two propositions –namely sequence actor versus action sequence–, he/she then addresses the results of the second level of analysis. The second level of analysis has been designed to determine the socio-cultural realities of the sequence actor relative to the outcome of his/her act of manipulation, hence pre- and post negotiation. As such the second level of analysis pertains to the social contexting of the sequence actor in relation to his/her autonomy of action vis-à-vis the two propositions (grid) and in connection with his/her 'perceived' status and 'actual' status with regards to the group-network operative in the action sequence (group).

In the consummation phase of the action sequence, a surprise may occur that will negate the sequence actor's proposition and radically shake, or destroy the reality myth of this actor. According to the Level 2 analysis, such a change in the sequence actor's socio-cultural identity occurs if the pre-outcome proposition and reality of the sequence actor *is negated* by the proposition of the action sequence:

> in every case (where the stipulated world conflicts with the actual world) surprises[...] will eventually tip the appropriate being out of one niche [i.e. socio-cultural reality] and into another.[18]

The Level 2 analysis, concluding with the Evaluation Typology, has thus been designed to determine whether, and what type of change in the sequence actor's reality has or, of necessity, must occur.

The analysis write-up should proceed in four stages. In the first stage, as *introduction*, the type of text treated is described. This description is followed by a brief recounting of the *textual data* analyzed so that a textual context is presented for the cultural data to follow. Next, the *cultural data*, as extracted and analyzed through the Cultural Inventory, is presented. After the cultural data is presented, the *cultural narrative* is discussed in detail focusing on the propositions and socio-cultural realities manifested through the text. Finally the student presents his/her *personal view* on the cultural narrative.

Sample Analysis Write-up of "Der Süße Brei" Action Sequence(2)

Introduction example:

Fairytales have been an effective tool throughout history to convey beliefs and values, the ideational products of culture, via lessons of life. Such lessons are recounted generationally to children who, in turn, internalize their beliefs and values as core assumptions and thereby become full members of the cultural community. Let us now proceed to examine such a lesson of life that contributes to the achievement of full membership.

Textual data example:

Mother and pious girl confront an emergency –hunger. The girl is given a solution to the problem in the form of a "pot" which she receives from an expert (the old woman in the woods) who knew of her troubles. Specific commands are necessary to make the pot produce food (sweet porridge). The old woman tells the girl the commands. The girl returns home operates the "pot" and the problem of hunger is solved.

One day, the mother becomes hungry. Believing she has mastered the commands to operate the "pot," the mother speaks the production command. The "pot" produces food; however, the mother fails to complete the routine as she does not know the command to stop the food production. Her inability to complete the routine leads to disaster (the town is filled with sweet porridge). No one is able to help. Finally, the girl returns and stops the "pot" with the appropriate cessation command.

Cultural data example:

At the beginning of the second action sequence, the mother is faced with the situation of exploiting the "pot". Having presumably watched the girl perform the routine, the mother believes she has mastered the learning necessary to perform the routine correctly. The mother's interaction indicates that she not only considers herself among those with an ability to exploit the "pot," but also that she has not perceived formal instruction, either from the girl or the old woman, as prerequisite to successful pot exploitation. The mother's operative proposition is therefore non-restrictive; for, her act of manipulation reveals a descriptive proposition that mastery through informal learning, such as observation, is possible and she has indeed observed the "pot" routine. As such, it is clear that the mother, as sequence actor, considers herself a non-ranked member of the text network. In terms of "pot" exploitation, it must be presumed that the mother equates her network status with that of the girl. Were this not so, she would not have attempted the routine to control the pot. As such, the mother represents an egalitarian socio-cultural reality. From her reality, she is aware of no warnings or restrictions on the performance of the routine, and she is a member of the group who has heard the words and who has access to the pot.

Thus the mother begins the routine only to realize that she has not, through lack of expert instruction, mastered the routine. For, she had neither received instructions from the girl, nor from the old woman. The mother's interaction results in a disaster that threatens the survival of the whole town and can only be rectified by the girl, an expert-trained authority. The second action sequence concludes with the town covered in sweet porridge, the "pot" still cooking. The action sequence(world) as stipulated by the mother's proposition is directly and drastically negated by the consummation phase of the action sequence. For, the consummation of the action sequence illustrates that informal learning of this particular routine is not possible.

The violent feedback of the action sequence reveals a stronger cultural message. Since neither the mother, nor the girl was ever warned about the potential danger resulting from possible routine mishaps, the action sequence reveals a tacitly restrictive normative proposition regarding learning. The cultural message of the action sequence is clear: limitations on one's abilities, even to obtain food, are directly related to one's formal training, and formal training is based on the choice from a higher authority (old woman) rather than on the desire to learn. Only those chosen to receive such training are qualified. Thus, the cultural message in short reads: do not attempt to perform any skill unless you have received the proper training from a designated expert. This proposition posits the mother, post her negotiation of the action sequence, within a fatalistic socio-cultural reality; for, she is severely restricted by the action sequence proposition as, not having been chosen to receive the training, she has no autonomy to exploit the food source. And, as she has no other means of obtaining food she is subject to the constraints of the action sequence proposition for survival. Thus, being subject to the restrictive proposition as an involuntary non-member of the text network places her, at the conclusion of the action sequence, in the socio-cultural reality of a fatalist.

Cultural narrative example:

Within the surface issues of environmental exploitation the text presents a cultural narrative in which beliefs and values on learning are negotiated. The sequence actor, operating within an egalitarian socio-cultural reality, holds the belief that learning a simple routine is subject to observation and trial and error, but not dependent on specialized training or particular attributes such as piety. She acts upon self-reliance and is self-confident in her ability to perform the routine. However, both her proposition and her reality are negated by those of the action sequence. The disastrous situation caused by the mother's own interaction directly negates her belief in herself as qualified and provides evidence for deducing the proposition operative for the action sequence which underscores the importance of formal training and particular attributes as necessary for the mastery of even simple routines. At the close of the action sequence, we can state that this action sequence exhibits a hierarchical socio-cultural reality with regards to the girl and old woman. However, the mother and town inhabitants, as subject to the restrictive proposition on formal training but having no access to such training, are thus forced into the fatalist socio-cultural reality.

Personal view example:

From my cultural perspective, the cultural narrative of this story is particularly disturbing as there were no safeguards built in to prevent the disaster. It is clear that the mother was totally unaware of the restrictions placed on the performance of the routine. The old woman gave no warnings when she issued the instructions to the girl. Under these circumstances the disastrous outcome was inevitable. Like the mother, I would have attempted the routine. I prefer the mother's cultural reality as an egalitarian.

Because culture provides the mediating principles of human interaction, social actors and, in relation to a Cultural Inventory analysis, sequence actors manifest their culture through interaction. When conducting a Cultural Inventory analysis on textual action sequences, the student employs the Cultural Inventory as a tool to translate the action sequence interactions as cultural communications. Textual interactions thus cease to be read by the student as behavioral events and instead are analyzed as cultural negotiations. The Cultural Inventory has been designed as a tool to facilitate this analysis process.

Having performed both the symbolic and social context analyses, the student is able to re-construct the narrative as translated through the Cultural Inventory. Thus employing the Cultural Inventory enables the student to both realize, and articulate the cultural narrative imbedded in the textual narrative. Upon completion of the analysis write-up, the student has achieved a cultural reading of the text. For, translating the sequence actor and action sequence as manifested propositions thus permits the conflict of the action sequence to be read, and described, at Level 1 as a conflict of propositions and at Level 2 as a conflict and/or change in socio-cultural realities. In this way, the method of analysis as translation facilitated by the Cultural Inventory enables the student analyst to discover the underlying culture of a textual narrative.

Notes

[1] Ostrander 17.

[2] See Chapter 2 *The Problem of Social Context: Elements of Socio-cultural Realities.*

[3] The symbolic analysis data are those data from Filters 1-4 and Applications 1-2.

[4] Ostrander 17.

[5] Thompson, Ellis, and Wildavsky 5. We have substituted our term propositions for their use of prescriptions.

[6] Douglas, *Cultural Bias* 7.

[7] Ostrander 17.

[8] Douglas, *Cultural Bias* 7.

[9] Gross and Rayner 9-10.

[10] Gross and Rayner 10.

[11] Gross and Rayner 8-9.

[12] Gross and Rayner 7-8.

[13] Thompson, Ellis, and Wildavsky 76.

[14] Gross and Rayner 7.

[15] Mary Douglas, *Cultural Bias.*

[16] Gross and Rayner 14.

[17] Thompson, Ellis and Wildavsky 28.

[18] Thompson, Ellis and Wildavsky 72.

Chapter 8:

Conclusion

The functional-relevance based revision suggested by this study addresses the expansion of culture pedagogy within foreign language programs; for, the future of language study necessitates a programatic shift which would fully establish culture pedagogy within the realm of foreign language study, altering the paradigm from foreign language study to foreign-language-culture study. Culture pedagogy, as presented in this study, focuses on critical analysis and addresses the individual interpretative and negotiational aspects of culture in the communication process. Its goal is to advance student-centered, critical reflection on the cultural narratives embedded in texts by developing strategies that teach students how to *read* and critically *assess* culture as the cognitive-core of ideological differences in communication. To meet this goal, we have suggested that Global-Information Age learners be taught a symbolic/cognitive conception of culture and an understanding of its semiotic function in communication. The culture pedagogy addressed in this study thus refocuses the foreign language approach to culture *from* behavior-based cultural knowledge *to* cognitive-based cultural awareness.

In a culture pedagogy which meets the functional aims of Global-Information-Age learners, methodologies based in symbolic-cognitive approaches to culture will aim to help learners develop an understanding of the foreign framework of ideas they have chosen to study. The method for analyzing 'culture' presented in this study is therefore grounded in symbolic and cognitive anthropological approaches.

We have worked to design and create a semiotic process of culture analysis as a method to promote the analysis and evaluation of culture as meaning systems contexted within socio-cultural realities. Our analytical process, presented as the Cultural Inventory, facilitates student-centered analysis and critical evaluation of the ideological content embedded in cultural phenomena.

The research goal for this study focused on developing the Cultural Inventory to be used to teach a cognitive-semiotic approach to culture. To this end, we have designed a pedagogical tool that will enable students to read, analyze and evaluate the 'deep' culture content of texts. The use of the Cultural Inventory will not only promote critical-analysis skills, but will also enable students to develop a symbolic-cognitive awareness of culture as the meaning systems by, and through which humans construct, and seek to maintain their respective socio-cultural realities.

The Cultural Inventory Worksheet

In the figure below we present a Cultural Inventory worksheet for further implementation and study.

Figure 8.1 The Cultural Inventory Worksheet
Situational Filter (1)

BASIC ARCHEPAL SITUAION	PHENOMENON	
	material	non-material
Territorial		
Temporal		
Subsistential		
Exploitational		
Recreational		
Instructional		
Protective		
Associational		
Economic		
Sexual		

Sequence Actor: _____
Phenomena: _____
B.A.S.: _____

Interactional Filter (2)

Sequence Phenomena Usage	YES	NO	Supporting Information	Symbolic Embodiment
Incitive Usage				Prompt
Systematic Usage				Routine
Informative Usage				Image
Evaluative Usage				Model

S.P.U._____

Symbolic Embodiment: _____

Sponsor Thought: _____

Application 1:

Belief or value of the sequence actor:

_____

Feedback Filter (3)

USAGE ADEQUACY MEASUREMENT	YES	NO	Supporting Information
Prompt Persuasive			
Routine Correct			
Image Convincing or Credible			
Model Prescriptively Effective			

U.A.M.: _____

Symbolic Outcome: _____

Application 2:

> Belief or value of the action sequence:
>
> _____

Notional Filter (4)

COGNITIVE ORIENTATION	PROPOSITION TYPE	
	descriptive	normative
Time		
Human Nature		
Nature		
Society		
Space		

> _____ **Proposition of the sequence actor:**
>
> _____
>
> _____ **Proposition of the action sequence:**
>
> _____

Synthesis 1:

Is the sequence actor proposition **restrictive** ?	**Pre**-Usage Outcome	
	Yes	No

Is the action sequence proposition **restrictive** ?	**Post**-Usage Outcome	
	Yes	No

> **Grid Determination (pre-outcome):**_____
> **Grid Determination (post-outcome):**_____
> [+ grid] = Proposition restrictive for actor(s)
> [− grid] = Proposition not restrictive for actor(s)

Interpersonal Filter (5)

INTERPERSONAL RELATIONS	Pre-Usage Outcome	Post-Usage Outcome
Ranked Member inclusion into ranked network		
Non-ranked Member inclusion into non-ranked network		
Involuntary Non-member involuntary exclusion from network		
Voluntary Non-member voluntary exclusion from network		

Synthesis 2:

> **Group Determination (pre-outcome)**_____
> **Group Determination (post-outcome):** _____
>   [+ group] = Member (ranked and non-ranked)
>   [– group] = Non-member (involuntary and voluntary)

Evaluation Typology:

	Pre-Usage Outcome	
	+ Grid	– Grid
+ Group	1	2
– Group	3	4

	Post-Usage Outcome	
	+ Grid	– Grid
+ Group	1	2
– Group	3	4

> **Typology Determination (pre-outcome):** _____
> **Typology Determination (post-outcome):** _____

BIBLIOGRAPHY

Primary:

Grimm. "Der Süße Brei." *Grimms Märchen Gesamtausgabe*. Ed.
Ludwig Richter. Vienna: Tosa Verlag, n.d. 366-367.

Secondary:

Abrams, M. H. *A Glossary of Literary Terms*. 5th ed. Chicago: Holt,
Rinehart and Winston, Inc, 1988.

Bales, Robert F. "Theoretical Framework." *Interaction Process
Analysis: A Method for the Study of Small Groups*. By Robert
F. Bales. Cambridge: Addison-Wesley Press, Inc., 1950. 30-
84.

Beaujour, Michael, and Jacques Ehrmann. "A Semiotic Approach to
Culture." *Foreign Language Annals* 1.2 (1967): 152-163.

Berger, Peter L., and Thomas Luckmann. *The Social Construction of
Reality*. New York: Anchor Books, 1966.

Blumer, Herbert. "Symbolic Interaction." *Culture and Cognition*. Ed.
James P. Spradley. Prospect Heights: Waveland Press, Inc.,
1972. 65-83.

---. *Symbolic Interactionism: Perspective and Method*. Berkeley and
Los Angeles: University of California Press, 1986.

Boulding, Kenneth E. "The Image." *Culture and Cognition*. Ed. James
P. Spradley. Prospect Heights: Waveland Press, Inc., 1972.
41-51.

Brooks, Nelson. "Teaching Culture in the Foreign Language
Classroom." *Foreign Language Annals* 1.3(1968): 204-217.

Byram, Michael, and Veronica Esarte-Sarries. *Investigating Cultural
Studies in Foreign Language Teaching: A Book for Teachers*.
Multilingual Matters 62. Philiadelphia: Multilingual Matters,
Ltd., 1991.

Byram, Michael. *Cultural Studies in Foreign Language Education*.
Multilingual Matters 46. Philadelphia: Multilingual Matters,
Ltd., 1989.

Cassirer, Ernst. *The Philosophy of Symbolic Forms*. Vols. 1-3. Trans.
Ralph Manheim. New Haven: Yale University Press, 1977.

Colapietro, Vincent M. *Glossary of Semiotics*. New York: Paragon
House, 1993.

Critchfield, Anne L. "A Primer for Teachers of German: Five lessons
    for the New Millennium." *Die Unterrichtspraxis* 27 (Spring
    1994): 11-17.
D'Andrade, Roy. "Cultural Meaning Systems." *Culture Theory Essays
    on Mind, Self, and Emotion.* Eds. Richard A. Shweder and
    Robert A. LeVine. New York: Cambridge University Press,
    1992. 88-119.
---. "A Folk Model of the Mind." *Cultural Models in Language and
    Thought.* Eds. Dorothy Holland and Naomi Quinn. New York:
    Cambridge University Press, 1987. 112-148.
Deely, John. *Basics of Semiotics.* Bloomington and Indianapolis:
    Indiana University Press, 1990.
---. *The Human Use of Signs or Elements of Anthroposemiosis.*
    Maryland: Rowman and Littlefield Publishers, Inc., 1994.
Douglas, Mary. "Introduction to Grid/Group Analysis." *Essays in the
    Sociology of Perception.* Ed. Mary Douglas. Boston:
    Routledge and Kegan Paul, 1982. 1-8.
---. *Cultural Bias.* Royal Anthropological Institute of Great Britain and
    Ireland no. 35. London: Royal Anthropological Institute, 1978.
---. Introduction. *Measuring Culture: A Paradigm for the Analysis of
    Social Organization.* By Jonathan L. Gross and Steve Rayner.
    New York: Columbia University Press, 1985. xvii-xxvii.
Eagleton, Terry. "What is Ideology." *An Introduction to Ideology.* New
    York: Verso, 1994. 1-31.
Eco, Umberto. "The Influence of Roman Jakobson on the Development
    of Semiotics." Eds. Martin Krampen, Klaus Oehler, Roland
    Posner, et.al. *Classics of Semiotics.* New York: Plenum Press,
    1987. 109-127.
---. *A Theory of Semiotics.* Bloomington: Indiana University Press,
    1979.
Erickson, Paul A. *A History of Anthropological Theory.* Ontario:
    Broadview Press, Ltd., 1999.
Firth, Raymond. *Symbols: Public and Private.* Ithaca: Cornell
    University Press, 1989.
Geertz, Clifford. *The Interpretation of Cultures.* New York: Basic
    Books, Inc. Publishers, 1973.
Gross, Jonathon L., and Steve Rayner. *Measuring Culture: A Paradigm
    for the Analysis of Social Organization.* New York: Columbia
    University Press, 1985.
Hall, Edward T. *Beyond Culture.* New York: Doubleday, 1989.
---. *The Hidden Dimension.* New York: Anchor Books, 1982.

---. *The Silent Language.* New York: Doubleday, 1990.

Hammer, Dean. "Achilles as Vagabond: The Culture of Autonomy in the *Illiad.*" *Classical World* 90.5 (1997) 341-366.

Hampton, James. "Giving the Grid/Group Dimensions an Operational Definition." *Essays in the Sociology of Perception.* Ed. Mary Douglas. Boston: Routledge and Kegan Paul, 1982. 64-82.

Harrell, Bill J. "Social Structure, World Hypotheses, and Change." July 6 2000. <http://sunyit.edu/~harrell/billyjack/socst_wh_chg.>

Hawkes, Terence. *Structuralism and Semiotics.* Berkely and Los Angeles: University of California Press, 1977.

Hedderich, Norbert. "When cultures Clash." *Die Unterrichtspraxis* 32.2 (Fall 1999): 158-165.

Henderson, Ingeborg. "Cultural Strategies in Elementary College Language Courses." *The Modern Language Journal* 64.2 (1980): 190-196.

Hodge, Robert, and Gunther Kress. *Social Semiotics.* Ithaca: Cornell University Press, 1995.

Holland, Dorothy, and Naomi Quinn. "Culture and Cognition." *Cultural Models in Language and Thought.* Eds. Dorothy Holland and Naomi Quinn. New York: Cambridge University Press, 1987. 3-40.

Holy, Ladislav, and Milan Stuchlik. *Actions, Norms and Representations: Foundations of Anthropological Inquiry.* New York: Cambridge University Press, 1983.

Hughes, George H. "An Argument for Culture Analysis in the Second Language classroom." *Culture Bound: Bridging the Cultural Gap in Language Teaching.* Ed. Joyce Merrill Valdes. New York: Cambridge University Press, 1995. 162-169.

Jenks, Chris. *Culture.* New York: Routledge, 1993.

Kearney, Michael. *World View.* Novato: Chandler and Sharp Publishers, Inc., 1984.

Keesing, Roger M. "Models, 'Folk' and 'Cultural': Paradigms Regained?" *Cultural Models in Language and Thought.* Eds. Dorothy Holland and Naomi Quinn. New York: Cambridge University Press, 1987. 369-393.

Koope, Pamala. "Hints from the Classroom: Teaching Culture and Language in the Beginning Foreign Language Class: Four strategies that Work." *Die Unterrichtspraxis* (Spring 1985): 158-169.

Kramsch, Claire, and Thomas Nolden. "Redefining Literacy in a Foreign Language." *Die Unterrichtspraxis* 27 (Fall 1994): 28-35.

---. "Culture and Constructs: Communicating Attitudes and Values in the Foreign Language Classroom." *Foreign Language Annals* 16.6 (1983): 437-448.

Lado, Robert. "How to Compare two Cultures." *Culture Bound: Bridging the Cultural Gap in Language Teaching*. Ed. Joyce Merrill Valdes. New York: Cambridge University Press, 1995. 52-63.

Landman, Michael. *Philosophische Anthropologie*. Berlin: Walter de Gruyter and Co., 1982.

Lang, Victor. "The Promises and Pitfalls of German Culture Studies." *Monatshefte* 71.3 (1979): 231-235.

Langness, L.L. *The Study of Culture*. Los Angeles: University of California, 1993.

Lett, James. *The Human Enterprise: A Critical Introduction to Anthropological Theory*. Boulder: Westview Press, 1987.

LeVine, Robert A. "Properties of Culture: An Ethnographic View." *Culture Theory Essays on Mind, Self, and Emotion*. Eds. Richard A. Shweder and Robert A. LeVine. New York: Cambridge University Press, 1992. 67-87.

Liedloff, Helmut. "Kulturthemen im Anfängerunterricht im College." *Die Unterrichtspraxis* 8 (Fall 1975): 21-27.

Littlejohn, Steven W. *Theories of Human Communication*. 5th ed. Belmont: Wadsworth Publishing Company,1996.

Morris, Charles W. *Signification and Significance*. Cambridge: Massachusetts Institute of Technology Press, 1964.

---. *Signs, Language, and Behavior*. New York: G. Braziller, 1955.

Nelson, G. E. "Focus on Undergraduate Programs: The German Major as Education." *Die Unterrichtspraxis* 7 (Spring 1974): 1-7.

Nollendorf, Valters. "Out of Germanistik: Thoughts on the Shape of Things to Come." *Die Unterrichtspraxis* 27 (Spring 1994): 1-10.

---. "The Whethers, Wherefores, and Whithers of German Culture Studies: Focus on Degree Programs." *Monatshefte* 71.3 (1979): 228-230.

Nöth, Winfried. *Handbook of Semiotics*. Indianapolis: Indiana University Press, 1995.

Oehler, Klaus. "An Outline of Peirce's Semiotics." Eds. Martin Krampen, Klaus Oehler, Roland Posner, et.al. *Classics of Semiotics*. New York: Plenum Press, 1987. 1-21.

Ostrander, David. "One- and Two-Dimensional Models of the Distribution of Beleifs." *Essays in the Sociology of*

Perception. Ed. Mary Douglas. Boston: Routledge and Kegan Paul, 1982. 14-30.

Pandian, Jacob. *Anthropology and the Western Tradition*. Illinois: Waveland Press, Inc., 1985.

Peirce, Charles. " v. 1897- C.P. 2-228-Division of signs." "76 Definitions of the Sign by C.S. Peirce." By Robert Marty. 29 June 1999. <http://www.door.net/arisbe/menu/library/rsources/76defs/76defs.htm>

---. "Logic as Semiotic: The Theory of Signs." *Philosophical Writings of Peirce*. Ed. Justus Buchler. New York: Dover Publications, Inc., 1959. 98-119.

---. "The Principles of Phenomenology." *Philosophical Writings of Peirce*. Ed. Justus Buchler. New York: Dover Publications, Inc., 1959. 74-97.

Petersen, Jim. *Lifestyle Discipleship: The Challenges of Following Jesus in Today's World*. Colorado: Navpress, 1994.

Pfister, Guenther G., and Yvonne Poser. *Culture, Proficiency, and Control in FL Teaching*. Lanham: University Press of America, Inc., 1987.

Pfister, Guenter G., and Patrick McGrath. "Theoretical Aspects and Possible Definition of Culture." Paper. University of Maryland: 1992. 18-19.

Posner, Roland. "Charles Morris and the Behavioral Foundations of Semiotics." Eds. Martin Krampen, Klaus Oehler, Roland Posner, et.al. *Classics of Semiotics*. New York: Plenum Press, 1987. 23-57.

Ray, Maruta L. "Teaching German Culture: An Alternative Approach." *Die Unterrichtspraxis* (Spring 1985): 135-139.

Rice, Kenneth A. *Geertz and Culture*. Anthropology Series: Studies in Cultural Analysis. Ann Arbor: The University of Michigan Press, 1980.

Richards, Jack C., and Theodore S. Rogers. *Approaches and Methods in Foreign Language Teaching: A Description and Analysis*. New York: Cambridge University Press, 1986.

Rimmon-Kenan, Shlomith. *Narrative Fiction: Contemporary Poetics*. New York: Methuen: 1983.

Ruttkowski, Wolfgang V. "Einige didaktische Überlegungen für den Kulturkunde-Unterricht." *Die Unterrichtspraxis* 9 (Spring 1976): 90-95.

Samovar, Larry A., and Richard E. Porter. *Intercultural Communication: A Reader.* 2nd ed. Belmont: Wadsworth Vincent Publishing Co, 1976.

---. *Intercultural Communication: A Reader.* 7th ed. Belmont: Wadsworth Publishing Co, 1994.

Savan, David "C.S. Peirce and American Semiotics." *The Peirce Seminar Papers.* Vol. 2. Ed. Michael Shapiro. Providence: Berg, 1994. 179-208.

Schein, Egar H. *Organizational Culture and Leadership.* 2nd ed. San Francisco: Jossey-Bass Publishers, 1992.

Scollon, Ron, and Suzanne Wong Scollon. "What is Culture? Intercultural Communication and Sterotyping." *Intercultural Communication: A Discourse Approach.* By Ron Scollon and Suzanne Wong Scollon. Cambridge: Blackwell Publishers, 1995. 122-163.

Seelye, Ned. *Teaching Culture: Strategies for Intercultural Communication.* Chicago: National Textbook Company, 1985.

Shweder, Richard A., and Robert A. LeVine. "Preview; A Colloquy of Culture Theorists." *Culture Theory.* Eds. Richard A. Shweder and Robert A. LeVine. New York: Cambridge University Press, 1992. 1-24.

Spiro, Melford E. "Cognition in Culture-and-Personality." *Culture and Cognition.* Ed. James P. Spradley. Prospect Heights: Waveland Press, Inc., 1972. 100-110.

---. "Collective Representations and Mental Representation in Religious Symbol and Systems." *Culture and Human Nature: Theoretical Papers of Melford E. Spiro.* Eds. Benjamin Kilborne and L. L. Langness. Chicago: University of Chicago Press, 1987. 161-184.

---. "Culture and Human Nature." *Culture and Human Nature: Theoretical Papers of Melford E. Spiro.* Eds. Benjamin Kilborne and L. L. Langness. Chicago: University of Chicago Press, 1987. 3-31.

---. "Some Reflections on Cultural Determinism and Relativism with Special Attention to Emotion and Reason." *Culture and Human Nature: Theoretical Papers of Melford E. Spiro.* Eds. Benjamin Kilborne and L. L. Langness. Chicago: University of Chicago Press, 1987. 32-58.

Spradley, James P. "Foundations of Cultural Knowledge." *Culture and Cognition.* Ed. James P. Spradley. Prospect Heights: Waveland Press, Inc., 1972. 3-38.

Steakley, James D. "Culture Studies and the B.A." *Monatshefte* 71.3 (1979): 236-243.

Sturtevant, William C. "Studies in Ethnoscience." *Culture and Cognition*. Ed. James P. Spradley. Prospect Heights: Waveland Press, Inc., 1972. 129-167.

The American Heritage Dictionary of the English Language. Ed. William Morris. Boston: Houghton Mifflin Company, 1981.

Thompson, Michael, Richard Ellis, and Aaron Wildavsky. *Cultural Theory*. Boulder: Westview Press, 1990.

Tinsley, Royal L. Jr. "An Alternative in German." *Die Unterrichtspraxis* 7 (Spring 1974): 10-13.

Tinsley, Royal L., and David J. Woloshin. "Approaching German Culture." *Die Unterrichtspraxis* 7 (Spring 1974): 125-136.

Vander Zanden, James W., and Ann J. Pace. *Educational Psychology in Theory and Practice*. 2nd ed. New York: Random House, 1984.

Wallace, Ruth A., and Alison Wolf. "Symbolic Interactionism." *Contemporary Sociological Theory: Continuing the Classical Tradition*. Englewood Cliffs: Prentice-Hall, Inc., 1986. 187-231.

Weber, Richard. "Re(de)fining the College Curriculum." *Die Unterrichtspraxis* 33 (Spring 2000): 50-61.

Webster's New Collegiate Dictionary. Ed. Henry Bosley Woolf. Springfield: G. and C. Merriam Company, 1981.

Wuthnow, Robert. *Meaning and Moral Order: Explorations in Cultural Analysis*. Berkeley: University of California Press, 1987.